HUGH DENNIS

BRITTY BRITTY BANG BANG

ONE MAN'S ATTEMPT TO UNDERSTAND HIS COUNTRY

headline

First published in 2013

by HEADLINE PUBLISHING GROUP

2

Cataloguing in Publication Data is available from the British Library

Trade paperback ISBN 978 0 7553 6429 9

Typeset in Myriad by Avon DataSet Ltd, Bidford-on-Avon, Warwickshire

Printed and bound by CPI Group (UK) Ltd, Croydon, CR0 4YY

Headline's policy is to use papers that are natural, renewable and
recyclable products and made from wood grown in sustainable forests.
The logging and manufacturing processes are expected to conform to the
environmental regulations of the country of origin.

HEADLINE PUBLISHING GROUP
An Hachette UK Company
338 Euston Road
London NW1 3BH

www.headline.co.uk
www.hachette.co.uk

BRITTY BRITTY BANG BANG

PRAISE FOR *BRITTY BRITTY BANG BANG*

'An archetypal British book: very funny, genuinely informative, and, most importantly, makes you forget what you're actually doing on the toilet.'
DAVID BADDIEL

'I wish people had written funny books like this about boring things when I was a kid. I might be a history professor by now.'
JO BRAND

'Writing about your own country is the hardest thing to do. Hugh Dennis has inspected our sceptred isle and remorselessly scoured it inside out and come up with a funny, hilariously satirical, but warm and brilliantly observed portrait of our complicated, ridiculous but loveable country. Utterly readable and laugh-out-loud funny.'
STEPHEN FRY

'Funny and interesting. The best guide to Britain since the 1976 *AA Road Atlas*.'
JOHN O'FARRELL

For Kate, Freddie and Meg

Author's Note

In the course of my research, most of which has been spent reading or sitting in front of a laptop in various locations – my office, my kitchen, the train, coffee shops and in the car waiting for my children to emerge from various sporting activities – I have consulted more web pages than I care to mention and followed leads and links to the innermost regions of the internet. And the thing about links is that as soon as you follow one, there is always another one waiting for you, ready to lead you down some other path in the crazy maze that makes up the World Wide Web. The astonishing thing is that each site you get to has been put together by enthusiasts; there are millions of pages, and almost every one has been written by someone who is genuinely interested in their subject and who wants to pass their expert knowledge on.

And the range of things that people are interested in is astounding in itself: there are pages on the development of the carburettor, on the empires of ancient India, on medieval foods, and the gruesome deaths of plant hunters. People have compiled lists of kings, vegetables and types of spanner. There are maps of diseases, football clubs and pressure in different types of weather system. And in chat rooms there are ongoing arguments about everything from democracy, to bicycles, to Paris Hilton. The internet is like a huge electronic Georgian coffee house, without the coffee, where information is given and exchanged without charge. It is a magnificent creation and I readily acknowledge the work and expertise of all those whose pages I have read and consulted, whether they be on Wikipedia, the BBC website, Physics Forum or any of a thousand others, and whether they were about fish, farms or pigeon fancying. I thank you and the authors of the other sources I have drawn on for a very interesting six months.

I have tried to be as accurate as possible, but mistakes will inevitably have crept in, and I apologise for those which have. Most will be down to my own shortcomings, but information from the internet can also occasionally be like a pink roast chicken: you don't know which bits to trust.

Thanks also to my agents, Samira and Paul, for being constantly supportive, and my editor Jonathan Taylor, for not throwing his hands up in horror.

Contents

INTRODUCTION

When I first decided to write this book, it was a different age, and we were living in a completely different Britain.

I had secretly been worried about what being 'British' meant for nearly a decade, ever since my friend Ardal had told me in passing that I was the most British person he had ever met. What did he mean? We were in a rehearsal room, and I had laughed, but underneath I was rather perplexed, searching for sub-text and unclear whether I was being praised, teased, vaguely insulted, or possibly all three – because it has always been very difficult to know how to feel about being British. For a long time it was a multiple-choice question, to which the answers

a. OK
b. depressed
c. ashamed
d. ecstatic

all seemed to be acceptable, depending on who the question master was. So I decided to explore the image of Britain, find out why we are so, well, British and then try to explain it to the 62,218,760 other people I share these islands with, or at least the ones who were prepared to buy a book about it, or had mistakenly downloaded it to their Kindle. But of course Britain was different then.

Let me explain.

To the outsider, Britain and what it means to be British had always been fairly obvious. Britain was a place of pomp, circumstance, democracy, a rather woolly established church and overpaid footballers. A nation that loved petty rules and regulations, that exercised a pointless and incomprehensible system of etiquette, and seemingly preferred to stand on the second step of the podium to winning and getting covered in all that champagne. None of which was particularly positive. It was a nation that appeared to be paralysed, obsessed with weather, aristocracy, dogs, gardening, moaning, and the class system, isolated in the corner of Europe and well past its best-before date.

And then came the Olympics.

A single month of Olympic and Paralympic Games seemed to change everything, to challenge every long-held belief about the British character, not least that the Australians are better than us at sport. For years we had been laughed at by them for only winning the so called 'sitting down sports' like rowing, cycling and sailing, but now we were beating them at everything, standing, running, squatting, punching and falling backwards from a 10-metre concrete platform. Not, incidentally, that only being good at sitting down sports had ever really bothered me. In fact, given that they are the only sports in which humans are genuinely the best in the world, I have always thought that they are the ones to win. Usain Bolt may be the fastest man who has ever lived, but he would still be pushed to match the straight-line speed of a domestic cat. Most gymnasts, however flexible, would be eased off the podium by a macaque, and I'm sure a gorilla would probably win the weightlifting, but you put a shark on a bicycle and Bradley Wiggins would still lead it home. In fact, the shock of it being there at all would probably make him go even faster. But I am off at a tangent . . .

The London Olympics surprised the world. Not only did we provide a Games much better than Mitt Romney expected, or the French hoped, as a nation we also presented a completely new face to the outside world, one which rebutted the idea that we're simply a nation of stuffed shirts, incapable of building anything on time or on budget, an island whose inhabitants have bad teeth, a terrible diet and a fixation with wearing long trousers even in hot weather. Instead we gave them a gleaming new vision of Britain: a smiling Britain of achievement, a Britain responsible for leading the world into the modern era through the Agrarian and Industrial Revolutions, a nation proud to embrace multi-culturalism, individuality and eccentricity. A country where a major politician can dangle helplessly from a zip wire like a discarded straw dolly and gain in popularity, and whose queen can send herself up and then descend by parachute. A country which brought the world railways, football and the World Wide Web – while Tim Berners-Lee was working in Switzerland, I think, but we can ignore that – and whose inhabitants have mediocre teeth and a fairly good diet and whose men have, unfortunately, embraced the three-quarter-length trouser, whatever the weather.

The unexpected legacy of the Games has been a Britain with a new-found self-confidence, in which we all know how to be British. A Britain that should be embarrassed by nothing and proud of everything, from sheep, to chimneys, to the Spice Girls, to industrial action and what had always previously been described as our 'ailing transport network'. A Britain which, having been pinned firmly in its own half, has dribbled the length of the field, nutmegged the defenders, unleashed a curling dipping shot into the top right-hand corner, scored a wonder goal and is now kissing the badge.

A Britain, reconstructed from the bits we knew were there but had slipped our minds. A country that has been rebuilt, re-buffed, and re-furbed.

Britty Britty Bang Bang.

OK, I will now switch off the national anthem currently playing in my head.

It is great. We are in a new Britain, and no-one is more shocked than we are.

How could the country we thought we knew so well suddenly nip up into the national loft and bring down so much we had all forgotten about?

To be honest, I've found it all a bit confusing. Should we now be proud of everything? Is there more to be proud of? What are our great traditions? Are we really good at inventing stuff? Are we obsessed by the weather? Did we invent democracy?

Are we obsessed with gardens? And who was Kenneth Branagh meant to be in that opening ceremony?

Crucially, if someone should ask about the good stuff this country has given to the world, would I be able to answer in an impressive and intelligent way?

Frankly, Britain has got some explaining to do, not least because allowing anyone, even a country, to wallow in its success without questioning its achievements simply wouldn't be British. Or wouldn't *have been* British. I think.

So I've decided to find out what I can. To ask the questions that matter, and many that simply don't, for the simple reason that the answers could be interesting, and even if they aren't, they could be useful in a pub quiz.

And the first question up: what actually is Britain?

AN ISLAND NATION

OK, I'm an hour in and I am already confused. I am going to have to forget any attempt at defining British achievements or tracing British traditions for now, because there is even debate about what Britain, Great or otherwise, actually is. As far as I can see, the situation is this: Britain is England and Wales; Great Britain is England, Wales and Scotland, although the Great might also simply be there to distinguish Britain from Brittany; the United Kingdom is England, Wales, Scotland and Northern Ireland; and the British Isles is a purely geographical term describing all the countries above with the addition of Eire, and is used only by geographers who want to have to eat their own corduroy and elbow patches the next time they go through customs at Dublin Airport.

What seems to be clear though is that Britain is, as the cliché goes, 'an Island Nation', although if you try to get an answer to how many islands there actually are, the internet gives you hundreds, all contradictory. Some websites say 1,000, some more than 2,000, while a man from the Ordnance Survey who answered the question 'How many islands are there in Great Britain?' on an internet forum said there are 6,289,which seems an incredibly large figure, but given that the Ordnance Survey draw the maps, and there is only the slimmest chance that this man doesn't work for them at all and is simply a freak who pretends to be a cartographer at weekends, I've decided to go with it.

This total is roughly one third of the number in Indonesia – a country so full of tiny islands that a map of the whole thing looks a blood-splatter pattern from *Silent Witness* – and 6,263 more than Switzerland, which surprisingly has 36, although they don't really count because they are all in lakes. The majority of the islands of Britain, however, are proper, honest-to-goodness islands surrounded by swell, approachable only by boat, causeway, sea tractor or, if you are a 1970s rock star who bought off Scotland because being a laird seemed like a good way to splash the cash, by helicopter. They range in size from the big one, that which contains England, Scotland and Wales, to fairly substantial isles like Wight, Sheppey and Skye, to marginally less bulky islands like Staffa, Lundy and Brownsea (try not to think too hard about how that one got its name), to simple lumps of rock that, whatever scale of map you are currently struggling to fold, really only merit a dot, far less a name.

They include islands that seem impossibly romantic, like Lindisfarne, which is connected to the north-east coast by a causeway described by Sir Walter Scott, and those that simply aren't romantic at all, like Portsea, the island on which

Portsmouth sits and which would isolate it from the south coast if it wasn't for a short bridge, only described by *The AA Book of the Road*, which guides the ferry-bound 36-wheelers over some tidal mudflats.

There are islands which appear to be islands but actually aren't, like the Isle of Purbeck and the Isle of Dogs. The first is simply a peninsula, where a medieval marketing consultant decided to improve tourist numbers by pretending there was water right round it, while the Isle of Dogs, the massive bend in the River Thames that forms the backdrop to the credits in *EastEnders*, and where I lived until I was ten, is just a bit ahead of the game. That is, it isn't an island yet, but will be in thousands of years if the river is left to do its natural thing and smooth out the massive meander that goes past Greenwich. Sadly, the point at which it would cut through to straighten its course – just like the diagram you half remember from GCSE Geography – is exactly where they have built Canary Wharf. With the current problems in global finance, you can't imagine any banks letting the River Thames surge through their trading rooms, however much the rest of us would like to see it.

There are islands you would think were ours but aren't, like the self-governing Crown dependency of the Isle of Man; Jersey in the Channel Islands; and the so-called Bailiwick of Guernsey, which encompasses a group of yet smaller islands, including Sark, Herm, Breqhou, Jethou, and Lihou, all of which seem to have been named by someone still recovering from dental anaesthetic.

There are islands which seem to have been named by a six-year–old, like the Isles of Scilly, a beautiful archipelago off the western-most tip of Cornwall. Made famous by the holiday-ing Harold Wilson and BBC's *An Island Parish*, the Scillies comprise St Mary's, St Martin's, Bryher, Tresco and its two neighbours, Tresco Metro and Tresco Express. OK, those last two don't really exist. The derivation of the word Scilly is the matter of some debate though – no surprise there: the internet doesn't really seem to deal in definite. The word could be from the Viking 'Syllorgar', which means . . . well, I don't know what it means, and nor did any source I looked at. Or it could be a corruption of the Roman name for the islands, Sully, mean-ing sun isles. Of the definitions, I lean towards the meaning-less Viking. Doubtless the islands do have a very good record for sunshine, but Romans calling any island off the coast of Britain 'sunny' seems a bit of a push. Perhaps they had never been to Sardinia, or Elba, or Capri. Perhaps they had never actually been outside.

There are islands that seem timeless, like the Hebrides, and islands where you step back through time to periods not that long gone. A trip to the Isle of Wight, for example, seems like taking a step back to the 1960s. Former London tube trains run on the railway network, and it was here that they tested the rockets for Britain's short-lived space programme and developed the first hovercraft. Best known for its festival, the last Jimi Hendrix played at, the island actually has a long and involved history. It was to here that Charles I escaped at the end of the English Civil War. Imprisoned at Hampton Court, and fearing for his life, he decided to make a run for it and set off down the A3 for the coast. Weighing up his options, he decided that escaping to France would be problematic, and plumped instead for Jersey. However, in the New Forest, en route to the port from which he would embark to begin his new life, he became lost in thick fog and missed the ferry to his chosen island. Unfortunately he had booked online and his ticket wasn't valid for the next sailing, so after a massive argument with his wife and his children, who were sitting in the back of the carriage and already filled to the eyeballs with Haribo, he swapped destinations to Carisbrooke in the Isle of Wight, where he was caught and thrown in prison again. What a great day out. None of this, incidentally, appears in Wikipedia, although it is of course accurate enough to be included.

There are even islands which haven't been built yet, like so-called Boris Island, wedged in the Thames between Kent and Essex, designed to contain several runways and, essential at every British international airport, a massive branch of Tie Rack. It may, of course, never be built, and the positioning does seem a bit dodgy. It is currently a haven for wild fowl and although airlines seem able to cope with strikes by cabin crew and baggage handlers, bird strikes are rather more deadly. Inconveniently, it also sits only a short distance from a Second World War wreck containing 4,000 tonnes of high explosives that are liable, as they say in movies, to 'blow at any time' and cause a fair degree of unexpected turbulence. My worry though is about possible temptation for the pilots. On a moonlit night, flying up the river towards the Thames Barrier, how much would you want to hum the theme to *The Dam Busters*, announce in a crackly voice, 'Baggage away', and then watch as a selection of Samsonite World Tourers bounces majestically upstream. OK, perhaps it is just me.

And there are islands like East and West Falkland, which, although they feel more British than Britain itself, are out of the equation entirely. Sitting in the South Atlantic, both are far closer to Antarctica than mainland Europe, although, metaphorically at least, the same would apply to the unfortunate Canvey Island in the Thames Estuary. In the 1950s the petrochemical industry put huge tanks there to store liquid gas, which had to be kept so cold that permafrost spread across the island, making it an extremely unattractive place to live except possibly for urban Arctic foxes and the odd polar bear.

So islands, yes there are plenty, and there used to be more, because a quick search of 'the geology of Britain' revealed that the island of Great Britain which, with the possible exception of Alex Salmond and Sean Connery, we think of as one unbroken landmass stretching from Cornwall to Caithness was once two separate pieces. And, as the best argument not yet used for Scottish independence, the break between the two bits was a massive crack called the Iapetus Suture, a line from the aforementioned Lindisfarne to the Solway Firth – exactly where an independent Scotland would build the border posts and the duty free.

Even more worrying for those of a unionist disposition, the geological separation between the two nations was fairly fundamental. Unlike England and France, separated by the English Channel but essentially part of the same chunk of land, England and Scotland actually started in completely different parts of the globe, some thousands of miles apart, which would have made any Land's End to John O'Groats cycle ride very difficult indeed.

Roughly 540 million years ago, in a geological period known as the Cambrian – or, if you prefer, 'just before the birth of Bruce Forsyth' – England, or at least the land we now think of as England, was somewhere down by the South Pole (a fact which enhances our claim to the Falklands, incidentally), while Scotland formed part of the eastern seaboard of North America, which was then known as the supercontinent of Laurentia (or wasn't, given that humans only started to develop language about 100,000 years ago). From these two starting positions, the two nations began slowly to float towards each other on their respective tectonic plates until at the end of the Silurian – another geological period and not, as you might think, an alien from *Doctor Who* set on the destruction of the earth – they crashed into each other and have been joined ever since. Who was responsible for the crash is unclear; police only arrived on the scene 400 million years later, and I don't want to add to Scottish grievances by suggesting that they could claim for whiplash injury or loss of earnings.

Given that the two modern nations were only travelling towards each other at 5–6cm per year, you'd think the damage would be minimal, but you would be wrong. Both seem to have had the tectonic version of a crumple zone, which bent and twisted as designed, leaving massive fold mountains from Norway to the Appalachians in North America, while the volcanoes that came as a bonus extra gave us ranges such as the Cairngorms.

Our transformation into an island nation, by the separation of Britain and the Continent, is much more recent though. It happened less than 10,000 years ago, a mere blinking of the eye in geological terms, when the land bridge that joined us to Denmark, Germany and Holland was finally flooded by a massive tsunami which had been set off by a huge lump of Norway falling into the sea. Obviously that isn't quite how the geologists put it – they call it 'the Storegga Slides', one of the largest landslips in history – but either way, the damage caused makes it one of the clearest examples of why 'bombing' is not allowed in public swimming pools.

Intriguingly, the land it flooded, essentially that between the coast of East Anglia and the Low Countries, has become known as 'Doggerland'. This is apparently because of its proximity to the Dogger Bank, made famous by *The Shipping Forecast*, although it still leaves me slightly suspicious of what Neolithic man was getting up to in public car parks.

But what has being an island nation brought us?

Well, for a start, the fact that we are fairly small and have been crumpled, crushed and twisted in practically every possible direction makes Britain one of the most geologically varied nations, by area, in the world. We have practically everything igneous, metamorphic and sedimentary; everything from chalk, to granite, to slate, to limestone is somewhere on the surface after the gigantic mash-up that has been our geological history. We have basalt extrusions, volcanic archipelagos, clints and grykes, soft downland, hard upland, peat, clay, coal, the lot. In fact, the only things we don't seem to have are an area of desert, although those living near Bracknell may care to differ, and glaciers, something we may shortly be sharing with the rest of the world.

In the not too distant past, if the movement of something was described as glacial it meant that it was going imperceptibly slowly. Now, though, the term would be better used to describe something that is moving backwards really quite fast. Which is why I would have preferred the hairdresser to have said something other than 'glacially' when I asked him how fast my hair was receding.

Anyway, back to Britain.

We have old bits which are being worn down, such as Scottish mountains which were once higher than the Alps, and new bits which are being built up, like the peat bogs of Somerset. We are also, it turns out, pivoting like a see-saw as Scotland, which was covered in ice up to 2km thick during the last ice age, reacts to having the enormous weight removed and springs joyfully upwards at up to 3mm a year, forcing the south of England down into the sea in a process known as isostatic recovery, or the attempted manslaughter of your nearest neighbour. Yes, Scotland is on the up, or on the rebound, depending which way you look at it.

We also have an enormously long coastline, stuffed full of estuaries, inlets, marshes, cliffs, fjords, platforms, bays, coves, creeks, arches and stacks. It is supposedly one and a half times longer than that of Italy and five times longer than that of France, although yet again no one can actually tell you how long it is. The estimates I read varied from 7,000 miles, to 11,072 miles, to the idea that it might actually be infinite. OK, I admit that at this point I had veered off into a website called PhysicsForum.com. Why is now beyond me. I think I must have been very tired. Anyway it turns out that the length of the British coastline was the subject of a paper by a famous mathematician called Mandelbrot, the so-called father of 'fractal geometry', which is a very odd name to give a child, entitled 'How long is the coast of Britain?', a label which left no one in any doubt, I guess, over what it was going to be about. His conclusion, which I haven't read the whole of but would be happy to if the lives of my family and children depended on it, was that the length measured depended on the size at which it was measured. That is, the more detailed a map, then the more little inlets you will see, the greater the intricacies that will be apparent and the longer the coastline you will record. This, according to some on the forum, suggested that the coastline could become infinitely long, while others thought that it couldn't actually get bigger than it is in real life, although ironically a real life appeared to be something very few of the people on the forum have.

Sorry, for the anti-physics thing. I don't really mean it. I've even voluntarily read a book on fractals. I know physics is a very important subject, practised by very clever people, on whom we as a society rely. It's just that I took it for A-level and got an E. I couldn't get the plasticine balls to swing properly in the practical. Don't ask. Just be grateful I'm not working at CERN.

The only really clear fact I picked up about our coastline at all is that, whichever way you look at it, it is much shorter than that of Greece, which has by far the longest coastline in the European Union. I can't imagine that will help in bail-out negotiations with Angela Merkel, but you never know, and what have they got to lose? Perhaps they should just throw it in and see what happens. Norway's is long too, and the people of Norway are a model of economic stability.

Anyway, for me at least, the picture seems clearer: Britain is 6,000 lumps of rock with a coastline which if stretched out into a single line might, and I only say *might*, get you from Basingstoke to Sydney. A rocky and dotty island kingdom, all governed as an uninterrupted whole, by a single uninterruptable monarch. There. All sorted. That is Britain.

Except, of course, if you count the foreign embassies, because I remember someone telling me that they aren't part of Britain at all, but count as part of the country they represent. There are more than 180 embassies or high commissions in London, and they are mostly in really nice houses in Notting Hill or somewhere. One of the greatest concentrations of them is on a road called Kensington Palace Gardens, and it would be a shame if every morning in the palace itself William and Kate pulled back the curtains to find that they were not looking at Britain at all, but at Norway, Nepal, Kuwait and Lebanon instead; although, with austerity in mind, it would at least make overseas trips a lot cheaper and more convenient. If the embassy is actually part of the country whose flag is on the roof, the royals could have an official trip to Romania and be back for breakfast. They could take a holiday to France, without the worry of paparazzi taking snaps of Kate without her top on, partially because the embassy isn't overlooked, but mainly because no one in their right mind would really want to go topless in a West London garden, even in August. Anyway it is a question worth asking: is Britain like the carpet in 1970s nightclub – does it have 180 Embassy-shaped holes in it?

The answer, you may be relieved to hear, is no. The embassies are part of Britain, whatever the brass plaque on the door says. The reason some people think they aren't is down to a misinterpretation of the 1961 Vienna Convention on Diplomatic Relations, a cracking read, which says that embassies are inviolate and must not be entered by the host country without the express permission of the head of mission. That is, you can get up to anything in an embassy and no one can get you for it. Policemen can't enter, and neither documents nor diplomats have to be surrendered to the British authorities. Which is, of course, why Julian Assange headed for the Embassy of Ecuador when he thought he might be extradited. It was either that or crossing his fingers behind his back and shouting, 'Fanites', which apparently does not guarantee immunity under international law, the rules of the CIA, or in the script of *Zero Dark Thirty*.

Within embassies, the laws of the countries they represent apply, except of course the natural ones. At the Australian Embassy, for example, the bath water still goes down clockwise, as it does for the rest of London, and when you look up at night, you see the stars of the northern hemisphere rather than their southern equivalents, like Kiri Te Kanawa or Ricky Ponting. Their status also means that diplomats are exempt from most local taxes, which isn't that shocking and simply brings them into line with rich people, and anyone who has Jimmy Carr's accountant.

Being an island nation is, of course, meant to be a key determinant of our national character. Historians have suggested that it has given us a more detached attitude to our neighbours, which given that we actually are detached from our neighbours, apart from that little bit along the border of

Northern Ireland, seems to make sense. It certainly means we have had to interact with the countries next door slightly less than semi-detached nations like Canada or Denmark, and far less than terraced countries like Belgium, whose neighbours keep coming through their garden and wrecking it, or indeed Monaco, which might be really nice but has France on both sides.

Certainly being an island does seem to lend islanders a certain unwillingness to be pushed around. When I was a child growing up on the Isle of Dogs, the Dockland Development Corporation so antagonized the locals by knocking their houses down that the islanders raised the bridges – well, raised one and swung the other – and declared UDI, a unilateral declaration of independence, just as Rhodesia had done five years earlier. My father was called on to mediate, I missed school, which was in Hackney, by then part of a hostile foreign nation, and the whole thing was terribly exciting. For a short time, we were heading for a Vatican City equivalent, a new country bang in the middle of the capital of another one. But perhaps it was the Vatican parallels which scuppered it. A tiny country would have been fine, but no one wanted to wear the silly costumes that seemed to go with it. And who can blame them? Imagine Phil Mitchell dressed as a Swiss Guard and you will see what I mean.

The whole debate about the effect of island dwelling on the psyche of a nation and its people is a fascinating one, and there are lots of historical Starkey-style questions that could be asked. Has it given us an inflated sense of self-importance? How has it affected our fractious relationship with Europe? Was the flooding of the Channel a watershed in the history of our nation?

Certainly lots of the sheds in Doggerland would have got very wet indeed. I, however, felt myself drawn to a question of a rather more basic nature.

Does island dwelling mean that we eat a lot of fish?

OK, it may not seem important now, but you never know when you are going to be on a plane sitting next to a man from the Department of Environment, Food and Rural Affairs.

It turns out that getting information on fish is very difficult indeed. A search under 'world fish consumption' gives you little: some recipes, an incomprehensible bar chart and a link to an advert for a fish-oil rich in Omega 3. Even my initial dealings with the website for the UN Food and Agriculture Organization (FAO) proved less than fruitful. Had I been after world pro- duction figures for asses, buffaloes or beehives, there would have been no problem at all. Likewise pigs, pigeons or rodents. You can even get figures for camelids, which I was relieved to find is the biological name for the family containing camels, llamas and alpacas, not, as you might think, the lid of a camel. Why a camel might have a lid I have no idea – possibly easier access to the food store. If it had two humps, it could have a different food in each, like a Müller Fruit Corner.

But figures for fish were a problem. Fortunately, enlighten- ment was not far away. Deep within the organization's internet offering, I found what can only be described as a 'fish com- parison website' which, by means of filling in drop-down boxes, a process not that different from fishing itself, allowed me to compare fish statistics from round the world. It would have been enough to give John West a wet dream, although as a fisherman he had probably had enough of those to last a lifetime. I set to my task. First, how did Britain match up with France, fish-wise? Surely, being entirely surrounded by water, we would eat more. I pressed enter and there was my answer, in a table entitled 'UK Seafood Supply – Quantity (1,000 tonnes) 2000–2010'.

Beneath it were two lines, one for France, one for Britain, weaving their way across the page, following the timeline along the bottom. Until 2002 we had a greater supply of fish than them, since when they have had a greater supply of fish than us. It is a ding-dong battle, fought out on the high seas, and all perfectly clear, except that I don't know what it means, because I discovered that 'supply' is simply how much you catch, rather than eat, and that seafood doesn't actually mean fish, it means all the other stuff as well. The category I was after was 'Fish: Demersal' – and, yes, I did have to look up what demersal means; don't try telling me that you wouldn't have had to. It means fish that feed on the bottom, and comes from the Latin *demergere*, meaning to sink, although obviously if that is all a fish can do, it is in a bit of trouble. Demersal fish include pretty well everything you and I would think of as fishy in a saltwater context – cod, sole, plaice, haddock and halibut – so it seemed the category to go for. I selected it and pressed enter, to find that in 2007 our fishing fleet provided 9.1kg of fish per head of our population, putting us ahead of Germany, level with France and well behind Spain, but then they have a massive fishing fleet which would trawl everything out of the ocean if no one stopped them, including all the fish, trans-atlantic cables and the wreck of the *Titanic*. At least I think that is what it said in the *Daily Mail*.

Hugh Dennis

In fish consumption, the situation is pretty much the same. We eat more fish than the Germans, less than the French and, at 21g per day, far, far less than the Spanish, who each eat on average 75g in every 24-hour period. Yes, it's not just football they're better at than us, it's cod-chomping as well. Incidentally, if you are interested, throughout Europe, with its largely Catholic heritage, Friday is the top fish-eating day, as you would expect, while in Sweden and Greece, it's a Tuesday. Answers on a postcard please. The amount of fish you eat also increases as you get older, and if you become a cat.

So, rather disappointingly, a nation of fish eaters we are not. In fact, our intake is really rather pathetic. This may, of course, be a modern phenomenon. Perhaps in the distant past we were like the current world champions of fish-eating, that other great island nation, Japan, who with an average per capita intake of 69kg of fish every year, eat one in ten of all the fish consumed in the world. In fact, they are eating so many, and so fast, that they often don't have time to cook them.

But of course Japan has an advantage in the world fish-eating league, in that the eating of four-legged animals was illegal for over 1,000 years, and fish therefore became the staple protein, and vastly important culturally. Although it is culturally important here too: throughout the nineteenth and twentieth centuries, fish and chips was the national dish, and we weren't going to give up that tradition to some foreign import, until we tasted chicken tikka masala.

For an island nation, in which no one lives more than 73 miles from the sea, it is still a bit surprising that we eat so few of its creatures, but statistics are statistics and, to be honest,

I have developed a new-found respect for the people who compile the fish ones. I just hope they also go salsa dancing or something.

Other aspects of our sea-faring culture have declined as well. It is now hard to believe that the Royal Navy, which now has only 36 capital ships, including a pedalo and two aircraft carriers on which the crew will have to run up and down the deck with their arms out pretending to be aeroplanes, was once the pre-eminent global naval force.

We are still obsessed by the sea though. Well, a lot of people on the internet seem to be worried about which place in Britain is furthest from it, although, once again, no one seems able to give a clear answer. Some say Coton in Cambridgeshire; some say Ashbourne in Derbyshire. It all seems to depend on where the coast actually is and how far the tide comes in. I say we phone Mandelbrot. Actually, *you* can phone Mandelbrot; I've got to get on and ask my next question.

Where did all that British etiquette come from?

PLEASE KNOCK BEFORE ENTERING

At the start of the Olympics, Transport for London placed a poster in their tube stations which was designed to encourage the thousands of foreign visitors to the capital to stand on the right of the escalators. There was a line drawing of a pair of feet standing on the correct side of the moving staircase, and next to it, in very large letters, the words, 'A little courtesy won't hurt you.'

A message suggesting that not only would our foreign visitors be standing on the wrong side, but that they would doing it deliberately. Indeed, that even before the Games had begun, they were already doing it, and that we had been pushed to the very limits of our tolerance. Did our uncivilized overseas visitors not realize that standing on the left of this essential piece of the urban transport network could hold up hard-working London commuters for periods as long as 30 seconds, make them late for work, and ruin the fragile British economy?

And yet, in spite of such posters, Britain has a global reputation for courtesy, decorum and its intricate system of etiquette.

It is a reputation that will have been enhanced by the Games themselves, and particularly by the Games Makers, whose willingness to help everyone and make sure that they had the best possible visit to these shores was nothing short of magnificent. Whether Mandeville will have equally impressed our overseas visitors is hard to say. He – or indeed she, I have never been clear on how to sex a mascot – seemed determined to overturn the stereotype of British reserve by practically assaulting the athletes as soon as they had finished their races, especially if they stood still to be interviewed, rather than using the clear advantage an Olympic athlete will have over the mutant child of Cyclops and a toothpaste tube, namely getaway speed.

Courtesy stands at the centre of British life. Economists don't agree, but I suspect that the reason we seem to be coming out of recession later than any of the other major industrialized nations may simply be politeness. We are just letting the others go first. To the uninitiated, the labyrinth that is British manners seems very daunting.

Foreign students, for example, worried about the culture shock of arriving in the UK and checking on the web for tips on how they should behave, are faced with a bewildering array of rules, although the websites do seem to be rather behind the times. One, in a section entitled 'Manners', gives very clear instructions on the making of tea, encouraging the user to use a strainer when pouring from the pot and to refill it with hot water when the tea becomes too strong. Quite right, and a useful tip if part of your journey has involved falling through a hole in the fabric of space–time to the Britain of Formica, china, and Bakelite. It is, however, rather more complicated than it needs to be, given that Tetley introduced the tea bag to the UK in 1953. Likewise there are instructions on the eating of a cream tea, where instead of a simple 'Eat it how you like, but be sure to pre-book an appointment with a cardiac unit' there are very complicated and frightening instructions on what the British will expect of the first-time cream tea eater. The scone – and, surprisingly, there are no instructions on how this should be pronounced – should first be halved with a knife horizontally. Jam should be added to each half, there is no need for butter, and finally cream added on the top. At this point, the two halves should be eaten separately. On no account should you put one on top of the other to make a sandwich, as that would be a dead giveaway that, frankly, you have no idea what you are doing. Stick to the instructions, however, and you will fit seamlessly into British life, until of course you try to pronounce the word 'scone'.

Even eating peas gets its own section, students being told that they should squash them against the reverse side of their fork, which seems a bit pointless to me. If you are going to squash them, why not cut out the middle man and go straight for the mushy ones?

The etiquette of tipping is also included. It is apparently essential to press the money subtly into the tippee's hand, thereby making even the most innocent transaction look like a covert drugs deal. Students are also advised never to talk about religion or politics at the table, which sounds reasonable, except that large numbers of them will have come here to study religion or politics, and never to gossip about acquaintances, even if they have made a complete hash of eating a scone. Surprisingly, they are also taught how to ask for the toilet, which is of course wrong. Toilet is a horrible word; in this house it is lavatory or loo, darling. We don't have a toilet, or a lounge, or a settee. Now pick up your serviette and start calling it a napkin.

Charming as it is, all this advice is, of course, largely irrelevant, unless the said students are hoping to be extras in an episode of *Miss Marple*, or have arranged to spend their three years of study living with an octogenarian spinster in a country vicarage. If they don't want to stand out as students, the advice they really need is that they should rarely wash, eat only Doritos, occasionally topped with something healthy like an old chicken nugget they've found at the back of the fridge, and watch every episode of *Loose Women* in tracky bottoms whilst drinking Red Bull. But then, even this advice will apply only fleetingly. As soon as tuition fees kick in properly, overseas students will only fit in with their British counterparts if they too are scavenging in the woods for food and burning their own furniture to keep warm.

Yet even though our system of etiquette is far simpler than it used to be, it is true that not quite knowing what to do can still be a nightmare. Who here can honestly say that they haven't at some point worried about how they should be holding a tea cup, which knife and fork to use, or whether it is socially acceptable just to leave in the morning? Even now there are genuine codes of conduct for certain social situations that become even more intricate as you progress up the social scale. Dealings with royalty are particularly tricky. For example, if you are leaving a room having met the queen, you are expected to reverse out towards the door you came in through, as you should never turn your back on the monarch. Why, I am not quite sure; she is after all very unlikely to nick anything. Likewise, you should never speak to the monarch unless you are spoken to, which is why I have a friend who still feels guilty about his one and only meeting with the queen. She came to open his school hall, the previous one having been destroyed by arson three years earlier. Nothing to do with him, I should add. As Head Boy, he was to be introduced to her in the Headmaster's study, but no one had told him about the etiquette of such an occasion and, introductions over, he turned on his heel and left. Realizing he had made a social gaffe, he was then unable to apologize for it, except by starting a conversation, which etiquette dictated he was not allowed to do. He has carried the guilt with him for 30 years.

Did I say 'friend'? All right, it was me.

So, as one of the politest nations on earth – the most polite seems to be Canada, but that is a title we have let them have for fear of appearing rude – and as the country whose etiquette seems to be most widely known across the globe, not least because *Downton Abbey* is on literally everywhere, including Iceland, Vladivostok and the Democratic Republic of Congo, the assumption must be that we pretty much invented the whole thing in the first place. Oh dear, I'm not sure how to put this without upsetting anyone: the truth is that we didn't.

Etiquette has been part of civilized society for thousands of years. Confucius mulled over it, and the correct manners for those serving a king merit a mention in *Beowolf*. Courtesy – in short, the conduct expected at court – became increasingly important during the Middle Ages, when knights decided that if they didn't behave decently no one would be able to call it the Age of Chivalry. There were, for example, rules covering who was allowed to speak first when knights met, and the situation was sometimes so unclear that no one said anything at all for fear of getting it wrong. At the Battle of Crecy in 1346, the King of France sent a team of knights on a reconnaissance of the English lines. When he asked them what they had found out, none of them could work out the correct order of preference or deference, and they just stood there like a group of teenagers accused of breaking a window. Eventually the king had to order one to speak, who then apologized to His Majesty for having turned his back on him earlier.

The church also played a key role. One of the first proper books of etiquette was written in 1204 by a Spanish priest, Pedro Alfonso, and was called *Disciplina Clericalis*. What it said, I am afraid I am unable to tell you, but I guess it tells clerics to beat themselves up about stuff, attend as many services as possible and stay away from nuns.

The word etiquette, however, is from French, as you may well have delighted Michael Gove by working out, and comes from the verb *etiqueter*, meaning to stick or label. Its transformation into the word we know comes from the habits of King Louis XIV, who apparently delighted in leaving little notices around the court telling his courtiers how to behave. Mostly these related to keeping out of his private bits of the Palace of Versailles, although I would like to think that at least some of them said, 'Please wash up your mug, no one else is going to do it!' Or, 'This milk is mine. If you want some, buy your own!'

To be fair, Louis did have a rather large court to administer. At its height, Versailles was home to some 19,000 people, made up of 1,000 noblemen, their 4,000 servants, Louis' own staff of 5,000 and 9,000 soldiers. For comparison, this gives it the same population as Worthing, Skegness or Truro, although I suspect it was rather more stylish than any of them. Louis XIV was, after all, 'the Sun King', not something we have now, although given the support he was given during his election campaigns and the fact that he is godparent to one of Rupert Murdoch's children, Tony Blair might lay claim to the title 'Sun Prime Minister'.

As his reign continued, Louis' system of etiquette developed beyond the copious use of multi-coloured Baroque post-it notes, and became a highly intricate system for controlling those noblemen who might otherwise plot against him.

Practically everything in the court was proscribed. No door was to be knocked upon, for example. Instead, those wishing to enter were expected to scratch at it with their little fingers until they were let in, which must have been terrible for the paintwork. Many courtiers grew extra-long nails to make the scratching easier, and along with a shellac finish, nail repair and rescue base coats became the most popular treatments at the Versailles Nail Bar.

Louis loved ballet and was apparently immensely proud of his own very shapely legs. So, to give him a chance to show off his beautifully honed calves and natural sense of rhythm, he developed various extreme dance-like forms of bowing and curtsying. Gentlemen were given set movements for sitting down in a chair: the left foot was to be slid behind the right before lowering oneself to the seat. There were even rules defining the types of chairs that the different ranks within the court were allowed. The king and queen, being the most important, each had an armchair, or *fauteuil*, which was throne-like and had plenty to grab on to. The next rank down, including the king's own brother, the Duc d'Orléans, were allowed only chairs with no arms, while the rank below that, plain old duchesses, for example, had to make do with stools. It was a rule that was rigidly enforced in all social situations. Thank goodness they never took a ride on a rollercoaster.

The most extreme form of court etiquette, however, was the gathering of the court to watch the king get out of bed in the morning and get dressed.

Watching monarchs rubbing their eyes and mumbling, 'What time is it? I think I'll just have another ten minutes' had long been a privilege granted to the closest courtiers, and was regarded by others as the best time to ask their king a favour. When he wasn't creating the Carolingian Empire, beating up the Saxons and the Bavarians, and unifying what is now the whole of Western Europe, Charlemagne liked to invite his advisors in to watch him put on his shoes. And every morning he would show the assembled crowd that there was a compass in the heel.

Louis XIV, however, took things a bit further. His morning routine was divided into two main sections. First came the *Petit Lever*, conducted within his own bedchamber. His physician, his surgeon and his nurse would nudge him into consciousness.

Most of us would be rather alarmed if the first thing we saw was a doctor and a nurse staring down at us, but this didn't seem to worry the Sun King at all. Once Louis had been woken, and kissed on the head by those present, a select group of noblemen was admitted, some because of their rank, and others because they had bought tickets. They then watched Louis getting undressed, while at least half of them wondered what had gone wrong, because they had thought they were off to the O2 to see Michael McIntyre. Roles in the undressing were clearly assigned. The Master of the Bedchamber removed the king's nightshirt, while the Grand Chamberlain of France presented him with his new day-shirt, which had been pre-warmed and wrung out from the previous wearing. Delightfully, Louis had a tendency to sweat profusely. Some accounts also suggest that a nobleman would be required to wipe the perspiration from the skin of the monarch, a job that had no effect at all on the future career path of the Duc du Garnier. Once dried, there was then a brief break during which the noblemen present could petition the monarch for favours, although not the favour they most wanted to ask: 'Would you mind just slipping some pants on, Your Majesty? We are all finding this a bit disconcerting.'

The dressing of the monarch then began. Louis liked to dress himself because, like dancing, he thought he was really good at it, and as he progressed through the many layers of apparel, struggling with a cuff here and a ruff there, further small groups of courtiers were admitted to the increasingly crowded chamber in a strictly controlled order. Ladies were only allowed to enter in the fifth group, and in the sixth, his many children could join their mothers and squeeze into any small spaces they could find in the corners, by the door and between people's legs. By the time Louis was putting on his socks, it must have been like dressing on a tube train in rush hour.

Once the king was fully dressed, he began the second stage of getting up, or *Grand Levee*. Louis left his bedchamber, shouting, 'Excuse me, excuse me, could I slip past please? This is my stop,' to enter the *Grande Galerie*, where the rest of the court was waiting for him in their hundreds.

By tying up their time with protocol and demanding that they be at Versailles if they were to extract any favours from him, Louis XIV effectively stopped the nobility from meddling in politics and kept them quiet. Over time, however, this method of control rather backfired. Those ordinary citizens disenfranchised by the system became more and more disenchanted with it. By 1789 the sight of grovelling, landed aristocrats whose special skills included monarchical sweat wiping, the *pas de deux* and never using a doorbell became too much to bear for the lower classes and the French Revolution began, taking with it the intricate etiquette of Versailles.

By then, however, some of its less extreme forms had spread across the world on a tide of fashion. The *levee* became popular in the British court and was introduced to North America by George Washington, where it took the form of a fully dressed morning social gathering. Washington, in fact, had shown a very early interest in etiquette, having written in his schoolbook a guide to social conduct entitled *Rules of Civility and Decent Behaviour in Company and Conversation*. He was 16 years old; what on earth was wrong with him?

It did, however, contain much advice that is relevant to social situations today. For example, 'When in company, put not your hands to parts of the body not usually discovered,' which is excellent advice for parents to give their young children, although I prefer the slightly more direct 'Get your hands out of there and stop fiddling.'

Those commuting will still appreciate the rule 'In the presence of others sing not to yourself with a humming noise.' No. Nor let your iPod do it for you, especially on trains, although this is merely the first phrase of that particular rule. Washington continues, 'Shake not the head, feet or legs, roll not the eyes. Lift not one eyebrow higher than the other.' How relieved must Roger Moore be that he wasn't born in Virginia in the late eighteenth century?

As a man who famously chose to wear a set of wooden dentures later in life, Washington was also remarkably definite about acceptable methods of dental hygiene. 'Cleanse not your teeth with a table cloth, napkin, or fork or knife, but if others do it then let it be done with a tooth pick.' Although that was only one of the cleansing methods open to George himself. He could also get off that nasty build-up of food, tartar and plaque with a plane, a chisel or a sander.

In Britain, unaffected by the revolution across the channel, the royal family continued to rather like the opulence, grandeur and manners that had so absorbed and fascinated their French counterparts, even if it had led to their downfall. For the Prince Regent, a man who despite the efforts of numerous contemporary portrait painters will still be thought of as looking like Hugh Laurie, a sense of style was particularly paramount. This was the age of dandyism. The age of Beau Brummell, the arbiter of high fashion, whose influence might not have been quite as great had anyone realized that his first name was actually plain old George – and worse still, his middle name was Bryan.

On these shores, though, the key period in the development of what we now think of as contemporary courtesy was the reign of Queen Victoria.

By the time Victoria came to the throne in 1837, the middle class was growing rapidly and saw correct manners and deportment as their passport to the social acceptance that merely having money could never bring them. Spotting the opportunity for a profit, publishers produced a continual stream of books on etiquette. Refinement became a measure of status, and gentility a means of showing disapproval for the boorish and promiscuous behaviour that had characterized the lifestyle of previous generations. The result was a set of rules so complex that those of cricket seemed like learning how to boil a kettle, and a female dress code so strict that it made wearing a burka feel a bit racy.

The new middle classes were told they needed enormous sets of cutlery, with different utensils for every possible culinary requirement. Cheese scoops, sugar tongs and fish knives were all eagerly adopted as a means of moving up in the world, even if, like the fish knife itself, they were simply pointless. As an eating implement, it has no possible advantage over any other kind of knife, although if teenagers could be convinced to carry something as blunt, stabbings would drop off markedly

Female ankles were never to be seen, women were never to turn to look back at someone in the street, to look around in church, or, if single, to be alone with an unmarried man. To be caught in such a way might be the ruin of the lady concerned. When Lady Dorothy Nevill, daughter of the third Earl of Oxford, was caught in a summerhouse with George Smythe MP, no one believed their story about checking on the tomatoes and assumed that she had been hoping to see his dibber. Nor were they convinced by Dorothy's argument that she had standards and that she had been having an illicit rendezvous she would have chosen a classier venue than a building you can buy in the Homebase Garden section. Dorothy was ruined and excluded from court by Victoria, whilst Smythe was able to carry on his parliamentary career as normal, and to have his moat cleaned at the taxpayers' expense and claim the summer-house as a second home. In fact, relieved of the constant worry that she might let herself down, by having already done so in the most spectacular way, Dorothy ended up having a rather more satisfying life than she might have done otherwise. She became a noted horticulturalist who supplied plants to Charles Darwin. She married a cousin twenty years her senior, and after he died, is rumoured to have had an illegitimate son with Benjamin Disraeli. Good on her.

The strictness of etiquette was so tight that it often made it difficult for couples to actually tell each other how they felt. Which is why the period became the golden age of floriography. Nowadays you might think that floriography is simply the way that geography students describe which course they are on after 12 pints in the Union bar, or that it is one of those degrees for which places are still available at the New Polytechnic University of the North West East Midlands, but in Victorian times, floriography, the art of communicating through flowers, was vital for couples who wanted to get it together, make up, or go their separate ways but simply couldn't tell each other in the modern manner. That is, by speaking.

To explain their feelings, gentlemen would send ladies small bouquets which held within them a coded message and, as you would expect of the Victorians, the language of flowers was very complicated indeed. If you think how ornate and twirly St Pancras station is, you won't be surprised at the intricacy of the messages carried in such small nosegays. Often they were just as incomprehensible to the unacquainted as a teenager's text message is now, although on the plus side, they did smell nice.

Some flowers had meanings stretching back into antiquity – rosemary, for example, had always signified remembrance – but now almost everything that was available came to mean something.

A red rose was true love, while a light pink rose meant desire, or in modern parlance, 'I really fancy you.' A red and yellow rose, however, meant joy or happiness, and not, as you might now think, 'This bouquet is patrolled by a lifeguard.' A red tulip carried the message 'hopeless love', which is either the kind of thing you might say to a lover you know you can never be with, or something a wife says to her husband after his latest attempt at DIY.

Viscaria (no, I had never heard of it either) was an invitation to dance; aloe meant grief, presumably that you had got so badly sunburned, you had to rub aloe on it; while asparagus meant fascination – possibly a fascination that someone had got together a really nice bouquet and then thought to stick asparagus in it.

A yellow carnation carried the simple message 'You have disappointed me,' which would make it a favourite flower of the Bond villain. A houseleek signified domestic economy, while cabbage, not something my own wife would be that thrilled to receive from Interflora, meant 'profit', which isn't surprising when you compare the price of a cabbage with the amount you would have to shell out on proper flowers. Strangely, coriander meant lust, although, thinking about it, I often feel a little frisky after a curry and beer.

With the burgeoning Empire, these British habits spread across the globe, bringing us the reputation of a nation mired in etiquette and grounded in courtesy. A nation whose people tended to do things rather differently from everyone else, and although we can't claim to have invented politeness, it does seem to remain in the national DNA. Last year I had my wallet taken in central London. It contained everything from cash, to credit cards, to photos of my wife and children, and crucially for this story, my photo driving licence with my address on it. Obviously, as soon as I was aware that it was missing, I cancelled everything and assumed that would be that, but no. Ten days later a neatly addressed envelope arrived in the post through my letterbox. In it was everything that had been taken, bar the cash and the wallet itself, all wrapped neatly in kitchen towel held together with Sellotape. It was as though the thief had thought, 'I may have robbed this man, but I have inconvenienced him enough, I will return to him the things I don't require, for that is the British way.'

Many early manners remain. Gentlemen are still expected to take their hats off indoors, especially if it is a motorbike helmet and they are in a building society, which is exactly what knights were required to do with their helmets when in the presence of the king, so as to show him that they were un-threatening and did not challenge his authority. I can't imagine they minded removing them very much. The weight of a helmet probably meant they had to sack a castle or two just to pay the chiropractor. Coats, likewise, are not generally to be worn indoors, and nor are shoes, according to that online student's guide to manners, 'unless your host tells you specific-ally that it is OK'. Personally, given what I have seen and smelled of other people's feet, I would rather my guests kept their shoes on.

In reality, though, a century after the death of Queen Victoria, Britain isn't that different from anywhere else. Most of the things that we regard as rude are also thought rude across the Western World. We are not the only people who shake hands, raise hats, or stand up when the host comes into the room. We don't seem to use any more cutlery than anyone else, or eat things in a way that no other country would consider acceptable, although, having said that, I did once attend a dining club at university where you were expected to eat an unshelled walnut with a knife and fork. It was very difficult and became much harder after drinking the various glasses of wine that were the real reason we were there. It is very awkward to spear a walnut shell, as a knife will slip easily on a hard, spherical object. Looking back, I should have used one designed for fish, but in a way I like the scars.

I am delighted to say that we do, however, do some things entirely differently from the rest of the West – driving, for example. After an Olympic opening ceremony that was quirky and mercifully different from anything any host city had produced before, one French newspaper said that they now understood why the British drive on the left. Actually, I don't think they do.

The reason for walking on the left side of the track is well documented. As most people are right-handed, it meant that if someone threatening came towards you, you would have your sword between you and them. Likewise, if you were driving a cart, you would want your whip in your right hand, so as to keep it accurate, and that meant sitting on the right side if you weren't going to get the whip tangled up in the load you were carrying. The downside, I guess, is that you might get it caught up in whoever had just gone past you in the other direction, at which point you would just drop your whip and get your sword out.

Originally, we weren't the only people to think that this made sense. There was no Highway Code as such for medieval taxi drivers to ignore, but driving on the left was fairly common throughout Europe. There is a claim that Roman armies marched on the left, but I've watched *Gladiator* and I tend to think that Roman armies marched where they bloody well liked. There is the suggestion that in AD 1300 or thereabouts Pope Boniface VIII issued an edict that pilgrims keep to the left when entering Rome. As all roads led there, it made sense to have some sort of system. And driving on the left makes still more sense, given that there is some medical evidence, admittedly questionable, that it is safer. As more people are right–handed, the non-dominant hand gets to change gear, while the dominant hand does the steering. As most people are right-eyed, the dominant eye tends to look for oncoming traffic, while the weaker eye concentrates on entirely non-dangerous things, like watching for people stepping out into the road and trying to get the radio tuned correctly, neither of which has ever been known to cause accidents.

So the question then isn't so much why do we drive on the left, as why doesn't everyone else?

For the French, the answer seems to be that Napoleon reversed everything for one of two reasons. Either because he was left-handed and preferred to steer with his left while keeping his right hand firmly in his jacket, like in all the pictures. Or, and this does seem more plausible, that French wagons were traditionally pulled by teams of horses driven by a man sitting on the rear left horse, which meant it was easier for him to pass other traffic on the left. Either way, the French standard was spread through their empire, and most of those countries didn't bother to change back once the French had gone and Napoleon was safely on St Helena, being poisoned by the paint in his own wallpaper.

Elsewhere, countries changed from left to right either because, like Austria and Czechoslovakia, they were forced to under German occupation, or because they wanted to be the same as their neighbours, who drove on the other side. Portugal swapped from left to right in 1928, Argentina in 1945, and China in 1946. Italy went right-sided as a nation in the 1920s. Prior to that, Rome, Turin, Naples and Florence were on the left, with much of the rest of the country driving on the right. In short, there was no actual rule, and having driven in Italy every summer, I'm not entirely convinced that there is even now.

In spite of the big switch to the opposite carriageway, a thrill we as Britons only get in a contraflow system, roughly one quarter of the globe still drives on the left. A large portion of these countries are former British colonies, but some, like Japan and Thailand, clearly aren't, although in the case of Japan, their choice was British-influenced, or so the story has it. During the opium wars of the nineteenth century, a brief period during which Britain did a passable impression of Stringer Bell from *The Wire* and turned drug pusher, Japan became key to our ambitions. It was at this time, with British gunboats off the coast, that our man in the Land of the Rising Sun, the magnificently named Sir Rutherford Alcock, convinced his hosts that driving on the left was superior, thereby paving the way, 150 years later, for the opening of a Nissan factory in Sunderland.

One of the main reasons for countries changing the side of the road they drive on is that border crossings can become accident black spots if neighbouring countries drive on the opposite side. Fortunately for Britain, most drivers have a whole ferry crossing to get used to the idea that on the other side of the Channel everything will be the wrong way round. For Britain then, there seems to be no good reason for swapping. Having to change the markings and signs on every road in the country might be exactly the kind of public works programme to lift us from recession, but who could live with a traffic network on which you have to take a hairpin bend at 70mph just to leave a motorway?

Hugh Dennis

And in a world that is increasingly similar, as cultures merge into one under the irresistible influence of digital technology, the fact that we are different is something to cling on to. If we have to change anything, I suggest it is escalators. That standing on the right thing, and letting people overtake you on the left – it seems, well, a bit foreign, doesn't it?

TOPIARY, TULIPS AND TITCHMARSH

Apparently, Cicero wrote, 'If a man has a garden and a library then he has everything.'

Which, from someone so bright, is obviously nonsense. A man with a garden and a library may not, for example, have a kitchen, a bedroom or a lavatory, all of which seem pretty important to me if you wish to sleep, eat, or the other thing which I can't mention due to my British sense of decorum. And, frankly, using up all that space on a library when all he had to do was buy a Kindle seems a bit odd. Still, who am I to argue with one of Rome's greatest orators when, as far as gardens go, it seems the British public agree with him?

Gardens play an enormous role in the life of the nation. Our Chelsea Flower Show, which in 2013 celebrates its centenary, is the most famous horticultural event in the world. For five days each May, 150,000 visitors take to the grounds of the Royal Hospital, while each night a further three million visit via the cameras of the BBC, keen to see Alan Titchmarsh interview the creators of the various show or artisan gardens and ask them the questions the nation wants answered. What do they think a garden should do or say? What is their attitude to pleaching, mulching and box-balls? And, most important of all, at least in the interviews I saw last year, how do they feel about the topiarizing of yew hedging?

New approaches to gardening are showcased and scrutinized. In 2012, for example, we saw Diarmuid Gavin's 'Sky Garden', a seven-storey scaffolding pyramid bedecked with plants and slides and a lift, designed to show the possibilities for a new type of urban gardening, one guaranteed to annoy the neighbours and be rejected by the planners.

We have a love affair with gardens – 90 per cent of households in Britain have one, and we spend upwards of £4 billion a year on things to put in them. Where, though, did it all begin?

As you might have guessed, like roads and aqueducts, proper gardening in Britain started with the Romans, whose legions brought with them box hedging, plums, garlic, walnuts, leeks, turnips, cabbages and roses. It is amazing what you can fit under a helmet. At the earliest recorded Roman garden at Fishbourne in Sussex, there is also evidence of topiary, suggesting that the garden was used for both cultivation and just pottering around in. In AD 278 Emperor Probus, the first Roman emperor to sound like a Toyota Hybrid, allowed the setting up of vineyards in Britain, an experiment which even nearly 2,000 years later has not proved entirely successful, particularly where they first tried it, in North Lincolnshire.

Once the Romans had left, however, gardening entered the Dark Ages, which was not a good thing at all for plants relying on photosynthesis. Only after the Norman Conquest did it start to bud and flower again, and begin the period of sustained growth that has continued until the modern era.

In the early medieval period, the major problem for gardens was that no one really stayed in one place long enough to make a go of them. The royal courts were peripatetic; the King and noblemen moved between a selection of royal palaces and castles, and couldn't really be bothered to think about getting out the trowel and popping a few bulbs in, just to make the moat look more attractive. Settlements or villages often moved location to find more fertile land, or to get away from fighting, so there too gardening was a low priority. Even now, temporary residents tend to care less about the garden than those who are permanent. I once lived next door to a house that had been subdivided into bedsits, and nothing much seemed to grow in the garden there except old fridges and bicycles.

To be honest, at this point, the British were a little behind the leaders of the European Gardening League, namely the Spanish. In Spain the Islamic influence of the Moors had made the creation of gardens rather more-ish. They had sprung up everywhere, including towns; the city of Cordoba was said to have over 50,000 of them. Of course, over the intervening millennium, we have caught up, which is encouraging for football. If the timescale operates in the same way in that arena, we will emulate Spain by winning the World Cup again at some point in the twenty-seventh century. Muslim gardens were religious and sensuous, laid out to symbolize the four quarters of the universe, and containing fragrant plants such as roses, jasmine and hyacinth. Indeed, in the Koran, the faithful are promised not only a supply of attractive women in eternity, but that it would be spent in a beautiful garden. Someone should tell that to terrorists. Telling a man he has virgins waiting for him is one thing. Telling him that there will also be a rake and a Flymo is something completely different.

Britain wasn't gardenless in this period, but there weren't many of them, and they were mainly restricted to monasteries, where the plants were grown for medicinal or culinary use. A monastery garden, incidentally, was known as a garth, and was a place both for cultivation and contemplation, which I will be pointing out to Garth Crooks should I ever be asked onto *Match of the Day 2*. And although at this point there was little to distinguish gardening from agriculture, there is also evidence that this was when the still recognizable shape of British gardens began to be established. Cottages might have had back and front gardens, the latter divided by a long, straight path, to make cultivation easier. And although most gardens were essentially big vegetable patches, there is evidence that not all time outside was spent in the back-breaking work of producing food. By the thirteenth century, there was a small pleasure garden at Smithfield, and on high days and holidays people would head out from the city of London to enjoy the fresh air of renowned local beauty spots such as Hackney and Hoxton.

And the royals were at it too. Henry II had a cloistered garden at Everswell in Oxfordshire, in which he also provided a home for all the gifts he had received from foreign rulers, including lynxes, camels, a porcupine and a crocodile, which must have made being a gardener there rather more exciting than it needed to be.

Even if it was mostly monks, monarchs and murderous reptiles scrabbling about in the medieval shrubbery, British gardening was on its way, although we were still way off the 12 minutes that the average British man now spends in the garden every day, or the seven minutes spent there by the average British woman. I do, by the way, doubt whether all of the 12 minutes spent by males in the garden is occupied by gardening. If the average British man is anything like me, a large proportion of the time will be spent fumbling in his bag, looking for his front-door key, unwilling to ring the bell for fear of being told that this is typical and that he is always losing them. Judged by this particular criterion of time spent in the garden, the greatest gardeners in Europe are Slovenian men, who spend roughly half an hour a day somewhere between the front door and the fence. My theory is they have very fierce wives.

Oddly, one of the biggest fillips to our national gardening obsession may have come with one of the most unpleasant episodes in our history, the Black Death.

In 1348–50 this plague wiped out roughly one third of the population of Europe, meaning there was more land for those who were left. Pretty much the only people on the Continent to be untouched were the Poles. Presumably God had decided he needed them fresh for the rebuilding work.

In 1440, or thereabouts, we saw the publication of one of the first English gardening manuals, *The Feate of Gardening* by 'John the Gardener', who I think had an affair with Gabrielle Solis in *Desperate Housewives*. By the end of the century kings were involved. In 1514 Cardinal Wolsey bought Hampton Court and began to create a garden there, and in 1525 Henry VIII decided he liked it so much that he nicked it from him. Thomas Cromwell, star of *Wolf Hall* and Wolsey's successor as most powerful minister of the crown, was apparently so annoyed at the small size of his London garden that, without asking, he dug out his neighbour's wooden house and had it picked up and moved 20 feet further away, to increase the size of his own plot.

Henry VIII, however, didn't only help the gardens of England on their way; he was also to play a role in the emergence of the county of Kent as the 'Garden of England'. Henry was partial to many things, among them other people's wives, beef and songwriting, although there is no truth in the rumour that he wrote *Greensleeves* on the day he had forgotten his hand-kerchief. He loved fruit, and he and Anne Boleyn often pigged out on strawberries, cherries and apples, in an attempt to get their five a day. For Henry, though, the grass was often greener than the sleeve he was holding next to it. He yearned for more and different fruits than England had to offer, and instructed his fruiterer, one Richard Harris (not the one who used to play Dumbledore), to travel to the Continent and bring back new varieties. When Harris returned, he planted 105 acres of apple and cherry trees at Teynham in Kent. From there, the fashion for orchard planting spread throughout the county, gaining Kent its soubriquet.

And Harris wasn't the only Tudor plant hunter for whom the world was opening up. Explorers such as Raleigh and Drake were soon scouring the world for plants that were not available on these shores. Raleigh is credited with the introduction of the potato to Britain, which suggests that etiquette had gone crazy even then –'Britain, can I introduce the potato? Potato, this is Britain.'

Unfortunately, it is a story that appears to be untrue. The potato was apparently already known in Britain via the Spanish, so it seems unlikely that Sir Walter would have risked asking Queen Elizabeth, 'Your majesty, do you know what this is?' for fear that she would answer, 'Yes, you idiot, that is a potato.' Unless, of course, he too wanted to be peeled, quartered and dropped in boiling water.

Either way, the potato soon caught on, and the spud, named after the spade-like tool used for planting them, became a staple of the British diet, available chipped, boiled, mashed or baked. Drake and Raleigh were soldiers, but many Tudor plant hunters had a greater devotion to horticulture. John Tradescant was the head gardener at Hatfield House, and in 1610 was asked by the Earl of Salisbury to travel to the Low Countries and gather fruit trees. The trip seemed to have given him the travel bug, and after it you couldn't stop him nipping off abroad to steal plants. He visited arctic Russia, Palestine and what was then known as Barbary, the lands along the west coast of North Africa. And from each expedition, he brought back specimens: strawberries from Brussels, plums from Turkey and hellebores from Russia. Such was his devotion to the future of British gardening that he even joined a fleet sent against murderous Barbary pirates in order to seek out an elusive apricot. Monty Don wouldn't do that, even if you bought him the ticket to Somalia.

With the dissolution of the monasteries under Henry, much of the land formerly owned by the orders had been grabbed by noblemen, and the former abbeys were turned into massive private houses with huge curtains and an enormous heating bill. The link between religion and gardening became broken and the design of gardens became slightly more frivolous. Mazes and knot gardens became popular, as did the idea of gardens as places for gentle exercise. Specially built banqueting houses were often constructed at the end of long paths, so dinner guests could head there for pudding and burn off some of the first course, which was eaten in the main house. Nice idea, but if it is exercise you are after, I still favour a large plastic goal on the lawn, or a basketball hoop attached to the garage. It is a lot cheaper.

Even at this point, Europe was still fonder of its plants than we were. By 1637 gardening across the Continent was so fashionable that the world experienced its one and only tulip mania. In Amsterdam single tulip bulbs were changing hands for the price of a one-bedroom flat, that being ten times the wage of a skilled craftsman. All over Holland young people were wondering how on earth they would get on the tulip ladder when the market abruptly collapsed. Bulb merchants at the traditional tulip auction in Haarlem were surprised that no one was there to buy their goods, and panicked. The simple explanation – that the people of the town were at that moment somewhat inconvenienced by a bout of the bubonic plague – did nothing to calm the market, and the tulip contagion spread. Fortunes were lost, businesses were ruined and bulbs became cheap enough for most of us to plant in our gardens.

England, meanwhile, was drifting towards civil war, as parliament turned against the king and Cavalier lined up against

Roundhead. Not much time for gardening, you would think, and yet for many there was. To avoiding taking sides in what was becoming an increasingly bitter conflict, many men decided the very best course was to keep their heads down and avoid all confrontation by spending a decade pottering in the garden, or sitting in the shed. This technique is still used today, as all men who head off to do the lawn when the children refuse to do their homework will testify.

Once restored to the throne, Charles II set about reintroducing the elaborate gardens that the Puritans had ripped out. Formality was in favour, and many of the styles that Charles had come to like during his exile in France were used, particularly that of the rigid, etiquette-bound Palace of Versailles, which sprang up in various mini versions throughout England. When William and Mary succeeded James II in 1689, they brought with them the Dutch style of parterres. It was total gardening, with greater use of water, and plants able to play in any position in the garden.

Our gardens were becoming a national pastime. Everyone was at it. As prosperity increased, our fingers got greener. There was barely an aristocratic home that didn't mimic greater estates elsewhere, barely a cottage, particularly in the south of England, that didn't compete with the house next door, and barely a rural shop that didn't fuss over the wilting display in its flowerpots. The whole place was beginning to look like the poster for a Britain in Bloom competition. The British obsession was developing nicely; a bit more nurturing and it would be fully rooted.

By the end of the seventeenth century it was also fashionable for Britain's young noblemen and sons of the landed gentry to head off on the Grand Tour. Designed to introduce the elite of Britain's youth to the treasures of the Renaissance and antiquity, and expose them to the sophistication of continental society, this was essentially the equivalent of a student gap year, but without the backpack, the girls, or the telephone call from Thailand to tell you that their credit card has been nicked.

Along with a tutor, a French-speaking guide and, if money allowed, a retinue of cooks and servants, each hapless young Grand Tourist would head for Calais, hire a coach and visit every museum, gallery, concert and garden that Europe could throw at him. Traditionally, the tour would take in the Spanish Netherlands, Belgium, Switzerland, Spain, Italy and Germany, before returning the exhausted young man to Dover, where he would throw away his 'Nobleman on Tour' T-Shirt and vow never to look at a bloody statue again. By then, of course, he would be a young sophisticate, ready to take his place in society, or so it was hoped.

In Paris he would have had lessons in dancing, fencing, riding and courtly behaviour, and possibly been shown the very room where the crowds had watched Louis XIV have his sweat wiped off with a Hyper-U sponge cloth. In Geneva he would have learned the intricacies of hiding gold and making triangular chocolate; in Florence he would have spent days wandering through the Uffizi Gallery, adjusting his headphones so it looked like he was listening to the gallery guide rather than his iPod; and in Rome he would have studied the ruins of the ancient city, taken in the architecture of the Renaissance, and marvelled at Vivaldi's *Four Seasons*, wondering whether it should have more cheese on top.

From Naples, some visited Pompeii and Herculaneum, and climbed Mount Vesuvius, active volcanoes being something of a rarity to those from England. Whilst in Venice, no young man was allowed to leave until he had seen the wonders of Byzantine architecture and mastered the music from the Cornetto adverts.

And the key rule of the Grand Tour was that whatever happened on the Grand Tour was not to stay on the Grand Tour. Returning to England, the young men would bring with them crates of statues, paintings, books and novelties that would then adorn their houses for years to come. Carrying all this stuff around the Continent made progress extremely slow, of course, which is why the clever thought they would just get all the presents at the airport on the way home.

For British gardening, the effect was marked, as stately homes began to take on some of the characteristics of classical antiquity. Ionic temples and amphitheatres appeared in the grounds, and statues of Diana and her nymphs bathing became all the rage. But change was afoot. In 1789 the French finally got fed up with the mathematics of working out which number the next Louis would be and decided to get rid of him and his mates instead by the use of Madame Guillotine. Some aristocrats tried to escape in disguise, but more often than not were given away by their dancing shoes, the elaborate flourish with which they lifted their hats and their habit of scratching the Dulux off doors with their little fingers. And with the French court went the garden designs it had championed. Formality suddenly took a nosedive. In Britain, a country that prided itself on its parliament, its free speech and its democracy, it was no longer thought appropriate to have gardens modelled on the autocratic regime of France.

Enter Capability Brown.

Capability Brown is probably the best remembered of all British garden designers, which just goes to show that everyone remembers a silly name. In truth, he was probably not that much better than his contemporaries, but they made the classic marketing error of going for names which were instantly forgettable, like Humphry Repton, William Kent, Ralph Allen and ... erm, I can't remember. Capability knew precisely what he was doing. My bet is that he also had a van with his name on the side, and put a board with his details on it at the front gate of every garden he worked on.

Capability reigned supreme. His idea was a simple one. Having lots of flower beds and intricate hedging near the front of your house meant a lot of expense, a lot of messy digging and a lot of maintenance afterwards. It would be far simpler and cheaper to do away with all that and just get people to look out of their windows to the far distance. It would be cheaper still, of course, if there were no windows, but he doesn't seem to have mentioned that.

His style, which was new to England, was therefore to run grass up to the house, dot the landscape with clumps of trees and lakes and make the countryside beyond look like you owned that as well, even if you didn't. In short, to make the house seamlessly integrate with the landscape that surrounded it, so that one naturally flowed into the other, without the fussiness of formality. I'm sorry, I seem to be channelling Kevin McCloud.

As a result, this was the age of the 'ha-ha', or deep-sided ditch. Worried that fences would catch one's eye as it gazed tear-filled and full of pride at the scenery that Brown and his contemporaries had created, landscape designers put in trenches instead, to keep the livestock in the correct bit of the garden. This was no problem unless you were coming back from the pub slightly worse for wear on a moonless night. Capability Brown would be fine, but Incapability Brown would more than likely be found face down in the trench, with his head in a sheep.

Brown's was a style that worked. He was responsible for the gardens of more than 170 stately homes in Britain which, given how long many of them took to finish, obviously means that he wasn't averse to saying he was just nipping off for some materials and then going to another job. The gardens he worked on include those of Blenheim Palace, Harewood House and Milton Abbey in Dorset. Subsequently, his style became criticized as rather bland, but many of his gardens remain largely unchanged, and his spirit lives on in anyone who has gone for a low-maintenance garden. Next time anyone tells you that you need more than a bit of lawn, a pond with a liner and a tree, refer them to Capabilty Brown. I reckon, given half the chance, he would have thrown away all those sashes and given Blenheim a full set of UPVC windows

Brown's trick had been to harness the landscape and, although it sounds unlikely, this is the period during which the term 'landscape gardener' seems to have originated. Although more commonly used in the nineteenth century than the eighteenth, it absolutely isn't as modern a term as it seems.

Strange, isn't it? I wonder if Brown had a personal Pilates coach and a man who sorted out his IT?

Brown's style gave way to Romanticism, which meant grottoes, I think, although there is nothing less romantic than grazing yourself while fumbling with your lover against the rough stone interior of a pretend cave. The aristocracy of Britain now wanted gardens which appeared wild, romantic and beautiful, which often meant that their gardens would have lumps of granite randomly thrown into them and dead trees deposited at discreet intervals, in order to achieve the effect. Even those of a somewhat more modest income had a go. Edward Jenner, now most famous for his work in eradicating smallpox, had a small romantic thatched shed built in his garden called 'the Temple of Vaccinia', into which he enticed the poor people of the village and inoculated them free of charge. It sounds far better than a normal surgery, doesn't it, but I bet you still couldn't ever get an appointment, and that the receptionist was really frightening.

Obviously this type of expansive, romantic gardening wasn't really open to the growing body of untitled or poorer gardeners that was emerging throughout Britain, but they might have been able to see examples of it. By the turn of the nineteenth century, it was possible to get yourself shown around the gardens of a stately home by slipping the owner or his staff a shilling or two, although without a tea room or a shop there was no chance to buy that National Trust picnic rug that you will never use.

Gardening was becoming a national pursuit and recreation. By the time Victoria began her reign, the taste for gardens in

England was firmly established, and the vast majority of newly built houses had them, which marked Britain out from the rest of Europe. In 1822 the then most successful garden designer of his generation, John Claudius Loudon, published his *Encyclopedia of Gardening*, probably the first book aimed at those with smallish town or village gardens, rather than those with the rolling acres of a rural estate. With the burgeoning urban population of the industrial age, and the growth of the middle class, suburbs and suburban villas were springing up around all the major conurbations, and gardening books took pride of place in bookcases all over Britain, as long as the volumes on etiquette said that was the correct place to put them. For authors, it was a lucrative area. Loudon, for example, was said to have written 66 million pieces of gardening advice in his lifetime. For town gardens, he provided a series of possible designs that were often followed religiously. He also gave tips on soil improvement, including one to bury the carcasses of dogs, deer, horses and partially rotted fish in your flower beds, suggesting that in Victorian London the smell was already so bad that having putrid, decaying animals by your back door would make no difference. Presumably they also had no worries about urban foxes digging up the petunias in search of a tasty snack.

The designs Loudon suggested are still recognizable. His 'Gardenesque' style worked on the principle that a plant would only make an impact if you made it stand out from the rest of the garden. He wasn't interested in mimicking nature, instead preferring tidy, precise beds, often circular, in which the plants could be shown. In other words, he created today's standard suburban garden. He was modern in many other ways too. Loudon advocated the idea of green belts and the creation of common green areas in cities, as long as they had dead animals buried under them, to improve the colour of the grass.

At the same time, innovations were beginning to make gardening easier and less labour-intensive. Until 1830 the cutting of grass had generally been done with a scythe, making the run of the ball on golf greens much more difficult to predict than Rory McIlroy would like. But then someone invented and patented the lawn mower. And, yes, put up the bunting, it was a British man that did it.

Edwin Budding worked in Stroud in Gloucestershire, a mill town and, somewhat bizarrely, a major centre for the production of the baize used on snooker tables. He noticed that in the finishing mills, small, rotating blades were used to remove bobbles from the cloth and leave it smooth, and wondered whether the same technology might be applied to grass. Whether he was looking at the green cloth used for snooker and thought it looked like grass, I don't know, but it would certainly explain his eureka moment. His first design was for a large mower that could be pushed only with some difficulty. This was soon followed by designs that could be pulled by animals and, towards the end of the century, by one that was powered by steam. Budding is also credited with the invention of the adjustable spanner, suggesting his early lawnmowers weren't quite as reliable as he had hoped. In case you are wondering, in the version pulled by animals, the horse or pony had to wear soft leather shoes to avoid damaging the grass before the mower got to it. The horse would also be warned that if there were any hoof marks, he or she would soon be included in the garden's soil-improvement programme.

Before you get too excited, although the lawn mower is ours, the Flymo isn't. Well, not entirely. It was designed by a Swede, who based it on the hovercraft, a mode of transport designed by British engineer Sir Christopher Cockerell. So we can at least claim the inspiration, if not the actual thing. It's a shame the hovercraft the Swede copied didn't have a thing on the back to catch grass-cuttings, because frankly the Flymo could have done with that too.

During the Victorian era, a market was also emerging for garden ornaments. In 1860 the first garden gnome went on sale in Britain. Don't panic. We, as a nation, weren't responsible. The origin of gnomes – well, the ceramic ones at least – appears to be German. House dwarves had been popular as ornaments from the late eighteenth century, but moving them outside was a new phenomenon. I suspect someone sensible was throwing one out, left it next to the wheelie bin slightly too long, and it became a permanent garden feature, just like last year's Christmas tree.

Whatever happened, the fashion for small, pointy-hatted, ceramic creatures who look as though they should live exclusively on Rice Krispies spread across Europe. Some have suggested that the gnome is the descendant of Priapus, the Greco–Roman god of fertility, whose statue often stood in gardens in Ancient Greece or Rome, sporting a monstrous erection. I'm not sure, although of course it would explain the angle of the fishing rod.

In Britain the attitude to the garden gnome has generally been hostile. Until a volte-face in 2013 the Chelsea Flower Show would not allow them in any designs and banned them from the site. In Germany, however, there are estimated to be 25 million of them, which makes gnomes their second biggest ethnic group, about which the gnomes are angry, because they still do not have the vote.

Throughout the nineteenth century, gardening was spreading through the whole population, not least because even in industrial areas, garden plots were common. A University of Cambridge study into five towns, Sheffield, Bradford, Preston, Northampton and Dorchester, has shown that gardens weren't simply the preserve of an urban elite. In Northampton, from as early as 1800, three-quarters of the skilled working class had private plots. This was due in part to the now discredited theory of miasma, or disease-filled fog.

If the Victorians had an obsession about anything, it was clean air. It was held, for example, that the London cholera outbreak of 1848–9 was down to noxious pollution emanating from a nasty concentration of rotting organic matter by the River Thames, and they didn't mean the House of Commons. The disease, it was believed, was not spread by contact with the individuals that had it, but was caught from the miasma or fog in which it had made its home. It was, of course, nonsense – we all now know that disease is spread by a conspiracy between the CIA and drug companies – but the Victorians lived in fear of this unhealthy fog, and belief in it drove major changes in sewer, house and garden design in the Victorian era.

After the so-called Great Stink of 1858, a summer when the smell of human waste in central London became so over-powering that parliament considered moving to Oxford or St Albans, just to get away from the stench, London's sewers were improved, and impetus was given to the development of innovations such as the dry earth closet, an advance which hasn't survived due to the difficulty of filling your cistern with mud. But legislation for housing and public health was also central to determining the shape and layout of Britain's rapidly growing number of houses. Closely built 'back to back' housing was thought to encourage and possibly trap miasma, which made the ideal model for Britain's new housing stock a terrace, with a garden at front and back, through which the lovely clean air from the factory chimney down the road could flow freely. Frankly, there also seems very little point in creating a miasma-free plot if Britain's foremost garden authority is then going to encourage you to bury a horse in it. Still, this basic house-and-garden layout is the model that has been followed ever since. It was copied for semi-detached housing, and gave us the springboard to be a nation of gardeners.

With new flowerbeds to fill and Loudon's plans to work with, Britain's legion of new gardeners was hungry for new and exotic plants. Fortunately, like the Tudors, Britain now had another generation of plant hunters ready to fill the holes they had prepared in their borders.

Plant hunting as an occupation had never really gone away. In 1797 Sir Joseph Banks, the great botanist who had been on the first voyage of Captain Cook, became the president of the Royal Botanical Gardens in Kew and began to dispatch explorers all over the world to gather plants for him. Not that he was any slouch himself. Roughly 80 species of plant are named after him, and he is credited with the introduction to Britain of acacia, eucalyptus and mimosa. Having visited that continent, he was also very keen on the colonization of Australia, leading a contemporary to suggest that what is now New South Wales be called Banksia, which would have made it sound like a penal colony for graffiti artists.

Joseph Banks was not, however, alone in his desire to gather plants and bring them home. There were many others smuggling them back in their hand baggage, and asking them for plants couldn't have been further removed from asking that nice guy in B&Q where the primulas are.

Plant hunters were the Indiana Joneses of the nineteenth century. They battled with disease, Indians, snow, desert and dangerous animals, all to make the garden centre a more fulfilling place to spend a Sunday afternoon in. They were the kind of men who really didn't worry about a pension plan, and quite rightly, for most of them didn't survive long enough to make it relevant.

David Douglas, the Scot after whom the Douglas fir is named, was one of first collectors for the Horticultural Society that Banks formed in 1804. On his first trip, in 1824, he went to the east coast of North America to pick up some fruit and vegetables, a task I now leave to Ocado. His second trip was to the west coast and the Columbia and Oregon Rivers, where he spent his time being chased by local tribes and occasionally falling into the current and losing all the plants he had collected. He died at the age of 35 in the Sandwich Islands, which we now call Hawaii, after tumbling into an animal trap already containing a bull. The bull wasn't happy at having to share and gored him to death, although Douglas's ability to fight back was somewhat hampered by the fact that he already had rheumatic fever and sight in only one eye. Ironically, bulls had only been introduced to the island 50 years before, by a previous scientific expedition.

Douglas's death wasn't that unusual, to be honest. Francis Masson had died equally nastily 30 years earlier. Dispatched by Banks to collect specimens in the West Indies, Masson had been imprisoned by the French, had his plants destroyed by a hurricane, been captured by privateers and starved in a prison, before finally being transported to New York. Thinking the worst must now surely be over, he decided to nip up to Canada to grab some more of the photosynthesizing green stuff and promptly froze to death somewhere near Montreal.

And in case you think it was just British plant collectors who were having trouble, the Americans didn't fare much better either. Meriwether Lewis, the man told by the third president of the United States, Thomas Jefferson, to find a route from the east of the continent to the Pacific Seaboard, and on the way to collect plants, log animals and note the geology, was shot through the buttocks when one of his under-explorers mistook him for an elk. He survived, but only to end his life miserably a few years later.

The list of unfortunate deaths is practically endless. George Vancouver, captain of HMS *Discovery*, died of renal failure at 40; John Gould Veitch, a man with the unlikely honour of being the imperial botanist on the first European ascent of Mount Fuji, died of a lung haemorrhage at 31. John Jeffrey, sent to collect the plants David Douglas had missed, died of frostbite or was killed by Indians aged just 28; while Jean Marie Delavay, a Jesuit missionary who collected 1,500 plants in northern Yunnan, made it to 57 years of age, but then contracted bubonic plague. Whoops.

That being said, some plant collectors had it easier. Archibald Menzies, who had sailed with Cook and Vancouver, was supposedly offered some pine nuts for dessert by the then governor of Chile. He didn't eat them, but pocketed them while his host wasn't looking and took them back to his ship, where he planted them in pots. He tended them during his voyage back to Britain and found, to the delight of designers of Victorian rectory gardens, that he had introduced the monkey puzzle tree. He died aged 88, with both of his eyes, a full complement of limbs and no scar tissue on either cheek of his bottom.

The efforts of the nineteenth-century plant collectors filled the great botanic collections at Kew and in Edinburgh, which were soon overflowing with rhododendrons, geraniums, lupins, lilies and camellias, and it wasn't long before those species that proved hardy enough for the British climate found themselves in Britain's back gardens, occasionally with unintended consequences.

The Monterey cypress is a native of the west coast of America and, doing what it says on the tin, is particularly abundant around Monterey, in the middle of the Californian coast. The Nootka cypress also grows in North America, although slightly further north, from just south of the border of Washington State to Alaska. Separated by some 400 miles, it seemed that the two trees were destined never to meet, and yet unfortunately, thanks to our intrepid plant hunters, they did, in a garden in mid Wales.

In 1847 John Naylor was given Leighton Hall in Powys by his uncle, Christopher Leyland, and decided to commission a garden. Beds were dug, paths were laid, shrubs were uprooted and the two heroes of our story, the cypresses Nookta and Monterey, found themselves planted next to each other. It was love at first sight and after a short courtship, they decided to exchange pollen, thereby unleashing on Britain the arboreal answer to Damien from *The Omen*, the leylandii tree. It is hard to imagine the shock for the parents of producing a child that was so uncouth, so fast-growing and so unpleasant to the neighbours. Growing to heights of 130 feet or more, blocking all available light and being as attractive as a set of massive, oversized, green roller brushes from a car wash, the leylandii was, for a time, the most popular plant in Britain's garden centres. You'd have a job finding the people who bought them now; they are living in the middle of a giant hedge, suffering from Vitamin D deficiency and having to keep the lights on just to see each other's faces. But I am being unfair. If planted with sympathy, leylandii can be a boon to any garden and now come in many different varieties, including Haggerston Grey, Leighton Green and Prunethathedgeorimgoingtopour bleachonyourcar.

By the turn of the twentieth century, gardening had become a fashionable occupation, and for the first time women came to the fore as gardeners and garden designers. The most famous was Gertrude Jekyll, who had a distinguished long-term collaboration with the architect Edwin Lutyens, although I'm fairly certain that if she'd had any sense of humour, she would have called him Mr Hyde. Jekyll's thing was radiant colour and her book *Gardens for Small Country Houses* was continually republished in the early years of the century.

In 1913 the Royal Horticultural Society held the first Chelsea Flower Show, which was so successful that it was soon added to Henley, Royal Ascot and debutantes' balls in the list of must-go events for the pre-war It Girl and It Boy.

But gardening wasn't just for the Edwardian cast of *Made in Chelsea*. For those who had no garden of their own, allotments were increasingly available. These were seen by the Victorians as a way of filling the time of the urban poor, giving them a sense of purpose, providing them with home-grown food and making sure that the only bottle they would be tempted to turn to was Baby Bio. By 1918, after the impetus given to them by wartime food shortages, there were 1.5 million plots throughout Great Britain. Gardening, whether for food or fun, was here to stay across all the social classes.

Gardening took to the airwaves with *In Your Garden*, a television programme broadcast in the very first month of the BBC's new service in 1936. Designed to encourage more people to buy televisions, it was presented by Mr Middleton, a well-established radio voice who spoke to the listeners in a relaxed way, as though they were 'old friends"; old friends whom he demanded call him Mr Middleton. Only 2,000 people had sets, no one watched and the programme still got higher figures than BBC Parliament does today. During the war, the BBC's fledgling television service was suspended and *In Your Garden* became a radio series. Roughly one third of the country tuned in for each broadcast, and it was used by the government to launch the 'Dig For Victory' campaign which encouraged the population to produce more of its own food. In 1942 research suggested that 70 per cent of those with wireless sets listened to advice about gardening.

In Mr Middleton, Britain finally had its first mass-market celebrity gardener, the root stock from which Alan Titchmarsh was grown. He died in 1945, but gardening programmes went from strength to strength, making stars of Percy Thrower, Geoff Hamilton and Charlie Dimmock, although in that last case it wasn't really the garden advice that most men were after.

In Your Garden was pensioned off when the BBC finally realized it sounded like a programme about stalkers. There were, however, replacements; *Gardeners' Question Time* started in 1947 and continues to the present day. Sadly, at no point have the BBC ever confused it with its political cousin, *Question Time,* and delivered David Dimbleby to the studio to answer questions about aphids or the best time to cut back a wisteria. It is a shame, because I suspect that he would know. Television's *Gardeners' World* joined the roster in 1968, and having pruned eight presenters, is still with us today, regularly drawing audiences of 2.5 million, which would be higher still if half the potential viewership weren't in their gardens.

So there you are, a brief history of gardening. Our love of it is down to the Romans, monks, Tudor explorers, a man who realized he needed a catchy name, another who advocated burying horses in the garden, plant explorers who thought begonias were to die for, and a radio presenter who shared his surname with our future queen. It is fair to say that no other country gardens with quite the zeal we do, with the possible exception of the Slovenians. And the Hungarians. Oh, and maybe the Belgians.

There is, of course, a worry that this tradition is under threat. According to what the *Daily Telegraph* described as 'secret Government forecasts' more than two million homes will be without gardens by the end of 2013, as developers grab land and people replace their front gardens with off-street parking. I'm not worried though; history shows that buddleias will break through tarmac, and that even if they don't want them, those gardenless Britons will have at least one flowering plant.

Britain's gardening obsession may not, however, be rooted in history at all. Looking out of the window at the vivid green of the British countryside, I can't help thinking that it may simply be that, as a temperate country, we can grow a greater variety of plants than most. And that is down to nothing more than another of our great obsessions, the weather.

AND NOW, THE WEATHER

Here is some UK travel advice from Trip Advisor. In a pub, queue or train 'an easy way to begin a discussion with a stranger is to talk about the weather. All British people have an opinion on the weather and most can tell you what the weather is due to do for the next four or five days. Being knowledgeable about the British weather is an essential part of living/visiting here. You will sometimes see people carrying umbrellas (brollies) on roasting-hot, sunny days because they know that it will rain intensely later in the afternoon for about 45 minutes. You ignore this expert knowledge at your own risk. Remember – in Britain, there is no such thing as bad weather: there are only the wrong clothes.'

Which is pretty much true, I guess, although the stuff about carrying umbrellas is a bit strange. I don't think I have ever seen anyone carry one on a roasting-hot day, and even if they were, how could they know that the rain would last about 45 minutes?

Hugh Dennis

I certainly don't like the idea of being stared at by tourists trying to work out clues to the weather from the clothes I am wearing. In fact, tourists should be warned that if they look at people in Britain for too long, especially in bars or pubs, and if those people say, 'What are you staring at?' the reply, 'I am interested in your umbrella' might well result in the umbrella being put to a use for which it was not originally intended. You ignore this expert knowledge at your own risk.

The sentiment of the piece, however, is good. As Dr Johnson observed, 'When two Englishmen meet, their first talk is of the weather,' although I do wonder whether in using it as an opening conversational gambit, we are showing actual interest in the weather itself or are simply being polite. I mean, what else are you going to say to a total stranger?

'What are you doing round here then?'

'Mmmm, nice shoes.'

'What is your view on monetary union across the Eurozone?'

None of them has the easy, undemanding good nature of a comment on the weather. Oscar Wilde may have described talking about the weather as 'the last refuge of the unimaginative', but if someone says, 'Nice day,' you can nod, you can grunt, you can answer in one word or thirty. All are acceptable, none is rude, and all may lead on to a more extensive conversation. As long, of course, as there is weather to comment on. Say, 'It'll probably clear up later' to someone 200 feet underground on a train to Morden via Bank, and it will generally mean they move several seats further away from you. In fact, the lack of weather to talk about, and the fact that it is too noisy to hear anyone properly, may be one of the many reasons no one does talk on the tube. It is also very difficult to hold a conversation when you are standing with your head in someone's armpit, about to play Twister in order to let someone get off before the doors close, or involuntarily testing your short sight by reading the *Evening Standard* which is constantly being folded and refolded in your face. Frankly, I would rather watch a sweaty French monarch get undressed.

The great advantage of comments about the weather is that they are easy and don't require much thought. For example, 'It'll probably clear up later' is simply a truism. Even Noah only had it rain on him for 40 days at a stretch. If it isn't going to clear up later, we are all going to drown. Essex will go the way of Doggerland, which apparently, in some car parks, after dark and after a fashion, it already has. Mind you, on childhood caravan holidays with my parents, it never seemed to clear up at all, however much my mother said it would. For want of anything better to do, I used to sit in the van doing my holiday homework and wondering why no one ever thought to include the question I really wanted answering in exams: 'If the mean annual temperature is two degrees and the mean annual rainfall is 150 inches, why on earth have you brought us here on holiday? Again.'

Mind you, other phrases aren't much better. For example, I would dispute that rain is, in any way, 'good weather for ducks'. Who has any proof that ducks like rain? Given that ducks spend a large portion of their lives sitting on water, I find it quite unlikely that they would want it pouring down on them from the top too. Good weather for fish, I could go for. Good weather for people who like to have their car cleaned without having to shell out for a car wash, I could go for too. But good weather for ducks, I just don't know.

Even good weather for wildebeest would be better, as it would save them from having to migrate in a massive circle, being stalked by lions, while David Attenborough provides a breathy commentary. No, when it rains, ducks are probably as pissed off as the rest of us.

OK, empirical evidence: we had ducks for a short time and when it was raining they stayed inside their little plywood house. On a rainy day I was also once chased by a goose, which bit me in the two softest parts of my anatomy. Admittedly, my children, then toddlers, had annoyed it, but I am convinced that the weather hadn't helped its mood. It certainly didn't help mine.

Sorry, I am beginning to ramble.

Yes, where were we? Right. I'll recap. There is a perception, put about by Trip Advisor and Dr Johnson, amongst others, that the British like to talk about the weather. There is a feeling that we are preoccupied with it, and that even if we aren't pre-occupied with it, per se, that we may be preoccupied with the fact that we could be preoccupied with it. Given that I am writing a chapter about that preoccupation, I should find it hard to disagree. However, I do. I think that our tendency to talk about the weather could simply be born of another British hobby horse: politeness. To be honest, though, there isn't much statistical evidence to help my argument. In fact, it points to a British weather obsession that goes much deeper than I had imagined.

In 2010, as part of a campaign to highlight the importance of British potatoes in their crisps, Walkers commissioned a survey of 2,000 people by YouGov. Its findings were as follows:

Only 50 per cent of us talk about the weather to facilitate social interaction.

You see, that is my case gone right there.

50 per cent of us talk about weather at least once every six hours.

Which is even worse for my argument.

Of those aged over 55, 88 per cent get a weather forecast every day, although for the 18–25 age group, this figure halves.

There seems to be no statistic for teenagers looking for a forecast, although I imagine that the numbers will be even lower, as the weather outside the bedroom window has a negligible effect on the operation of the Xbox or the possible kill scores for *Call of Duty* or *Halo 4*. The fact that bad weather might be approaching would be of no interest at all, even if it was a parental storm.

Interestingly, the survey also found that among those questioned, men tended to be more optimistic about weather prospects than women, which could simply be because they tend to have less hair to go frizzy when it gets damp.

Now, obviously a small survey for a crisp manufacturer conducted as part of a PR exercise isn't necessarily that reliable, and I will also admit that I have a slight problem with polls carried out by YouGov because their name just reminds me of cockney banter. Every time I hear it, I want to reply, 'Yes, squire.'

Fortunately then, the suggestion of obsession is borne out elsewhere. In November 2008 the *Daily Telegraph* published the results of a poll designed to identify 'the top 50 British traits'. Top, obviously, was 'talking about the weather', second was 'queuing' and third was 'sarcasm', which was a problem because I was then unsure whether I should believe the rest of the survey. An uncertainty which was exacerbated by finding that the 29th most British trait was 'not saying what we mean'. Luckily, there is also the evidence of music.

In 2011 *Weather*, a journal whose very existence indicates that we are quite fond of the subject, published a paper by Dr Karen Aplin of the University of Oxford and her colleague, Dr Paul Williams, entitled 'Meteorological Phenomena in Western Classical Orchestral Music'.

Yes, you read it right. Don't tell me that I haven't been to the furthest reaches of the internet to research this stuff. Essentially, it was a survey of which composers most mimicked the sound of weather phenomena in their music, and its conclusion was that composers from the UK are more enthusiastic about the weather than their colleagues elsewhere. You know how I was saying that this book could be useful for pub quizzes? Well, get this: three of the seven composers depicting frontal storms are from the UK. That is, as a country, we account for 43 per cent of storms depicted in Western music.

OK, to be useful in a pub quiz, there would have to be a round about music and weather, including the specific question 'What percentage of storms in Western music have been depicted by British composers?' but you know what I mean. Imagine if you had played your joker on it.

It is good to know that there are aspects to British weather, like storms, which can be inspiring to those of a creative bent.

Obviously it is each to his own, but I can't imagine anyone uncovering Britten's great lost *Drizzle Symphony* or Handel's musical tribute to British meteorology, *The Scattered Showers – Clearing Later*.

If celebrating storms is indicative of our weather obsession, then we also have the evidence of our own Olympics, of course, for no one from Antwerp in 1920 to Beijing in 2008 had even considered including a mistaken weather forecast in their opening ceremony until the British did it at London 2012. Yet, for us, it was obvious, so there it was. And there he was, poor old Michael Fish, in front of a global audience of one billion people, delivering his forecast before the 'Great Storm' of 1987, skilfully reminding us of previous summer Games by being an twerp himself.

'Earlier on today a woman rang the BBC to say she'd heard there was a hurricane on the way,' he began. 'Well, if you're watching, don't worry, there isn't.'

Cue the biggest storm to hit south-east England since 1703.

To be fair to Michael Fish, it wasn't technically a hurricane, which to be given that title needs to have originated in the North Atlantic or North Pacific, which this one didn't. It simply had hurricane-force winds. Hurricanes, incidentally, may be named for the Mayan god Huracan who, among other achievements, is credited with destroying 'the wooden people'. I'm not sure what that means, but to be safe, I think the cast of *The Only Way is Essex* would do well to stay in if they hear the wind getting up.

To help Michael's cause further, they got the forecast wrong in France as well, where the devastation was on roughly the same scale. He did also predict that there would be very heavy winds, although unsurprisingly they tend not to broadcast that bit on clips programmes, or in Olympic opening ceremonies.

I actually slept through the great storm altogether. The morning after the devastation, I had a breakfast meeting in the West End of London, so I got up as normal and wandered down to Camden Town to get the tube, not really taking in the fallen trees and branches that were scattered across the road, or the fact that there seemed to be very few people about. Just short of the tube station, there was a bus stop, and I remember thinking how disgusting it was that overnight some vandals seemed to have moved the bus shelter that used to be next to it.

When I got to work, I seemed to be the only one in, so I turned on the news and discovered what had happened. In terms of an ability to sleep through noise, I had always thought it fairly spectacular, until I met my parents-in-law. They had managed to sleep through the alarm in their house going off, in spite of the fact that there were two bells, one internal and one directly beneath their bedroom window. As if that wasn't enough, they had also managed to remain unconscious while their next-door neighbours knocked noisily on the door, let themselves in, checked everything was OK, turned the alarm off and scribbled a note to tell them what had happened, leaving it on the kitchen table. The next-door neighbours lived nearly 80 yards away, and assumed that my parents-in-law must be away for the night.

That the 'Great Storm' is thought of as a major event at all is, of course, indicative of how mild our climate generally is, although with global climate change, this pattern may be altering. I suspect that whoever is in charge of the weather upstairs, he, or indeed she, probably regards Britain as a bit of a training exercise, a region where, for example, rain can learn the rudiments of falling before it becomes involved in the more demanding stuff, like a monsoon, or tropical storm. A place where wind puts on the L-plates before being given a name like Nancy or Hubert and unleashed fully qualified on the Eastern Seaboard of the United States. A country where the sun is on short shifts or flexible working, readying itself for those long hours, without even so much as a lunch break, when it finally gets posted to Spain or Equatorial Guinea. A nation where snow begins building up to the 90 or so different types that will be required in Greenland by practising with just two: 'snow' and 'the wrong type of snow'. What we have is changeability, a little bit of everything, and perhaps this is the cause of what I must now admit is our obsession with the weather.

If often amuses me that when expats are asked why they moved to Spain or Portugal or Cyprus, or indeed anywhere in the sunbelt of the Mediterranean, that they will usually say, 'For the weather.' Because patently it is for the complete opposite: they have actually moved for the unbroken, unrelenting blue skies that indicate an utter lack of weather. By contrast, the British climate seems to have Attention Deficit Disorder. Like a small child fed exclusively on sugar and E-numbers, it can't concentrate on anything long enough to make it stick. And that is why we like it. Nothing seems to go on too long. Nothing is too disheartening. There's enough happening to keep our interest. God knows what it is like for forecasters in Svalbard or

Vladivostok, but in Britain, thank God, you are very unlikely to hear the news anchor hand over for the forecast like this: 'Well, with the cold snap into its third month, let's go over to Carol on the roof of Television Centre. She's not meant to be there. She's just a bit depressed.'

The reasons for the changeability in our weather are fairly obvious. These islands sit exactly at the point where cold air whipping in from Siberia and the north meets warmer air and warmer sea heading up from the south, the latter in the form of the North Atlantic Drift or Gulf Stream. This is why palm trees can be grown in the south-west (although they shouldn't be because they look a bit ridiculous) and you often need thermal underwear in East Anglia in August.

The smorgasbord of meteorological possibilities that the meeting of these air masses throws up is further added to by the presence of the Northern Hemisphere Polar Jet Stream, which whips across Britain at the cruising height for aircraft and which is formed, once again, where colder air meets warmer. The balance between the factors determines the weather we have. If, for example, the Jet Stream forms too far south, we freeze our nuts off. If it forms slightly further north, the tabloids are full of pictures of sunburned holidaymakers to whom wearing cream means letting some of the 99 with flake that the photographer has made sure they are holding dribble down their chins.

The overall result of the airborne battle is that we have a temperate maritime climate, where the weather can change at any minute, and then just as fast change back again. There is a constant fight between the high and low pressure systems in the atmosphere around us. The west is generally mildest; the north and Scotland are generally coldest and wettest; and the south and east tend to be the driest and most likely to have a hosepipe ban. As far as I know, we do not hold any global weather records. And in spite of the perception overseas that it rains all the time in Britain, the country only gets about 1,200 mm of rainfall, on average, every year, which is a long way from the 22,000 mm which fall on the Khasi Hills of India. I love that name. I'm sorry, but the 12-year-old in me still finds it funny.

What the changeable weather seems to have done for us, though, is put us at the forefront of developments in weather forecasting. It makes sense. Forecasting isn't something you really need if it is just going to be sunny again.

Admittedly, we didn't lead the way at first. The Babylonians and Indians did that, finding ways both to predict and measure the weather. Sometime in the fourth century BC, Kautilya, an administrator of India's Maurya Empire, is credited with accurately measuring rainfall for the first time. For his ideas on administration, Kautilya is now often referred to as 'India's Machiavelli', and you can see why. He proposed that, as the amount of rain falling on the land was generally a measure of how productive the soil would be, and therefore how much money farmers could make, it would encourage them to do a good job if he introduced a tax on rainfall. Which he did; the more wet stuff that fell out of the clouds, the more farmers had to pay to the empire. If you are employed in agriculture and reading this book, I suggest you now black this section out, or eat it, in case George Osborne ever calls round, picks this copy up and gets a few ideas.

I am also certain, incidentally, that the argument that rain is always a good thing would gain very little sympathy with the farmers of Gloucester or Tewkesbury, especially if the helicopter they thought was about to rescue them from the roof of their house was actually from HMRC and the man on the winch had a loudhailer telling them to self-assess by the end of December.

I do, however, have a rather happy picture in my head of Kautilya greeting strangers on rainy days by raising his hat and saying, 'Good day for tax. No, not ducks, tax!'

Kautilya's epic treatise, *Arthashastra*, which contained his radical ideas on statecraft and fiscal, monetary and military policies, became a bestseller, although it disappeared for thousands of years and was only rediscovered in 1915. My theory is that it had been hidden by a flooded farmer, who had reached his overdraft limit.

Next on the meteorological scene was Aristotle, who pretty much nailed the hydrological cycle, realizing that it was dependent on solar energy from the sun.

And then even Jesus had a go. Well, I say had a go. Matthew XVI: 2–3 has him saying this: 'When in evening, ye say, it will be fair weather: for the sky is red. And in the morning, it will be foul weather today: for the sky is red and lowering.' Which is, essentially, 'Red sky at night, shepherd's delight. Red sky in the morning, shepherd's warning,' only without the rhymes. In a way, it is a shame he stopped at that, because there must have been a lot more he could do.

'Angel hovering in air, shepherds really, really scared.'

'Burning bush has caught on fire, drought and heatwave really dire.'

'Moses parted the Red Sea, hosepipe ban in Galilee.'

Yes, quite wisely he chose to leave it at the one.

I'm afraid that the next meteorological pioneers on the scene weren't British either; they were from Italy, where the Renaissance had extended its reach into a study of the atmosphere. Galileo invented the thermoscope, essentially a thermometer but with a cooler name, while his one-time pupil Evangelista Torricelli invented the mercury barometer, having first been called in to fix a problematic pump for the Duke of Tuscany.

Now, obviously, in most circumstances, those called in to solve a pump problem would simply go, 'Yeah, sorry, Duke, your pump has gone. You need a new one. Unfortunately I haven't got one in the van, so I'm just going to have to nip off to the plumber's merchants. Sorry about that,' before disappearing to the nearest café for two hours and then returning with the wrong pump, fitting it and giving you a bill for a whole day's work.

Torricelli, however, wasn't like that at all. No. He looked at the pump, worked out why it wasn't working and thereby made one of the great scientific discoveries of the age, namely the existence of atmospheric pressure. The problem had been this: the Duke of Tuscany thought his castle might be attacked and realized that if that happened the pump he used to get water from his well would be vulnerable. So he had moved it higher up the walls, where he thought no one could get at it. Unfortunately, in this new position, the pump was useless. It didn't seem to be able to pump water any higher than 10 metres, however hard his workmen tried, which probably wasn't very hard at all. Toricelli looked at the pump, then looked at the workmen, to assess what they might do to him if he sounded too geeky, and suggested that the maximum height that the water could reach was determined by the pressure of the atmosphere pushing down on it. When the column of water was 10 metres high, the force of the water upwards balanced the force of the atmosphere downwards, and therefore it could go no higher. Fortunately, the Duke looked rather impressed, saving Torricelli from having to deliver his back-up explanation, that it just needed a new washer or something, and as a consequence, the footage never made it onto *Rogue Traders*.

To prove his theory, Torricelli then investigated what would happen to a column of mercury in an inverted tube when it too was exposed to the pressure of the atmosphere, and found that he had invented the mercury barometer, the instrument that is key to the interpretation of weather data through its ability to detect high and low atmospheric pressure. Torricelli also correctly noted that the gap above the mercury in the inverted tube was a vacuum. Previously, Galileo had denied that the vacuum existed, despite the fact that his flatmates had shown him thousands of times that it was in the cupboard under the stairs. That's boys for you. Dirty tyke.

In spite of his achievements, Torricelli has never really been rewarded to the same extent as many other scientists. He has a unit named after him, the torr, but as it is a unit of pressure in a vacuum, it isn't one that many of us will be using that often. He also has an asteroid named after him, number 7,437, meaning that 7,436 people got that particular honour before he did. Frankly, I think I would be a bit annoyed were I him, especially since Mr Fahrenheit has a unit in common usage, and Mr Celsius, who has the same honour, didn't even suggest the scale that his units are named after. The one he suggested was upside down, with O degrees as the boiling point of water and 100 degrees as the point at which it froze. It took Linnaeus, the man who developed the system of plant classification, to flip it over the right way. Perhaps I'm being unfair. Celsius was Swedish and it is possible that whoever built his first thermometer simply read the instructions wrong, or didn't have the right Allen key.

Anyway, in the Renaissance, the accurate gradation of temperature was still way off, leaving time for the first meteorological foray by a major British scientist, in the person of Sir Christopher Wren. Given that the Italians were thinking of the scientific and philosophical attributes of the atmosphere, you would think that Wren would be desperate to come out with something equally impressive, just to keep up. Sadly, you would be wrong. What Sir Christopher Wren first gave to the world was the automatic, self-emptying, tipping-bucket rain gauge. You can only assume that wasn't on the CV when he applied to rebuild St Paul's Cathedral.

'So, Sir Christopher, tell us of your plans for the Great Cathedral.'

'Thank you, sir. I intend to reconcile the Gothic with the harmony of the Renaissance, to provide a cathedral that will dominate the skyline of this great city and form a lasting tribute to the Glory of God.'

'Right, and what else have you done? What qualifies you for this great project?'

'Well, er, I have designed a rain gauge.'

'Right.'

'But no ordinary rain gauge, sir. An automatic, self-emptying, tipping-bucket rain gauge.'

'Thank you, Sir Christopher. Could you please close the door on your way out?'

The rain gauge was, in fact, a very clever idea. In previous methods of measuring rainfall, someone had to empty the bowl or bucket that was being used to collect the water before it all spilled over the top. If the rainfall was fairly constant, say like Britain in August, that meant emptying it and recording the findings while it was still raining, which, unless you were well ahead of the curve and had a Mac some 150 years before they were invented, would have been quite unpleasant. Sir Christopher, however, designed a mechanism whereby the rainfall was collected in two scoops, which formed the two ends of a tiny seesaw. When one scoop was full, the water poured over the end of it into a massive bucket below. Now much lighter, that scoop then swung up, moving the other scoop into position, and so on. Each time a scoop emptied itself, the rain gauge recorded it, although, from the small sketch that survives, it isn't quite clear how this was done. No one had to be there at all. They could be somewhere else completely, spending the day with their feet up, reading the paper and having a cup of tea. Every now and then, when the sun was out, they could nip over to the tipping buckets and note how many times they had tipped on a nice, dry piece of paper. Very civilized. Not surprisingly, the design, later modified by Hooke, spread as a standard through the rainfall-measuring world.

To be honest, that wasn't all Wren had done by the time he took on the building of London's great cathedral. He had already designed 50 city churches, and made advances in physics, optics, maths and astronomy. He was also a founder member of the Royal Society. Amazing what you can achieve if you don't have a television.

Shortly after Wren's rain gauge, although I am guessing not inspired by it, came the meteorological observations of Edmond Halley, of Comet fame, by which I mean he had one named after him, not that he worked there. Although that would have definitely upped the average intellectual attainments of the Saturday staff.

'So, you want a 42-inch Samsung or Panasonic, HD–ready, with built-in Freeview box? No problem. I'll get Sir Edmond to come and help you. Sir Edmond! Sir Edmond! Sorry, he'll be with you in a minute; he's just timing the transit of Venus. You know, to determine the size of the solar system.'

Halley's contribution was to postulate that the trade winds, on which sailors relied, were dependent upon solar energy, and that as hot air rose at the equator, where the sun was directly overhead, it would be replaced by air from higher latitudes arriving in the form of winds. The trade winds were, therefore, part of this huge cell of circulating air. Unfortunately, he wasn't entirely correct, in that the actual direction of the trade winds didn't seem to fit the pattern that his thesis suggested. The solution to this came 49 years later, when a scientist called Hadley adapted Halley's theory slightly, and his name slightly, and proposed that the winds were also skewed by the rotation of the earth.

The trade winds had originally been discovered by Christopher Columbus on his transatlantic voyage in 1492. He had used them as a sort of nautical travelator to get his three ships across the widest point of that ocean in only 36 days, which, given that he was supposedly the first person to do it at all, then constituted a world record.

On such voyages, however, sailors didn't only have to understand the trade winds, they also had to get to grips with that other great determinant of the British weather, the Gulf Stream. As the Gulf Stream heads north from America to Europe, it splits into two branches, like an aquatic northern line. One branch turns right and south towards Spain, while the other branch continues east and north towards the coast of Britain. This is the North Atlantic Drift, the reason why children in Devon feel persecuted in winter when schools everywhere else are closed due to the cold weather. Not surprisingly, the story of the mapping of the Gulf Stream, and understanding how it works, also has a British angle

For a short time, Benjamin Franklin, one of the founding fathers of the United States, a man famous for his revolutionary sentiments, and second only to George Washington as the driving force behind independence, had what now seems the extremely unlikely job of deputy postmaster to the British American colonies. It's a bit like finding that Robespierre was a Christmas postman, or Che Guevara worked for UPS. Anyway, as postmaster, and this is less surprising, he received a lot of complaints, one being from the Colonial Board of Customs, who asked why boats carrying the mail from Falmouth in Cornwall to New York were taking several weeks longer to cross the ocean than merchantmen sailing to Rhode Island from London, in spite of the fact that the distance from Falmouth was shorter. This intrigued Franklin, who set about trying to find an answer as to why the mailmen were slower, beyond the obvious, that they had much longer lunch breaks and they drank tea all the time. His cousin was a whaler, who worked with Bob Marley (don't worry, I've made that bit up), so he asked him if he had an explanation. And his cousin, Timothy Folger, did. The merchantmen realized that if they chose the most direct route, there was a strong current running against them and always crossed it to go a slightly different way, while the mail boats turned straight into it and kept going, extremely slowly.

As a regular on transatlantic crossings, Franklin then set about mapping the current, the width of which could be worked out by noting the water temperature, the speed of surface bubbles and the whereabouts of whales, who liked to lunch on the plankton that the current carried, and who seemed to treat it like the conveyor belt at Yo Sushi. To help his colonial masters, he then sent his findings to the post office, who decided that they didn't amount to much and that they should be ignored. I am proud to say that delivering mail late is a tradition that the Royal Mail still follow to this day.

Perhaps I am being unfair. Franklin also had form. The post office officials may have thought, 'Benjamin Franklin, I wouldn't listen to a word he says. He flew a kite into the middle of a thunderstorm? What an idiot. I mean, you could get electrocuted doing that.' And, in a way, they would have had a point, for Franklin was obviously mildly eccentric. During his career, he also decided to develop an alphabet which did away with all the letters he considered redundant – c, j, q, w, x and y – and replaced them with new letters which made sounds that he considered under-represented. Famous for playing chess, Franklin obviously didn't watch *Countdown*.

After his view of a lunar eclipse was ruined by storm clouds, Franklin also worked out that storms may move contrary to the direction of the prevailing wind. And if watching clouds is proof of an obsession with the weather, it is perhaps fitting that this very activity provided the British with their next major contribution to the science of helping people understand the weather we all have to live with.

Luke Howard may sound like a golfer or a member of Take That, but was in fact a nineteenth-century pharmacist living and working in London, who in 1802 published his paper 'On the Modification of Clouds'. He had been obsessed with the fluffy white things since childhood, when the gigantic ash cloud caused by the eruption of an Icelandic volcano caused vibrant skies and sunsets over Western Europe, and the cancellation of thousands of flights bringing early Georgian families back from skiing for the start of term. After this, Howard decided to study and draw clouds. Except possibly those he thought might be caused by miasma. Everyone tried to stay away from them if they had any sense at all. He recognized that clouds came in three basic types: dumpy clouds with a flat top, which he termed cumulus, after the Latin for heap; wispy ones high up, which he termed cirrus, after the Latin for a curl of hair; and flat, broad ones called stratus, which often obscured the sun and made cloud-gazing about as inspiring as watching *The Blue*

Planet on a black and white television. He also coined a term for rain-bearing clouds, calling them nimbus, not to be confused with nimbys, which are clouds that don't want any other precipitation near them. These names then formed building blocks, and could be joined together to describe different types of cloud: cirrostratus, stratocumulus or cumulonimbus. Yes, week by week, Howard's descriptions built into a picture of the sky above you. Each type of cloud was associated with particular weather conditions, and the art of weather forecasting was born.

I think it is fair to say that Luke Howard would have begun most of his conversations by talking about the weather. Indeed, the majority of his conversations would have been about nothing but the weather. In addition to the now universally accepted system of cloud classification, he also delivered scientific papers on 'The Average Barometer' and 'The Theories of Rain', and with the time he had left over, identified what is now known as the 'urban heat island', whereby towns are warmer than their surrounding countryside due to the heat given off by buildings, an effect cows should point to when their emissions are blamed for global warming. And whatever Oscar Wilde may have later thought of weather and weather investigation, it certainly wasn't perceived as unimaginative in the early years of the nineteenth century. Howard had poems dedicated to him by Goethe, and his work inspired the landscapes and seascapes of both J. M. W. Turner and John Constable. He lived in one of the roughest parts of Tottenham, testament to the fact that if you spend most of your life looking up, you are not really going to worry what your street looks like.

As Howard developed his system of weather classification, so others on these islands, equally obsessed by what the weather could throw at them, were developing theirs. One such was Francis Beaufort, whom we have to thank for the classification of wind speed that bears his name – the Beaufort scale. And it was a scale that we might not have had at all, had it not been for an unfortunate accident suffered by Francis during the early years of his naval career. Trying to escape from pirates in the eastern Mediterranean, he was shot in the groin with a musket ball that shattered his hip. The records do not relate if the pirates had an apricot, or if the sniper who fired the shot thought Beaufort was an elk. Beaufort was sent back to England to convalesce, and although he didn't retire from the navy until the age of 81, he was apparently never again considered for a combat role, leaving him plenty of free time to assess and measure the wind.

The scale Beaufort decided upon initially measured the force of the wind by the effect it had on the sails of a frigate. However, the navy was in the process of switching to steam – 'The Navy Sail. Everything Must Go' – so a new gradation had to be found. He decided, therefore, to focus on the effects that the wind had on the sea. The scale ranged from 'calm: sea like mirror' to 'storm: very long waves. High, overhanging crests'.

And it proved very useful. Until that point, there had been no common standard and sailors had to rely on subjective methods, such as the reaction of their passengers, to work out how bad conditions had got. Among these were: 'calm: everyone happy', 'strong breeze: several of them burping a lot, but claiming it is just the lunch' and 'storm: everyone sitting with their heads in their hands, muttering, "Bollocks, bollocks, bollocks. I think I am going to die," before being sick on the deck again'.

At the age of 55, Beaufort became the man responsible for the provision of accurate sea charts to ships of the fleet, the official hydrographer of the Royal Navy. In this capacity, he provided charts for HMS *Beagle*, the ship on which Charles Darwin would later formulate his theories of evolution, as well as training its captain, Robert Fitzroy, soon to become the father of modern weather forecasting.

Fitzroy's command of the *Beagle* began in rather tragic circumstances, when the ship's previous captain, Pringle Stokes, shot himself during a bout of severe depression, a condition which cannot have been helped by people constantly saying, 'Oi, Pringle. Once you pop, you can't stop,' and then running away laughing. Frankly, in his delicate state of mind, he would have preferred them just to talk about the weather. A name like Pringle Stokes would not have seemed even remotely laughable to Robert Fitzroy, however. The *Beagle* was, at that period, on a hydrographic survey of the Pacific, around Tierra del Fuego, during the course of which some locals had made off with one of the *Beagle*'s boats, while members of the ship's company were asleep on an island. Fitzroy gave chase, caught the natives, and to encourage them never to commit such a crime again, decided that the very best thing would be to rip up his Save the Children membership card and keep some of their children as hostages. Indeed, he decided to take them back to England, and because they would be on board long-term, to give them names. The names he chose for them were: Fuegia

Basket – named after local landmark, Basket Island; Jeremy Button – because he had been exchanged for mother-of-pearl buttons; York Minster – because Fitzroy was plainly a bit mad; and Boat Memory – because he was channelling Frank Zappa, or Bob Geldof, or Gwyneth Paltrow, or someone.

Not surprisingly, the children's visit to Britain didn't turn out that well. Boat Memory died of smallpox, and when the other three returned 'civilized' from their trip some years later, Fuegia Basket became a prostitute, while Jeremy Button was implicated in the murder of a group of missionaries in the so-called 'Wulaia Bay Massacre'.

Although this part of his career didn't work out that well for Fitzroy, it had unexpected benefits for Charles Darwin. Having to get his three misbehaving young hostages out of London rather rapidly, Fitzroy apparently invited Darwin onboard the *Beagle* to keep him company, as he was unable to face the trip back with them alone. The rest, as they say, is biology.

Such a hiccough didn't seem to hold Fitzroy back though. He subsequently became the governor of New Zealand, where he failed to prevent a war with the Maoris. Then, in 1854, having returned to London, and helped by his connection to Beaufort, he became head of a new government department within the Board of Trade devoted to the collection of weather data at sea. It was the forerunner of the Met Office. He gathered data from ships, and from the new barometers that he had installed at ports. The system was incomplete, but in 1859, after the loss of 459 lives on *The Royal Charter*, a steam clipper that was wrecked off the coast of Anglesey by a massive storm, he decided to widen his data-gathering, in the hope that such bad weather could be predicted in future. To the data gathered from ships, he added that from 15 land stations. Using the new telegraph system, barometric readings were then relayed to a central office and a map was drawn showing the pressures at the places the readings were taken. By joining the dots of equal pressure, Fitzroy had created the synoptic chart and the pressure contours that Carol Kirkwood points at on the days when they don't make her stand outside being rained on. As a result, storm warnings could now be given, which made Fitzroy very unpopular with the owners of fishing fleets, who wanted their boats to go out in all weathers, and very popular with the fishermen, who didn't fancy dying for a netfull of cod.

In 1861 the first weather forecast was published in *The Times*. And, I imagine, two days later, the first complaint was received, a lady writing in to say that she had been promised sunshine and had put her washing out, only for it to rain all day, and that it simply wasn't good enough. BBC radio weather broadcasts began in 1922, and those on television in 1936. The first in-vision weather forecaster, George Cowling, didn't make it to our screens until 1954 when, in a moment of brilliance, the BBC realized that it would be much better for the organization if the public had an individual to blame.

And that is about it for these small islands, in terms of the men who measure the weather. But, perhaps unsurprisingly, given the 1,200 mm of rainfall we enjoy every year, we seem to have nurtured an equally large number of men and women who instead of predicting when the heavens might open, simply took steps to ensure that we didn't get soaked when it did. As a result, we have been home to the world's leading manufacturer of waxy jackets, raincoat entrepreneurs and the inventor of the steel frame for umbrellas.

Until the mid-eighteenth century, the British didn't really bother with umbrellas as a protection in wet weather. This was largely because they were made with a wooden or whale-bone frame, which was very difficult to fold, and were covered in a type of oiled cotton which was heavy to start with and even heavier when it got wet – which it did, that being pretty much the job description of an umbrella. The French used them, but the British of the late 1700s regarded them with the same suspicion we had for baguettes or Bonne Maman jam before they were stocked by Tesco. Indeed, if you were using one at this time, you were likely to be the target of ridicule, and possibly the chant, 'Frenchman, Frenchman, why don't you call a coach?' which was probably shouted by the cab drivers themselves, who thought that umbrellas threatened their trade. In rain, the numbers using cabs went up, as umbrella-less pedestrians traded the inconvenience of being wet for the unpleasantness of being hauled around town by a Europhobe – or if it was a sedan chair, two Europhobes, one front, one back – who shouted at people indiscriminately. In 1852, though, Samuel Fox, a steel manufacturer from Sheffield, on a mission to use up his unwanted stocks of steel stays for women's corsets, hit upon the idea of a lightweight metal umbrella frame, and the modern umbrella, brolly, parapluie or bumbershoot came into being.

Since then, we have had telescopic umbrellas, storm umbrellas, golf umbrellas and umbrella hats, which to me always make the wearer look like he has lost a rather vicious argument with a cocktail waiter. The umbrella is an essential bit of kit in Britain, to be carried if it is raining, if it threatens to rain, or if you are planning to assassinate a Bulgarian dissident on Waterloo Bridge by poking him with a poisoned tip.

Not surprisingly, as a nation, we have also had a leading role in the development of the raincoat. The British colonies in the East provided ample supplies of rubber, and inventors all over Britain tried to work out what they could do with it. Some decided it would be the perfect covering for electrical and telegraph cables, including those running under the Atlantic. Some concentrated on overshoes, whilst others, such as the textile manufacturers Charles Macintosh of Glasgow and Thomas Hancock of Manchester, thought that what the world really needed was a waterproof fabric to wear when it was chucking it down.

The early attempts were not that successful. The fabrics that they made were heavy and stiff; if you wore a coat in conjunction with an early umbrella, you had as much free movement as a medieval knight in armour who had lost his WD-40. The rubber also showed an alarming tendency to melt in hot weather, so if you left the coat on marginally too long before taking it off, you ran the risk of looking like you had been mugged by a man with a puncture repair kit.

Fortunately, when the companies of Messrs Macintosh and Hancock merged in 1830, Hancock found a way of vulcanizing the rubber, which solved the problem and, in addition, made the rubber emotionless, logical and capable of using the Vulcan death grip.

Macintoshes aren't, of course, the only type of rainwear loved by the British; there are also parkas, cagoules and anoraks. Parka is an Inuit word, used in English since 1625 and worn by mods; the cagoule comes from a French word meaning 'hood' and is worn by ramblers; and the anorak comes from Greenland and is worn, well, by anoraks.

The Macintosh soon became a generic name for rainwear, leaving many other manufacturers frustrated that the raincoats they had so carefully crafted and branded could not escape being called Macs. One, however, did: the Gannex.

The Gannex raincoat was the creation of British entrepreneur Ernest Kagan in 1961. Its success was down to two key factors. First, it had a layer of waterproof material that was separated from a layer of wool by an envelope of air, thus making it warm, waterproof and breathable. Secondly, and of rather greater importance, Kagan convinced the prime minister to wear one. The Gannex factory was sited in Elland, just a few miles from Huddersfield, where Harold Wilson had been born. Keen to support local manufacturing, Wilson, then in opposition, wore one of the coats on a world tour, a stroke of luck for Kagan that turned his raincoat into a world brand. As Wilson globetrotted, a selection of world leaders admired his rainwear. US president Lyndon Johnson took a shine to it; Kruschev thought it would be just the thing for those 'will it, won't it' rainy days at the Kremlin; Mao Tse-tung thought it would coordinate perfectly with his boiler suit, while not being too showy; and single men living on their own in bedsits throughout the world thought it would be the perfect thing to go flashing in.

Wilson, a short, slightly dumpy man, who had been an Oxford don and the youngest cabinet minister of his generation, became a fashion icon, while Kagan became a millionaire, was ennobled, and became the occupant of a plush, red leather seat in the House of Lords. For a while.

After Wilson resigned, it was found that Kagan had committed tax fraud. He was stripped of his place in the Upper Chamber, although he kept his knighthood, and he served several years at Her Majesty's pleasure. None of which really surprised him – after all, that had been the key to his fortune. It never rains but it pours. Sir Harold probably wished he had worn a Burberry. Mind you, he wasn't wearing a raincoat at all when he came to give the prizes at my school in the late 1970s. I was disappointed, but probably not as disappointed as he was in me. I had won the fourth form prize, and not really understanding that you should choose a book that made you seem properly intellectual and clever, like *The Iliad*, or Kenneth Clark's *Civilisation*, or something, I allowed Sir Harold, a man with a brain the size of a small planet, to present me with *The Reader's Digest Book of Home Improvement*. It had a small section on bicycle maintenance at the back, which I was particularly keen on. You think I would have learned my lesson, but no. The very next year, the Duke of Norfolk presented me with *The AA Book of the Car*.

So, raincoats, rain gauges, umbrellas and the classification of wind and clouds; they all speak of a country in which the weather and talking about it is indeed a national obsession, but also of a people that have put that obsession to good use. As for forecasts, well, we may have been making them longer than anyone else, but they are often still wrong, and the Met Office is still regularly threatened with legal action by disgruntled holidaymakers, hoteliers and theme park owners seeking financial recompense for unexpected conditions, or the fact that the weather wasn't quite as bad as the forecast had said it would be. In 2012 it was the turn of an attraction in Bideford in Devon called 'the Big Sheep', which you'd think would be fine in all weathers, but apparently not.

Weather remains unpredictable, even with satellite technology, let alone all the effort the BBC have put into their 3D weather map, and with global climate change, it seems set to become less straightforward still. The gentle warming up of southern England that we were promised, giving us a landscape swathed in vines, seems to have been replaced with alternate drought and flood, giving us a landscape covered in mud and drowning Brussels sprouts. Still, broadcasters at least can be cheered by the fact that, to my knowledge, no weather broadcaster has ever been sacked for an incorrect forecast. In 2009 R4's *Shipping Forecast* presenter, the freelance Peter Jefferson, was told that he would not be having his contract renewed just days after making a mistake on air, but his crime was not failing to predict a squall, low pressure, or spotting a non-existent occluded front. His crime was letting the high pressure get to him. Having tripped over his words and crashed into the pips before the news, Peter Jefferson used a word beginning with F that wasn't fog, front, fisher or forties. He had thought that the microphone was off. The BBC claimed that the incident was unrelated to the end of his employment at Broadcasting House, but that may simply be them exhibiting British trait number 29 again: not saying what we mean.

But for those who are upset by the lack of forecasting accuracy, I would like the forecasts to be more honest too, and look forward to the day that I hear this: 'At 0200 hours, the Met Office issued a severe weather warning. They told the weather never, ever to do that again. But has it taken any notice? Has it heck!'

A BATTLE WITH THE BOTTLE

British achievements in the arena of alcohol are not hard to find.

We seem to love it. We consume, on average, 74 litres of beer a year, and 13.37 litres of pure alcohol. Around 30 per cent of our teenage boys have been drunk ten or more times in the last 12 months, and our teenage girls are the greatest binge-drinkers in Europe.

Yes, if you are slightly depressed by our European standing in other areas, drinking really does provide something to cling on to, a proper antidote to always coming last in the Eurovision Song Contest. All right, to be fair, Engelbert Humperdinck only came second last with 'Love Will Set You Free', and would probably have done even better if he hadn't been 76 and hadn't had a name that sounded like he was taking the piss out of all the Germanic viewers. The original Engelbert Humperdinck, from whom our Engelbert nicked his identity, was a famous German composer, best known for his opera

Hansel and Gretel. He only died in 1921. Having Engelbert as our representative for Eurovision was about as clever as the Austrians entering a band called Ralph Vaughan Williams and the Benjamin Brittenettes for the Brit Awards and then moaning about not winning.

Anyway, alcohol. Yes, for binge-drinking both female and male, we are firmly in the European top five, and yet for overall alcohol consumption, things aren't quite so rosy, or bleak, depending on which way you look at it.

For all the scare stories about 'Broken Britain', we are in fact only the 15th largest per capita consumers of alcohol in the world, a statistic I have no reason to query. It was provided by the WHO, and whether that is the World Health Organisation or the rock band fronted by Roger Daltrey, I reckon they are going to know about excessive alcohol consumption.

From the published data, it is obvious that although we can just about keep up with the best of the West, namely our near neighbours France, Ireland and Portugal, we are going to have to change the whole structure of our game and training methods if we are even going to begin to compete with the 'drink you under the table' republics of Eastern Europe, who occupy the top six positions in the league. In reverse order they are: Estonia, Ukraine, Russia, Hungary and the Czech Republic. And top of the pile of empty glasses, bottles and cans: Moldova.

It is almost as if the countries of the former Warsaw Pact, fed up with being thought of as a faceless confederation, suddenly realized the status they could each achieve individually, turned to each other and demanded the toppling of the Berlin Wall.

'What will we use to knock it down?'

'We have plenty of vodka bottles!'

In fact, with Croatia, Belarus and Romania also pushing for a place under the top table, Eastern Europe would occupy all top ten positions, were it not for the valiant efforts of Western Europe's top devotee of drinking – Andorra, the tiny, duty-free, high-altitude tax haven clinging to the peaks of the Pyrenees. And, paradoxically, even encouragingly, all that drinking seems to do the Andorrans very little harm at all, as in addition to copious volumes of beer, *vin chaud* and whisky, they also enjoy the fourth highest life expectancy in the world. Strangely, no government has ever used this as the starting point for an investigation into whether taxes are a bigger killer than alcohol.

The WHO data also breaks down the types of drink that each country enjoys. Southern Europe and France tend towards wine, as you might expect, while Eastern Europe has an understandable cold-weather, grain-and-potato-growing bias towards spirits. The Czech Republic, however, owes second place in the table to its massive consumption of beer, of which their average citizen consumes 132 litres a year, nearly twice that consumed by the average Brit. It isn't that surprising really. Not only did they give the world proper Budweiser and Pilsner, but it is very cheap there. When I visited Prague, a pint cost 9 pence. In the United States, cheap gas has produced gas-guzzling cars; in the Czech Republic, cheap pints have produced beer-guzzling people.

The one surprise for me about the top 15, other than the fact that we don't feature in it, was that Belgium doesn't seem to appear either, in spite of that nation's own reputation for beer production, and the fact that all the Belgians I have met, and admittedly that isn't very many, seem to like a drink. Perhaps that is just a misplaced personal observation. You see, I once went to a Belgian Trappist monastery, to buy some of their famous *bière blonde*. It was a grey, wet day, and as I was queuing in the car for my turn at what was essentially a drive-through monastic off-licence, a monk in his full garb knocked on the window, which I wound down.

'How is your trip?' he asked.

'Well, it's a bit miserable today,' I replied, resorting to talking about the weather, just to make it clear that I was British.

'Oh, never mind,' he said. 'With Trappist beer, you always have a happy feeling.'

To be honest, I was a bit shocked. I surmised that his habit wasn't simply the thing he was wearing, and began to wonder how strong the beer I was buying was. It was only nine in the morning, but this monk seemed to have drunk so much already that he had forgotten that the Trappists take a vow of silence. He wasn't right about the happy feeling either. The beer I bought was 8 per cent and, having drunk it, the only feeling I can remember was one of nausea. But maybe I'm being unfair to the Belgians. I have never seen Poirot touch a drop, and Tintin gives very disapproving looks to Captain Haddock, even if his own hair is the same shape as an opened ring pull.

However, before we begin to celebrate our mid-table mediocrity and decide that there is really no need to stand up in that meeting and declare, 'My name is Britain and I am an alcoholic,' it must be said that there are worrying aspects to the British attitude to alcohol. For a start, we seem to drink in a different way from those countries that out-perform us in the boozing stakes. So, while the French tend to drink slowly and with food, and the Ukrainians tend to drink very heavily indeed for periods of 2–3 days, fall face down in the snow and then not really touch it until the next bender, the British tend to drink very fast, without any food at all, and far more frequently than practically anyone. We also often 'pre-load' at home, in order to make getting off our faces quicker and cheaper. We seem to treat a can of booze in the same way as predatory animals treat their kill, getting through it really quickly in case someone else comes and tries to take it away. I bet if they were sober enough, some British drinkers would be happiest taking their drinks up trees.

I apologize. I think I should probably explain pre-loading. It means getting fairly drunk before you go out for the evening to get very drunk. When I bought the computer that I am writing this on, I was told that it too was 'pre-loaded', but I am fairly confident that is not what the salesman meant. The spell-checker seems to get the grammar right and none of the words are slurred.

The worrying thing for the inhabitants of the rest of Europe is that our drinking style seems to be becoming fashionable where they live. For all the column inches here devoted to why we can't develop the same drinking style as the French, France seems to be veering to the British model, and it isn't even any classier. Given their culture, you would hope that the teenagers who collapse in the shop doorways of French town centres would be there thanks to the effects of Sancerre Super, Beaujolais Extra, or absinthe, at the very least, but no. In La Belle France they are off their faces on cheap international booze brands, just like the UK.

Hugh Dennis

Initially, in Britain, the blame for binge-drinking was put at the door of alcopops, alcoholic beverages so sweet and pop-like that children wouldn't understand what they were drinking until it was too late, leaving their parents to find them snoring in one of the folds of the bouncy castle. And possibly they do have a role. The United States, which is the world leader in teenage drunkenness, did indeed invent the alcopop, although not by that name. In America the original, consisting of wine mixed with fruit juice, was known as a 'wine-cooler', which is very confusing this side of the Atlantic, although possibly quite helpful in the drive for abstinence. If you are planning to get drunk as quickly as possible, it is going to be a blow both to the budget and the speed with which you can do it if the barman gives you a tray full of empty wine-bottle-sized terracotta flower pots in response to your drinks order.

In the UK binge-drinking is also routinely blamed on super-markets, because drink is much cheaper there than in pubs. Most of the price difference is, however, down to duty, the tax imposed on alcohol by the government. It is interesting then that, by convention, during the budget speech, the chancellor of the exchequer is the only man in the chamber who is allowed to have a drink, and usually it is obvious why. 'It is all right, I don't need it. I'm only having it now because I'm making it massively more expensive after midnight. Hang on! This isn't my house.'

And however keen the government seems to be on reducing alcohol consumption and alcohol-related health problems, there does seem to be some irony in the fact that parliament is one of the most alcohol-soaked institutions in the country, with four subsidized bars for its 650 MPs. I have occasionally wondered if MPs who wrongly claimed for a second home did so because they always saw two of them, although they only had one. Certainly, those working on behalf of parliament don't provide a very good role model for those we are trying to stop from binge-drinking. If they are so against waking up and not being able to remember anything, why did they let James Murdoch get away with it at the Leveson Inquiry?

The problem, it seems to me, is that people think you have to be drunk to have a good time, when actually that is really only necessary if you are watching the stage version of *Les Misérables* or the school's Christmas carol concert. It is a link that needs to be broken, much as the link between having a tan and having had a good holiday needs to be broken too. Over the years, I have become fed up with people saying, 'Well, you're not very brown' when I have just told them what a fantastic holiday I have just had. The fact is that I don't tan very easily and however long I lie on the beach, my stomach stays the colour of natural yoghurt, but that doesn't mean I haven't enjoyed myself. Getting a tan is not the sole determinant of holiday pleasure. If it were, the Scottish tourist board would be wasting their time. But if you think that it is, be my guest, book yourself two weeks on a sun bed and enjoy popping the blisters.

Sorry about that outburst. I think I need a drink. But not a big one, and drunk very slowly, in the presence of food.

Look, one thing is for certain. However long it takes us to sort out binge-drinking (and youngsters are already drinking less than they did a few years ago), we shouldn't allow it to cloud the contribution we as a nation have made to brewing, distilling and mixing. Nor should we panic that the antics of the group of children currently vandalizing your local bus stop means that society is on the verge of collapse. Binge-drinking is just the latest phase in the 12,000-year-long relationship between human and alcohol. What is more, the British have been here before, some 300 years ago, during what is now known as the Gin Craze.

In 1688, when William of Orange arrived from Holland, having seen off his two main rivals, Norman of Vodafone and Philip of O2, he brought with him – hidden in his luggage and undeclared to customs – a love of gin. It was perfect timing. After years of war with France, the government was annoyed that people were still drinking their brandy so, seeing an opportunity to wean the population off it, they slapped more tax on the French import and allowed grain deemed unfit for the production of beer to be used in the distillation of unlicensed gin. It was a masterstroke which the French couldn't fail to notice, and they didn't. Soon the average Londoner was drinking 112 pints of gin a year, which really isn't a very good idea, especially as no one thought to add tonic for at least another 100 years.

London, in particular, went gin crazy, plunging into an epidemic of drunkenness and debauchery; gin became blamed for rising crime, neglect of the young, mental illness and increasing prostitution. And the *Daily Mail* wasn't even being published then. The whole city was awash with the paralytic. Hogarth decided to sketch the effects in his satirical Gin Lane, figuring that if you can't get hold of a vase and some flowers, no still life will ever be easier than comatose gin addicts lying face-down on a city pavement. By 1730, the capital had 7,000 gin shops and was producing six times more gin than beer.

Faced with an ever-worsening situation, the government decided to legislate in a series of Gin Acts. The first slapped a massive tax on it and required sellers of gin to buy a licence. Unfortunately, only two sellers ever applied and the whole industry went underground. Indeed, if anything, the situation became worse, as bootleggers often doctored their gin with turpentine, which is a poison. The only advantage was that painters could ask drunks to breathe on their brushes in order to get them clean.

It seemed to be a craze that simply wouldn't go away, and yet a mere 71 years after its genesis, the problem all but disappeared. Mindful of the fact that 76,000 soldiers would shortly be returning to Britain after the Austrian War of Succession, and panicked by what they might do when brimful of gin, the government finally passed effective legislation to limit the trade. This, combined with an inflated price for grain, made the drink too expensive for normal people to afford. London became calm and the tabloids switched their attention to genetically modified vegetables or something.

It is strange that gin, the drink now most closely associated with moral outrage, was the drink that first caused it. Next time you are sitting in the golf club bemoaning the behaviour of all those who drink WKD, just consider that less than 300 years ago acceptable behaviour for those supping your particular drink was stealing and shouting and having sex in doorways. The actual effects of excessive gin-drinking must also have come as a shock to the man first credited with discovering it, Dr Sylvius, a seventeenth-century German chemist who intended it as a medicine, with benefits for those with kidney problems. Ironically, the re-emergence of gin as an internationally acceptable drink was down to its mixing with a fluid with actual beneficial qualities, namely tonic, and for that we do have the British to thank. Well, them and the mosquitos of India.

It had been realized, from around the time of the Gin Craze, that quinine was effective in the prevention of malaria, and the British East India Company were keen that their soldiers should take it. Unfortunately, like the wife of an unfaithful MP who took his points for speeding, it was extremely bitter and left a nasty aftertaste. Eventually, however, the soldiers realized that they were very happy to drink it by the bucketload if it was mixed with gin, ice and a slice. Soon the medicinal tonic with gin, became gin and tonic, and malaria plummeted, as any mosquito drinking the blood of a British officer became far too pissed to bite anyone else. G&T became the drink of the Empire, and the favourite tipple of the English-speaking world.

Using alcohol to cover the taste of quinine wasn't an exclusively British trick, mind you. The French also had a malarial problem in the Foreign Legion and ran a competition to find a better way of getting their soldiers to take their daily prophylactic. One of the entrants was Dubonnet. Another French blended aperitif wine also contains quinine, although it has limited popularity in the UK, down to the obvious problem of asking for a Lillet with ice.

That gin and tonic was originally medicinal comes as no surprise to me. I look forward to a G&T as much as I look forward to a cup of Benylin, but it is a definite tick in the plus column of British alcoholic achievement, however much it grieves me.

Unfortunately, the same cannot be said of the nation's favourite tipple, beer, for although it was the first alcoholic drink made in these islands, we were by no means the first people to brew it. Indeed, beer may well have been around since before the advent of language, and is a pillar in the development of many societies and cultures, from Mesopotamia to Ancient Egypt, much of its success being down to the fact that the process of fermentation made it safer to drink than water. But while we may not have invented it, we certainly like it. By the late Middle Ages, average per capita consumption in England was of the order of 528 pints a year, with beer being served at every meal. Oddly, this didn't seem to promote a debate about binge-drinking, but then the alternative was catching cholera.

In fact, the government's main concern during the Middle Ages was not to discourage people from drinking beer, but just to make sure that the quality was all right. Nowadays, the role of Quality Control seems to be to put a small white sticker on things to show that they have passed the rigorous 'it looks all right, I'll put a sticker on it' test. In the Middle Ages, however, the tests in the brewing industry were far more rigorous. The local court would appoint an ale-conner, whose job it was to test the wholesomeness of local bread, beer and ale, and to check their pricing. The test for beer was somewhat unusual. Instead of using the obvious method of tasting it, the conner would pour some beer onto a bench and sit in the puddle in a pair of leather trousers. Obviously, as this is a ludicrous way of testing anything, except possibly the suitability of leather trousers for salmon fishing, or the gullibility of potential ale-conners, historians have disputed that this ever happened. I obviously would like to think that it did, so I'm sticking with it. And sticking with it is very much the point, because it was the degree of stickiness of the ale and the extent to which it stuck the leather to the bench that the ale-conner was measuring. Again, there is some dispute over what conclusions could be drawn from this test, even among those who think that the test existed. Some say that if the conner stuck to the bench, then the ale was impure and had too much sugar in it, whilst others claim that if he could stand up, with the bench stuck firmly to him, this was the sign of the best brew. I don't suppose the conner minded much either way about the quality. He wasn't drinking the beer, but as long as the pub door was wide enough, the stickier it was, the more likely he would walk out with a free bench. True or not, I have great admiration for ale-conners. Unless you know precisely what you are doing, it can be a very dangerous business to go into any pub in a pair of leather trousers.

While we may not have been in on the birth of brewing, we have proved to be rather good at it, producing new types on a regular basis. In the eighteenth century, London breweries produced the first porter, a dark, hoppy beer made from brown malt and named for its popularity with porters in London's markets and on the Thames. It was cheaper than other beers and didn't go off so quickly. From porter came stout, tradition-ally the strongest version of the same thing, and from stout came Guinness, once the method had crossed the Irish Sea.

We also developed IPA or India pale ale, a well-hopped beer brewed in London for export to the British colonies and able to survive the long sea voyage to, yes, you've guessed it, India. It was originally brewed in Hodgson's Brewery in Bow, and Hodgson was apparently soon responsible for half the beer drunk in the subcontinent. Now, of course, a different Hodgson is continuing the tradition by being responsible for half the beer drunk during England football internationals, as supporters the length and breadth of the country shout, 'Oh my God, he has brought Shelvey on,' and reach for the nearest can.

But Britain's relationship with beer has also been a rocky one. By the beginning of the nineteenth century, gin was on the comeback trail, and as gin palaces once again began to spring up across the country, it was spoiling for another fight with the legislators. To try and stop another Gin Craze in its tracks, the government decided that the best thing would be to give the people a cheaper, more benign alternative, one approved of even by the temperance movement: namely, beer. For much of the early nineteenth century, beer was believed to be entirely healthy, nutritious and suitable for children, so with the Beerhouse Act of 1830, the government made it possible for any householder to brew and sell beer from their own front room, once they had paid a fee of two guineas. And the British public absolutely went for it, just as they had a century before.

Given that the express aim of the act was to reduce public drunkenness, you would have to say that it was about as good at its job as a penguin at an inter-bird flying competition. The act threw Britain into a never-ending Happy Hour. Homeowners the length and breadth of the country realized there were enormous profits to be made by turning their lounges into lounge bars, and soon 46,000 so-called beerhouses had sprung up. Their total was larger than all other drinking establishments combined, and in some streets there was one in every other home. Seeing that almost no one could now walk in a straight line, the government decided it would not be thought odd if they did a massive U-turn themselves. So they did, and introduced licensing laws, much as we have today. Some beerhouses still survive, and the fact that that William IV was on the throne when the beerhouse legislation was passed is apparently why so many British pubs are named after him.

The British have also had a hand in the history of sherry, port and, of course, Scotch.

The first record of whisky being distilled in Scotland seems to be in 1494, although it is likely that it had been around for 1,000 years before that.

Its global popularity, however, is much more recent. It only started to be produced legally for export in 1823, and it took the devastation of French vineyards to turn it into an international brand. In the late nineteenth century, vines across France were attacked and destroyed by the phylloxera aphid, which caused them to wither and die. French wine and brandy production were decimated, and scotch whisky stepped in to fill the gap. It is also possible that phylloxera itself was exported to France via Britain, as it first came to Europe when Victorian botanists and plant hunters brought American vines back from their travels. If talking to a Frenchman, it is, of course, best to blame the United States.

Sherry, which was first brought to Britain by Sir Francis Drake, is, rather fittingly, a slurred pronunciation of Jerez, the Spanish town from which it comes. Determined not to let the Spanish build the Armada and threaten an invasion of Britain, Drake sailed into the port of Cadiz on a pre-emptive strike and set it alight, but not before loading 2,000 barrels of sherry that he had seen sitting on the quayside, and which he had decided to bring home with him. You have to admire him; rolling barrel after barrel of booze up a gangplank is not the sort of tactic of which the SAS would now approve during a stealth attack.

The Spanish were understandably furious, not least because the key ingredient of the massive trifle they were planning to make was now heading for Plymouth across the Bay of Biscay, but in the long run it was very much to the benefit of both nations. The British developed a taste for Fino, Manzanilla and Amontillado, and the Spanish discovered that they had a ready-made export market, once the hostilities were over. The drink became a favourite at the English court, and its popularity spread through the wider population until eventually it became the favourite tipple of almost every elderly female victim in *Midsomer Murders*. Britain soon accounted for the lion's share of Spanish sherry exports, and Britsh importers bought into sherry producers such as Domecq and Gonzalez Byass, realizing they were on to a good thing.

Although we still drink a fair amount, sherry consumption has fallen in recent years, as the drink struggles to be thought of as a tipple for the younger generation. The producers think this may well be down to advertising. Certainly, the fact that one of the leading brands is called Dry Sack suggests that it isn't going to taste very nice, unless you just love the odour of hessian. Attempts have been made to bring it up to date. The Spanish themselves often drink it with lemonade and ice, in a drink called the Rebujito, although this is apparently just a recast of a popular British tipple of Victorian times, the Sherry Cobbler. Again, I am sensing a marketing problem.

Once Francis Drake had sacked Cadiz, he thought he would give his crew a bit of well-earned rest and relaxation by stopping off at Faro in Portugal and sending them ashore with a box of matches, so they could set fire to that too. His boats were already too full of sherry to bring home any port, but that wasn't to stop it too becoming a great British favourite. In 1703 the British government signed what is known as the Methuen Treaty, effectively a deal with Portugal that as long as they didn't impose duty on any of our woollen cloth, we in turn would keep duty on port below that on French wines, which we couldn't really get at that point anyway, because we were at war with them again. As a result, port, wine that had been fortified to survive the trip, became very popular in Britain.

Initially, like gin and tonic and beer, it was thought of as a medicine. As a teenager, Pitt the Younger, soon to be our 24-year-old prime minister, was on a bottle a day as a cure for gout, which is about as effective a medical treatment as suggesting you might want to cure your headache by smashing your forehead against a lamppost. Since the seventeenth century, most of the companies exporting port have been English.

Traditionally, the British also claim a starring role in the development of the drink that sits in the fridge, in the limo and on the bedside table of every self-respecting WAG: Champagne. Obviously, we didn't have anything to do with naming it, because that is simply the name of the French wine-growing region from which it comes, but we do have a claim to the development of the recipe, to the technology for making the bottles and the design of the corks. I know, but hear me out.

Traditionally, Champagne is thought to have been invented by French monk Dom Pérignon at some point in the late 1600s – but, get this: it wasn't. Allegedly. Sparkling wine had already existed for over a century; the oldest is Blanquette de Limoux, developed at Carcassonne's Abbey of Saint-Hilaire and sold with the tagline 'with Hilaire, everything is hilarious', or at least one would hope so. What is more, nearly 40 years before Champagne is supposed to have been invented, a British physicist called Christopher Merritt documented the method of second fermentation used in Champagne production. Apparently, there was even a paper containing the method sent to the Royal Society.

As to the bottles, well, explosions dogged the sparkling wine producers of Champagne, as the glass they used was unable to stand the internal pressure from the bubbles in the bubbly. The British solved the problem by using coal ovens to produce sturdier glass than the feeble stuff the lower temperature, wood-fired French ovens could turn out.

The French also had the habit of stopping their bottles with rags soaked in oil, and while this was a good method if you were planning to throw lighted bottles at policemen during a strike or riot, it wasn't ideal for the long-distance transport of

Champagne. The British, however, had been using corks since the time of Shakespeare, and their use in Champagne made the business internationally viable.

Incidentally, we also lay claim to the world's first patented corkscrew, developed by the Revd Samuel Henshall in 1795. How we had got corks out of the bottles for the previous hundred years isn't altogether clear. I guess we just pushed them down with a thumb, or if there was a French aristocrat around, with his extremely well-developed little finger.

That Champagne became popular on our shores at all, though, is down to a French nobleman called Charles de Saint-Evremond. Banished to England in 1661 for his views on the so-called 'peace of the Pyrenees', which got me pretty worked up too, he brought with him still wine from the Champagne region. The aristocracy developed a taste for it, so when the sparkling version emerged, the British public were willing partakers. Britain is still Champagne's largest export market, and we drink more per capita than any non-French-speaking country. Brut Champagne was developed specifically because we liked it, although I don't. It is never a good idea to mix sparkling wine and aftershave.

Our influence on drink hasn't only been noticed in alcoholic beverages though. In 1767 English chemist Joseph Priestley, the man credited with the discovery of oxygen, made another advance at least as important to British and American teenagers: how to make carbonated drinks. Finding there was carbon dioxide above the fermenting tanks in a Leeds brewery, he recreated some at home, dissolved it in H_2O and made soda water. This method was adopted in Germany by one Dr

Schweppe, who later moved to London to establish Schweppes and exploit the new fizzy drinks he was then making.

Given the vast numbers of Costas, Starbucks and Caffe Neros that now fill our high streets you might also harbour a hope that these islands played an integral part in the development of coffee, the world's favourite stimulant. Sadly, we didn't, but perhaps we could have done if someone had realized the opportunity 300 years ago. Initially coffee had been a drink popular in the Orient and Arabia. English travellers reported that it seemed to reduce the desire for sleep, to promote discussion and argument, and was consumed all day and all night, especially by men in the middle of an essay crisis. Like every alcoholic drink I have so far named, it was also ascribed with medicinal qualities. In this case, it was thought to be good for gout (again), smallpox, scurvy and so-called 'head melancholy', a condition caused by melancholic juices in the brain, which I am almost certain Wallander has got.

The first English coffee house was established in Oxford in 1650 as a place for discourse, scholarship and, of course, coffee. It was attended, amongst others, by Sir Christopher Wren, who had to sit on his own in the corner, because no one could bear him droning on about his rain gauge, self-tipping or not.

Soon coffee houses spread to London, although the format remained the same. They were places for discourse, politics, philosophy, gossip, social interaction and discussion about the scandalous price of a latte. They became centres for news, where pamphlets and newspapers such as the *Tatler* and *Spectator* were circulated, and forums for egalitarian debate, where the social standing of those taking part was unimportant, although gender was crucial. Women were generally excluded.

Some coffee houses also offered lessons in academic pursuits such as astronomy and Latin, and gentlemanly ones such as fencing and dancing. Different coffee houses catered for different professions. Men in the shipping industry met at that run by Edward Lloyd, hence the foundation of Lloyd's of London, while doctors and surgeons gathered in another, so that only they would know how much the coffee was making their hands shake. Men off their faces on gin went to whichever they could crawl into, desperate for a quick caffeine fix.

But just as their future looked secure, coffee houses went into a rapid decline. The intellectual elite who had established and championed them decided that they were now a bit too common and went off to set up gentlemen's clubs instead. There seemed to be nothing they could do to reverse the trend. Sir Christopher Wren suggested that they all change their name to Starbucks, install Wi-Fi, introduce strange saucers where the cup isn't in the middle and locate near primary schools so all the mothers could gather after they had dropped their kids off. No one listened to him. The possibility of global coffee domination disappeared, and those who mourned the lost opportunity sat down and cheered themselves up with a nice cup of tea.

Which isn't that far from the truth, as tea was taking over as the more popular drink. Coffee relied on supplies from Arabia and, like oil in the 1970s, this was subject to unexpected price hikes and interruptions in production. Coffee became more expensive to buy and more difficult to get hold of, and Britain weathered the crisis by having a cuppa. And thank goodness we did, because tea, both the making and the drinking of, is what the British are supremely good at.

As a popular drink, tea was first introduced to these shores by Catherine of Braganza, the Portuguese wife of Charles II, the Portuguese having acquired the taste for it through their empire in the East. It was an immediate hit and, realizing that without it there would be no tea breaks, British workers demanded more and more. At last the populace seemed to have settled on a drink that was harmless, fairly cheap and socially acceptable, so the government moved immediately into action. Preferring to promote only those drinks that left you comatose and with liver ache, like gin and beer, they hit tea with an enormously high level of tax. By the late eighteenth century it stood at 119 per cent, forcing British tea dealers to bring the stuff in illegally. Having to smuggle tea is, of course, ridiculous; tea-making is as great a danger to society as the cauliflower trade or gangs of teenagers carrying Q-tips, and yet that is what happened. By the late 1700s seven million pounds of tea was arriving illegally in Britain every year, until finally Pitt the Younger reduced the tax to one-fifth of its former level. He had realized that neither port nor coffee were having any effect on his gout and thought that tea might be worth a try.

Once the tax obstacle was cleared, the British and tea embarked on a full-blown love affair. The Victorians liked it so much they started taking high tea and invented the tea dance – not a rain dance to encourage the bringing of tea, but an early evening social gathering. They developed new plantations in India to supplement those in China from which the East India

Company had been supplying the British market, and they built new tea clippers, such as the *Cutty Sark*, which raced to bring the tea back as quickly as possible, even if it is now a brand of whisky.

We now drink 160 million cups of tea a day, against a mere 70 million cups of coffee. Although, having said that, a cup in coffee terms ranges from the ones they use for espresso to the reinforced paper water-butt that is the receptacle for a grande flat white. Yet, surprisingly, we are not the largest consumers of tea in the world. That honour goes to the United Arab Emirates, whose people get through nearly three times as much per capita as we do. Indeed, we are only seventh in the list of tea-drinking nations, behind others such as Morocco and Mauritania. Of course they don't drink their tea in the same way, having it black, but for those of you thinking, 'Well, that doesn't count then. I bet you no one beats us in the consumption of tea the way it should be drunk, that is with milk,' I'm afraid you are wrong in that too, as that particular accolade goes to the Irish Republic. Why we drink tea with milk is also up for debate. Some say it is because without milk the heat of the tea would have cracked the china cups of early tea-drinkers, and others that milk was added to tea by to make it a less costly drink. With the British obsession with etiquette, it also seems entirely possible that tea was served with milk just so the upper classes, who put it in the cup first, could laugh at the poor misguided lower orders, who put it in afterwards, not realizing the terrible faux pas.

Although we didn't introduce the tea bag, which was first marketed by Thomas Sullivan of New York around 1904, we have led the way in changing its shape. This has been a largely futile attempt to convince the British public that what counts when making a cup of tea is neither the temperature of the water, nor the length of time the bag is left in, but the design of the paper wrapper that surrounds the leaves.

First, in 1989, Tetley replaced the square tea bags the public had had to put up with for decades with a tea bag that was round, and which therefore mirrored the base of the mug you were making it in, although not the shape of the mug you were if you really believed the tea would taste any better. Millions bought them, and Tetley duly knocked PG Tips from the number one position in the market. But PG Tips weren't going to surrender the industry they had dominated since 1958 without a fight. It took them seven years of planning and development, but in 1996 they hit back with a tea bag in the shape of a pyramid. Not the size of a pyramid, or the age of a pyramid, but the shape of a pyramid. This design, they claimed, allowed the tea to move around more freely and achieve swifter infusion – a speed of infusion that had only been achieved in the past by getting a spoon and swirling the tea bag round a bit.

The more complicated shape did it. PG Tips went straight back to the number one spot, leaving Tetley to wonder whether there was any mileage in a tea bag in the shape of a cuboid, a cone, or a trapezoid in three dimensions.

Lipton's Yellow Label, the world's bestselling tea, doesn't come in a circle or a pyramid, but it is British, although, strangely, not sold in Britain. Owned by the same company that has PG Tips, Yellow Label comes in the fourth tea bag shape:

oblong, with a string and a tag on it. This is designed to enable easy removal of the bag once the correct strength has been reached, but once the water you pour on it has forced the whole thing under the surface, you usually have a cup of tea that just tastes vaguely of string and tag.

While we can take credit in the arena of drinks, it is difficult to claim any global influence for Britain in the area of cuisine. Indeed, our cooking seems to have become something of a global joke, although just occasionally the joke has worked against the people making it. According to Sebastian Coe, a few days before the meeting which would decide which city was to host the 2012 Olympics, Jacques Chirac, the French president, attended a G8 summit at Gleneagles in Scotland. On being served haggis, the traditional Scottish delicacy of sheep heart, liver, lungs, oatmeal and onion, described by *Larousse Gastronomique* as having 'a delicious savoury flavour', Chirac decided to ignore the opinion of his nation's own culinary bible and go for a cheap joke. He turned to his fellow world leaders and said, rather too loudly, 'How can you trust people who cook like that?' Which is a bit rich coming from a man who has probably eaten brains, snails and the legs pulled from frogs, and been given a two-year suspended sentence for corruption, fraud and the misuse of public funds.

Hearing of the remark, Cherie Blair, the haggis-loving wife of our own prime minister, became incensed and decided to take Chirac to task. The opportunity presented itself at the crucial Olympic meeting in Singapore. Seeing the French president enter a gathering at which the bidding countries would try to garner the last few votes of the IOC delegates, she headed across the room to talk to him, and he, seeing her coming, fled the room in an Olympic qualifying time, having failed to talk to anyone he had planned to. Result: the IOC vote went in favour of London, and all the carefully crafted French plans went to waste, including a radical one to use haggis in the shot put.

But Chirac doesn't seem to be alone in his attitude to our national culinary offerings. To be honest, no one else really seems to like what we cook.

Unlike the French, Chinese, Italian or Indians, there are practically no restaurants serving our national cuisine anywhere else on the planet, and no one, to my knowledge, has ever said, 'Where's the takeaway menu? I really fancy a British.'

Apart from roast beef and fish and chips, which are both more popular here than anywhere else, our sole gastronomic export seems to have been the sandwich, and that isn't even really cooking, just a means of packaging food so you have to spend less time eating it, the kind of thing you would do if the food you were eating wasn't very nice in the first place. By repute, the sandwich was invented by the fourth Earl of Sandwich, who asked for roast beef and bread to be brought in sandwich form, so he could eat without putting down his cards while gambling. Lesser known is the fact that the earl was apparently also a member of the Hellfire Club, a group set up for the purpose of performing immoral acts and rumoured to take part in black masses. If true, it may just be luck that Britain's favourite sandwich fillings are now beef, chicken and salad, and tuna and sweet corn, rather than goat, goat and virgin, and defiled virgin with mayonnaise.

The reputation we have for terrible food is, however, relatively new. During the Middle Ages and the Enlightenment, British food didn't suffer much in comparison with that of other nations. Indeed, those who visited these shores seemed to envy the amount of meat we had to eat. In Victorian and Edwardian Britain too our cuisine was regarded as perfectly acceptable, if not particularly tasty, as sauces were regarded with suspicion and garlic thought to be too 'Catholic' to be used as a flavouring in a Protestant country. Recipes were wholesome and complicated, and required the Mrs Patmores in charge to sweat profusely over a range the size of a small house. Cholesterol was certainly not an issue, and nor it seems was giving dishes attractive names. Traditional recipes of the era included the somewhat cannibalistic-sounding Bath chap, a pig's head in brine, and the stagnant-sounding Sussex pond pudding, a big lump of suet encasing a whole lemon – a sort of Scotch egg for fruit lovers.

Many dishes seemed to be named after animals, real or imagined, such as Welsh rabbit, toad-in-the-hole and the Bedfordshire clanger. Goodness knows how they got hold of the last one; perhaps Neil Armstrong wasn't the first man on the moon. The clanger was, in fact, a suppertime one-stop shop, a suet Swiss roll, filled at one end with steak and kidney, and at the other with apple and raisins, so you didn't have to go to the bother of pausing between courses, and could just plough straight on. If they had put another compartment in containing Coke or a coffee, they could have sold it as a 'Meal Deal'. Can't say I would have fancied it very much, although I might have had nibble at Berkshire Bagpuss, Suffolk Sir Prancelot or Peterborough Pugwash, had they been available.

However, as great English country houses began their decline amid the austerity at the end of the First World War, many of these recipes fell into disuse and British cuisine began its long parallel decline. Somewhere between the end of the First World War and the formation of Duran Duran, British cookery went off the rails, leaving the rest of the world to look at the wreck on the plate in front of them and say, albeit apologetically, 'Do you know, I'm feeling a bit full, I think I will grab a snack later.'

By 1945 it was obvious that the British government needed to sort out the mess that was British agriculture. Keen to feed the population rather than delight it with tastes and flavours, they put the emphasis firmly on self-sufficiency and higher yields for the indigenous crops that we could grow. Farms became far more mechanised, and hedgerows, those havens for wildlife which had made the pre-war landscape a picturesque patchwork of fields, were pulled up to ease the passage of tractors and combine harvesters. More difficult and expensive varieties of crops disappeared, and with them went the last vestige of tastiness in British cooking. We became a country where bland carrots, massive potatoes, low-quality grain and apples with the taste and texture of cardboard became abundantly available.

The emphasis was on food security, the idea being that, should we go to war again, we would at least be able to feed ourselves without being reliant on outside help. At least, they say that was the idea. Having lived through the era when a salad was half a hardboiled egg, a slice of beetroot and a stick of celery, it seems at least as likely that our food was being used as a deterrent to our enemies, a way of telling other nations not to bother invading us, because all they were going to get was suet, cauliflower, custard powder and watery tomatoes the size of a space hopper. If that was the case, the strategy was both misplaced and counterproductive; for much of the 1970s, facing yet another bowl of Smash, I would personally have welcomed direct invasion by France.

Once started, the freefall in our culinary standing seemed impossible to stop.

Determined to find ways of making our food even less enticing, our food scientists worked night and day for a breakthrough, and then in 1961, at the Chorleywood Laboratories of the Flour Milling and Bakery Research Association, they did just that, discovering a method of making our bread more cheaply and quickly than any other country in the world. Using high-speed mixers and shaking the dough violently to speed up fermentation, the Chorleywood Process sounded like a low-grade Len Deighton novel and made bread that tasted as though you were eating one. The journey from flour to loaf took only three hours. It could be done with low-quality, low-protein British wheat, and it guaranteed that each slice in every finished article would be exactly the same size. The soft, spongy, uniformly taste-free, polythene-wrapped, mass-produced loaf had arrived in thin, medium and thick sliced, and it had been conceived, developed and delivered by British knowhow. With the techniques now adopted by over 80 countries, we can claim to have fathered the most consistently awful bread on the planet. It makes you proud, doesn't it? Thank God it wasn't available earlier, because I'm not sure the Earl of Sandwich would have bothered.

Our willingness to accept such low quality and such lack of choice as a means of clawing our way back to prosperity showed a certain grim British determination. Sadly, it seemed to become more of an ingrained habit than a necessity, and one which was very hard to break.

If I were to judge now, though, I would say that British cuisine, like Mr Chirac himself, should get a suspended sentence. Determined to rid itself of the salad cream and wet lettuce nightmares of the post-war years, British cuisine has rediscovered its mojo. Television channels are awash with cookery programmes: *Ready Steady Cook, River Cottage, Masterchef, The Great British Bake Off, Hell's Kitchen, Jamie's Ministry of Food* and *Saturday Kitchen*, to name just a few. Chefs have become intent on improving the food in schools, introducing previously untried combinations of taste through molecular gastronomy, and becoming famous by swearing a lot for no apparent reason. British restaurants are now among the best in the world, with Heston Blumenthal's The Fat Duck in Bray holding the title as the very best for a short time. In terms of the number of restaurants with three Michelin stars, we do admittedly still lag behind the French, who have 26 to our four, but I'm not sure I trust the Michelin system anyway. When all is said and done, Michelin is a tyre manufacturer. Would we, I ask myself, pay so much attention to a restaurant guide published by Lucas Car Parts?

And with the rise of British cookery has come the return to older traditional foodstuffs. We have put Chorleywood bread to one side, where all the additives in it will stop it going mouldy for up to three weeks, and rediscovered the art of artisanal baking. We have started to produce fantastic cheese. We have stopped buying only the mass-produced and started to turn to farmers' markets, and food fairs. And, most notably in the person of Heston Blumenthal, we have started to be experimental with taste again. Spurred on by the fact that he shares his first name with one of gastronomy's most loathed eateries, a motorway service station, Heston has devoted his career to producing new culinary experiences such as egg and bacon ice cream, snail porridge and meat fruit, combinations so revolutionary they were only ever going to be thought of by Heston or hungry drunk men returning from the pub and consuming whatever they could find in the fridge.

'Eat your heart out, Heston, I'm having half a pork pie, infused with yoghurt, a vine tomato and some cat food. I can't afford to go hungry. I have a budget speech to make tomorrow.'

Not that new tastes and flavours are completely alien to us anyway. Throughout our culinary decline, we have always had curry. The first curry house appeared in London in 1810, and curries became increasingly popular throughout the time of the British Raj. However, it wasn't until the 1970s and mass immigration from the Indian subcontinent, particularly Bangladesh, that the curry became part of the fabric of British life. Frankly, it arrived just in time, its styles and varieties filling a yawning taste gap for the British public. Many new dishes were created just for us. Chicken tikka masala is an Anglo–Indian fusion dish, as possibly is balti, which may or may not have been developed in Birmingham.

We may also owe Worcestershire sauce to an attempt in the 1830s by local chemists to recreate a curry powder that a client had encountered in India. The powder that Mr Lea and Mr Perrin produced as a result was so powerful as to be inedible, but luckily someone thought it might work in a sauce, which it didn't, at least initially. It was so unpleasant that the barrel of it they made was abandoned in the cellar of their building. Rediscovering it a year or so later, they had a quick taste, which was foolhardy in the extreme, and guess what? It was delicious. They decided to make more and, for some inexplicable reason, name it after the county they were living in, rather than acknowledge its rather more Eastern origins. Presumably, with British food being rather more acceptable in the 1830s, they were playing on our wholesome agricultural heritage. And they weren't the last to pull that trick. For those of you seeking good old British fayre when you go to the pub, the ploughman's lunch is by some accounts a meal invented for an advertising campaign by the Milk Marketing Board in the 1960s.

Who knows, with our culinary new wave, we may finally have found something exportable, but some British tastes will surely remain our own. For example, Hugh Fearnley-Whittingstall's love of road kill doesn't seem likely to set the world alight. For a television programme, I once ate a selection of foods scraped from the A38: otter in the form of a risotto and therefore called 'risotter', blackbird pie and badger stew. It tasted fine-ish, although I was a bit suspicious to start with, particularly as I had to sign a disclaimer for the BBC that if I died, it was nothing at all to do with them. I was, however, left with a lingering worry about how an otter and a blackbird had ended up on the major trunk route into Devon, when a river and the sky would seem far more sensible travel options for them. Got lost, I guess, or sent the wrong way by their sat-navs.

Still, we do now have fantastic young cooks, and some fantastic older ones. We should take pride in the fact that we could all quite reasonably line up along the south coast and chant, 'We've got Mary Berry and you ain't!' towards any former French presidents who happened to be in earshot.

Monsieur Chirac, and yes I do mean him, would also do well to remember that cuisine doesn't just mean the three eight-course meals a day that every French president is doubtless served. Oh no, it can also mean the snacks that we are not meant to eat in between, and here the British Isles has been a lot more successful, particularly in the area of chocolate.

Chocolate has been with us for millennia. The chocolate residue found in pots from Honduras suggests that cacao beans, the seeds of the Theobroma cacao tree, have been culti-vated for at least 3,000 years, while South American evidence from AD 400 suggests that the Terry's Chocolate Orange advert should really have gone 'It's not Terry's. It's Mayan.'

The Aztecs were at it too. Montezuma had 50 mugs of drinking chocolate every day, apparently, which couldn't have been good for him and may well explain why 'Montezuma's revenge' has become travellers' slang for diarrhoea. In Aztec culture, the cacao beans were also used as currency, which doesn't work here. I once tried to buy something in Sainsbury's with chocolate money and got thrown out of the shop.

Given their South American empire, it isn't surprising that chocolate came to Europe with the Spanish, who then managed to keep it all to themselves for a hundred years, before it spread,

Nutella-like, across the Continent and to Britain. At this point, chocolate was simply for drinking, as no one had yet worked out how to make it in solid form. Usually this drinking chocolate took the form of diluted sweetened chocolate powder mixed with water, but in 1689 the collector and scientist Hans Sloane, after whom Sloane Square is named, travelled to Jamaica and brought back with him a recipe for a drinking chocolate based on milk. Initially used simply by apothecaries, this was subsequently sold to Cadbury's. Cup hands, here come profits.

Yes, you may have boeuf Bourgignon, Mr Chirac, you may have dauphinoise potatoes, but we developed drinking chocolate.

By the early 1700s, the chocolate houses, effectively cafés, had become very popular in London, alongside the new coffee shops and gin dens. The choices for Londoners wanting a drink and a bite to eat had never been so great, although, to be honest, most people still went to a Wagamama, a Zizzi, or a Frankie and Benny's if they were in slightly less of a hurry.

It took nearly 200 years from its introduction to Europe for chocolate to find its way into the bars we know today. Initially, the Italians had a go, then the Dutch improved the recipe, but it wasn't until 1847 that J. S. Fry and Company, of Bristol, England, found a way of mixing cocoa butter, sugar and chocolate into a form that meant it was possible to mould a bar of chocolate that we would recognize.

Yes, Mr Chirac, you may have cassoulet, salade Niçoise and duck à l'orange, but you have us to thank for Chocolate Cream.

And that is not to be sniffed at, because Cadbury's Dairy Milk bars and Kit Kats, the other great star of British chocolate manufacturing, are now two of the top ten chocolate brands in the world. Both from British companies, Mr Chirac. British companies owned by the Americans and a Swiss multi-national. And here is some more for you. The Flake is ours, as are Maltesers, probably, and the Mars Bar, which is a bit more of a surprise to us all.

In the early 1930s Forrest Mars, son of the company's founder, decided to leave the USA, where he was finding working with his father rather difficult, and come to the UK. He set up in Slough, which if it was a more pleasant place to be than with his own parents must mean that his relationship with them was very bad indeed. There he invented the Mars Bar. All right, essentially it was like the Milky Way bars his dad was already selling in America, but I don't think we should dwell on that too much. Later, he invented Maltesers, although he might already have gone back to the USA by that time. OK, my research may be shaky, but it isn't so bad that *Newsnight* wouldn't broadcast it.

And don't think you can stop reading yet, Mr Chirac, because we haven't told you about our cereal and biscuits.

No, we can't claim Rice Krispies, or Corn Flakes, or Sugar Puffs, or Frosties, or anything from Kellogg's. Nor can we claim to have invented Weetabix, which I was fairly certain we could, because it is, in fact, Australian. Where we have hit the international jackpot is with . . . wait for it . . . wait for it . . . Alpen.

Yes, for a short time in the 1970s, Alpen, a Swiss-style muesli developed and manufactured in Northamptonshire only a few miles from the town of my birth, was the bestselling branded muesli in North America. And it only stopped being bestselling because we had underestimated the demand and couldn't get supplies across the Atlantic quick enough.

Stick that in your pipe and smoke it, Mr Chirac. I did as a teenager, and it isn't very nice at all. The oats are OK, but the raisins don't really burn properly.

And what of biscuits? Well, we have the Digestive, first produced in 1876; the Rich Tea, developed in seventeenth-century Yorkshire; and we also manufactured the first ever packet of Animal Crackers, a biscuit I'm not really familiar with, but I thought I would mention anyway. All of them are globally successful, apparently. The crumpet is also ours. I know that may sound a bit desperate, but give me a break here; it looks like a biscuit, and it may be Anglo-Saxon.

Crisps are a bit of a weak spot for us, I will admit. In fact, we have had almost nothing to do with them. They are American, first made in Saratoga Springs in New York, although flavoured crisps, such as salt and vinegar, are down to the Irish company Tayto, who were determined that no other country would replace Ireland as the world's leading potato experts and patented a way of seasoning them.

As for other snacks, we can claim neither peanuts nor pork scratchings, but don't worry, for the Twiglet seems to be ours, developed by biscuit company Peak Freans in the 1920s, although by a French technical manager called Rondalin. I am sure that must be wrong. Admittedly, it does sound French, but you spell it Ron Dalin, and he is as British as they come.

And finally, Mr Chirac, which country do you think made the first banoffee pie?

That's right. Britain. In 1972 a restaurant called the Hungry Monk in Jevington, East Sussex, took the inspiration of an American coffee toffee pudding and made the first toffee-coffee-cream-banana-artery-clogging pie on the planet.

And if that isn't enough, Mr Chirac, if you still feel that you can disparage our global contribution to food or drink, don't forget that the combination of the two has given us that uniquely British institution, the pub, described by Samuel Pepys as the 'Heart of England'.

Sure, other countries have bars and roadside inns, but only we have decided to name them after the heads, and arms, of dead royalty, or a selection of mismatched objects so bizarre you feel they must have been chosen by the drunk people sitting at the bar. Yes, Mr Chirac, only we would choose objects that simply don't go together, so think on that next time you are sitting in the Ferret and Firkin, the Dog and Trumpet or the Election Promise and Liberal Democrat.

VOTE NOW

Wikipedia lists over 30 possible ways of running a country including:

Aristocracy – rule by elite citizens
Kakistocracy – rule by the stupid
Kleptocracy – rule by thieves
Bankocracy – rule by banks
Magocracy – rule by magicians

All of which seem to apply to modern Britain. Well, all except the last one, unless Paul Daniels has become more powerful than we could possibly imagine.

None of them, however, describes our over-arching system of governance, for if there is one thing we British can surely all take pride in, it is our democratic system, which in the form of a bicameral (two-chamber) representative democracy – a phrase I have just learnt and will be using a lot at dinner parties – we have exported around the world. After all, as every schoolchild that was paying attention in that lesson knows, 'Westminster is the mother of all parliaments.'

Except that no one ever actually said it was. Sadly, whoever was listening to John Bright MP at the meeting where he supposedly coined the phrase in Birmingham in 1860 was hard of hearing, lacking concentration, or not as bright as Mr Bright was, because the whole thing turns out to be a misquote.

Bright didn't even mention Westminster, and actually said that England was the mother of all parliaments, a phrase which makes considerably less sense, and doesn't quite cut it in terms of memorability. Possibly the journalists present simply tweaked it, in the knowledge that although putting words in someone's mouth was dodgy, Lord Leveson wouldn't be born for another 100 years.

The second slight problem in believing that our democracy must be the envy of the world is that – well, how can I put this? – we aren't actually that democratic.

A quick scan of the *Economist* magazine's 2011 index of the levels of democracy in 167 countries reveals that we are, in fact, one of the least democratic nations in Europe. Don't worry, we are still in the global premiership, a group of 25 countries regarded as full democracies, but we are in 19th position, hovering precariously above the relegation zone and fearing the drop to the division below, the so-called 'flawed democracies', which rather comfortingly includes both France and Italy.

The positions are based on five criteria: electoral process, civil liberties, functioning of government, political process and political culture. And for those bored even by that short list, you are one of the reasons for our lowly position. An increasingly large number of people in this country seem to be bored by politics. Nobody really wants to get involved and, as witnessed by the total of four people who elected our police commissioners, not very many of us vote except on *The X-Factor*. In hindsight, of course, the police election would have been easy to make more exciting and attractive. Why none of the potential commissioners pledged to use a Bat Signal is beyond me.

Britain's other democratic failing, as far as the index is concerned, is that we seem to be clinging to our unelected second chamber, the House of Lords. By giving undue weight to the views of peers, this makes us a partial aristocracy, or perhaps more accurately, a geri-napocrocy, rule by the elderly who fall asleep a lot. To me, marking us down for this democratic imperfection seems unfair. The Lords cannot overturn legislation passed by the Commons, and we are reforming the second chamber anyway. The process has simply hit a bit of an impasse. An impasse it has been in since 1911.

The French ranking as a 'flawed democracy' seems to have been caused by a large immigrant population who do not feel fully integrated into the democratic process; while the fact that Italy is also in that division can be explained by two simple words – Silvio Berlusconi. If you want to be seen as fully democratic, it is apparently not on to have the prime minister also controlling large tracts of the press and television, and granting himself immunity from prosecution. Although, to be fair to Silvio, he did score well on the number of women in the cabinet, in the bathroom and anywhere else he could hide them, and on the long discussions he had with female teenage voters at his Bunga Bunga parties. I have often wondered if Silvio is quite well. Any man of 76 who thinks that 19-year-old girls might find him attractive must surely be suffering from some sort of senile, if not penile, dementia.

According to the index, the most democratic countries in the world are all Scandinavian, with Norway, Denmark, Iceland and Sweden occupying the top four places This seems a remarkable turnaround, given their history. Bowing to the will of the people seems like one of the last things a Viking would consider.

'Damn. Put out the burning torch, Olaf, the pillaging is off – 40 per cent of these villagers would rather we just left them alone. We'll have to hope for better luck in the next hamlet.'

'But 40 per cent is not a majority, Sven.'

'It is if you count the 25 per cent who spoiled their ballot papers. Perhaps I shouldn't have frightened them quite so much.'

Scandinavian democracy is now supremely well established, so however it came about, the Vikings seem to have burnt their boats on that one. No, I agree, that joke wasn't really worth it. All we can hope is that Danish democracy, in particular, doesn't become too flawless, and have faith that most Danes would welcome a small residue of governmental corruption if it meant there were still plotlines for *The Killing*

Another dent to potential British pride is that we had nothing to do with inventing democracy in the first place. That, as everyone who understands the origin of the word knows, has traditionally been credited to the Ancient Greeks. Although, given that their descendants have spent most of the last 2,000 years under a dictatorship of one form or another and that their most recent bout of democracy has coincided with a complete financial meltdown, they could be forgiven for wondering whether inventing it had really worked in their favour.

OK, here's the history.

Oh, I should probably explain here that I never learned Greek at school and gave up Latin when I was 12 in order to do German, so you will have to bear with my lack of classical education.

In the 6th century BC traditional aristocracies such as Athens began to be disrupted by occasional revolts, as the people rose against their rulers. At which point, we meet the Ancient World's version of Ban Ki-moon, the poet and lawmaker Solon. His solution, and one which he hoped would satisfy rich and poor alike, was to divide the Athenians into four groups, each with different rights and roles. All citizens were able to vote in the assembly, or Ecclesia, a name which makes it sound like a rebranded insurance company.

Unfortunately, Solon's reforms failed to stop the bitter power battles between the aristocrats for the Archonship, the position of greatest power within the city state, which then fell into the hands of the tyrant Pisistratus – who sounds like a cloud I haven't heard of before – and his sons Hippias and Hipparchus – who, with the rather murderous requirements of tyranny, probably weren't hip at all.

To save the situation, enter Cleisthenes, son of Megacles, brother of Bicycles, and cousin of Spectacles, an Athenian nobleman of the Alcmaeonid family – which makes him sound like some kind of beetle – who beat Hippias and undertook a complete revamp of the system of government. For this, he rather than Solon is often described as the father of Athenian democracy, although if history is anything to go by, that is probably a misquote written down when Cleisthenes made a speech in Birmingham. Incidentally after defeating Hippias, Cleisthenes then took on Isagoras, who was, and I'm guessing here, the most tax-free of Hippias's allies.

To ensure peace and good governance, Cleisthenes then divided Athens into ten tribes, eight more than the number Frankie Goes to Hollywood thought might go to war, and introduced the principle of equality of rights for all, or 'insomonia', a word just one letter different from the sleeping condition that I find reading political biographies is the perfect cure for. It was during this period that the word democracy, meaning literally 'rule by the people' first appears in Athenian usage.

It wasn't entirely the democracy we would recognize today. There was no representation for women and full citizenship was apparently based on the individual's ability to fight in wars, but in many other aspects, it wasn't that far away from our modern version. For example, to ensure there was no corruption, government posts were apparently allocated randomly to ordinary citizens by the drawing of lots, which meant that then, as now, you could end up with people in power who had no idea what they were talking about.

Likewise, being a direct democracy – that is, one in which citizens voted directly on issues rather than electing representatives to do that for them – the system meant that there were no real leaders, a principle still followed by the Labour Party.

Other aspects of the Athenian system simply wouldn't work in modern Britain however. For example, Solon – who, now that I write the name again, could easily be a brand of sun cream – took it upon himself to democratize the availability of pleasure through a network of publicly funded brothels. A sort of sexual benefits system that would now be politically impossible, or require you to be a very Liberal Democrat indeed.

Nor did the democratic system protect its founding father, Cleisthenes. In addition to his other reforms, he also introduced ostracism, whereby anyone threatening the democratic system would be sent away from Athens for ten years. Big mistake. Having told everyone how it worked, he was then ostracized himself. No one is quite sure where he spent his exile. My bet is Coventry.

Still, it all seemed to work for Athens, which added further reforms under Pericles and developed a philosophy of political liberty through the works of Socrates, Plato and Aristotle. The city entered a golden age of art and literature, during which its great playwrights, Sophocles and Euripides, produced a string of hits such as *Oedipus the King, Orestes, Are you Being Served?* and *Dad's Army*.

It would be wrong, however, to think of Athens as the only cradle of modern democracy. Although Athens' near neighbour Sparta was technically an oligarchy – a system of government where power rests in the hands of a few powerful individuals, mostly Russian, some of whom own football clubs – it was at the same time developing many systems which were democratic in form. Inspired by the lawmaker Lycurgus, it had an education system where all citizens received the same teaching, irrespective of status or wealth, and a general assembly of all Spartans called the Apella. And an upper house, or Acapella, in which all citizens had to sing in close harmony.

The structures of Athenian democracy were not, however, to survive successive invasions, and by the time of the city-state's absorption into the Roman Empire, the system was effectively moribund. Although the Romans had elements of government which have subsequently been mimicked by modern democracies too – the idea of a senate, for example – it seems to be that many of the influences for British and Western democracy lie elsewhere. The desire for the participation of the people in government was certainly not restricted to the civilizations of southern Europe.

In the Middle Ages any sort of democracy in Europe was pretty thin on the ground. The Anglo-Saxon kingdoms in Britain had the Witenagemot, a council of noblemen who would advise the king, although that hardly counts as universal suffrage. The Isle of Man had the Tynwald, supposedly established in the tenth century, and Iceland had the Althing.

Although its name makes it sound as though Icelanders have forgotten what its proper name is, Iceland's parliament, the – oh, what is it called, you know – the Althing, is one of the oldest parliamentary institutions anywhere. Founded in AD 930, it has survived for 12 centuries, which is remarkable, especially as it began as an outdoor assembly in a country where, as the name suggests, conditions are rarely suitable for a picnic. Although the assemblies were seemingly open to all, power still resided in the hands of the most powerful, which I take to mean those who had the warmest tents. At much the same time, the Faroe Islanders had a parliament called the Logting. I think they were trying to remember the name of a ride at Thorpe Park.

The city-state of Venice also enjoyed a form of democracy in the early Middle Ages, which was perhaps partially due to the way the place was founded. The Venetians had initially established their settlements on dry land, but when faced by the marauding hordes of Attila the Hun in the fifth century AD, they decided that the best way to avoid him would be to run into a nearby lagoon, hide there, and hope that the Huns had forgotten to bring their waders. The Venetians then decided to build a city where they had ended up, which obviously, given the rather wet conditions, required them to cooperate with each other to get the job done. Indeed, they seem to have been so polite that no one dared mention that probably, on balance, each building would need a damp course.

Semi-democratic models also emerged relatively early in countries as far apart, and as unexpected, as Mali and the Ukraine.

The Kouroukan Fouga, the thirteenth-century constitution of the Mali Empire, is one of the earliest declarations of human rights found anywhere. Under it, society was divided into ruling clans, with each represented at a Great Assembly. Society was also structured by age group, an age group being those born in a three-year period. If any big decision had to be made, the young and the old were then excluded from the process, leaving only those in their middle age with any power. Fine by me, although it wouldn't go down very well in the House of Lords. The constitution aimed to get everyone living harmoniously and suggested how it might be done, with edicts such as 'Never offend the talented' – which might work, I guess, although it would make judging *Strictly*

Come Dancing almost impossible – and 'Lies that have lived for 40 years should be considered truths,' which I am all for. By the laws of medieval Mali, I would now have got away with hitting my brother around the head with a golf putter and saying it was an accident.

The constitution also tried to protect the traditional relationships between the people of the empire. These were of two types. The first was a blood pact, and the second what was called a 'joking relationship', whereby two people might express their friendship by exchanging insults. The type of relationship tribesmen had with one another seemed to depend on their relative status, but only one man, the chief mediator, was allowed to joke with everyone, including the royal family, which may be why the Malian Royal Variety Performance never really took off.

By the seventeenth century, the Ukrainian Cossacks had also established a system with some of the hallmarks of a modern democracy. Under the leadership of the 'Hetman', a role with Jason Statham written all over it, the Cossack 'Hetmanate' included self-governing towns and allowed the wealthy to buy offices and titles. At last, as you can see, we are getting close to the British way of doing things.

The first proper modern democracy, however, was that of the Corsican Republic. In 1755 the Corsicans, led by Pasquale Paoli, declared independence from the Republic of Genoa and wrote a constitution that extended suffrage to men over the age of 25 and, by some accounts, to women. It wasn't to last. The French invaded the island in 1768, took most of the newfound rights away and didn't give them back, even after the toppling of their own system of government. You might think that a revolution designed to overthrow monarchy, aristocracy and religious authority and replace them with new ideas of citizenship and human rights would extend the voting franchise to women, but no. Even after La Revolution, French women still didn't have a vote, an oversight which wasn't rectified until 1944. Robespierre and the others stuck firmly to their guiding principles.

For men: 'Liberté. Egalité. Fraternité.'

And for women: 'Liberté. Egalité. Make the tea.'

Why, then, should Britain be seen as a beacon of democracy?

Well, first, although we haven't been at it as long as the Norse nations, we seem to have been muddling our way to full representation of the people for an awfully long time. The Palace of Westminster has been there for over 900 years, as has the oldest member of the House of Lords, and the word parliament has been in use in these islands since 1236, when it was used to describe the meetings between the English king, bishops and noblemen.

Admittedly, these early parliaments were purely for the benefit of the monarch. They were held wherever and when-ever he demanded and could last as long as he wanted them to. But by the thirteenth century, the barons, annoyed at being called away just when they were in the middle of doing something important, like polishing their swords, doing Sudoku, or tithing serfs, decided that they wanted a bit more of the decision-making for themselves and forced the king to sign the first document ever to limit the power of the monarch.

And that is why we have the parchment that sets us apart from all other nations.

Magna Carta.

Yes, you can now get out the flag and start waving it, because Magna Carta is without doubt 'the greatest constitutional document of all times – providing the foundation of the freedom of the individual against the arbitrary authority of the despot'. At least that is what Lord Denning said, and I don't think that even being on Radio 4 occasionally gives me the authority to question it. It is the foundation of British democracy and was an inspiration to those who drafted the constitution of the United States. Yet, to be honest, I'm not sure that many of us actually quite know what it was, including our own prime minister.

In fact, I know that David Cameron doesn't. On a trip to the United States, the prime minister decided, somewhat ill-advisedly, to go on *The David Letterman Show*, where he was ambushed. Having been welcomed into the studio by dry ice, which was meant to replicate those pea-souper fogs we so regularly get in London, Cameron was then asked a series of questions of which he had no forewarning. They were all about Britain. First, who wrote 'Rule Britannia'? To which Cameron replied, incorrectly, Elgar. The music was, in fact, composed by Thomas Arne in1740, and set to a poem by James Thomson. No, I wouldn't have got that either.

And then the next question: what does Magna Carta mean? Well, I suppose we have to be grateful he didn't think it was the name of an ice-cream, like the other Magna, Magna Classic and Magna Mint, but the fact that he said that he wasn't quite sure was embarrassing enough in itself. Even those of us without an

Etonian classical education could have made a fairly good guess that it means 'Big Charter'. The Latin was just used to make it sound more impressive and to prevent any possible confusion with Big Yellow Storage. I'm guessing that when he finally made it back to Downing Street, Michael Gove gave Cameron a detention, told him to pull his socks up and that the correct answer to Letterman's question would have been: 'What Magna Carta means, Mr Letterman, is that we had the beginnings of a free society at least two centuries before America was even discovered.'

The Big Charter in question was signed, or at least sealed with wax by one of those big stamp things, in 1215 by King John, who had really been hoping that he wouldn't have to do it at all. King John's problem was that he wasn't very popular with his barons. He had managed to lose most of their land in France for them, and then followed that up with a plan to impose higher taxes. Under normal circumstances, the barons would simply have tried to replace John as king, but luckily for him, there were no obvious candidates. With their whole rebellion in danger of becoming a bit embarrassing, the barons decided they had to do something and set about curbing John's power by drawing up Magna Carta. It was a long list of royal dos and don'ts, and rights and freedoms for everyone else, including a clause that meant that the barons could overrule the king and seize his possessions if he failed to stick to the conditions. Looking to buy time so he could rebuild his military strength, John told his servants to warm the wax.

So, just as the NASA space programme brought with it the unexpected bonuses of the roll-on, the biro and the non-stick saucepan, the liberties enshrined in the Great Charter were an unexpected benefit of a different project entirely

For all its historical significance, Magna Carta remained effective for only three months. King John had had his fingers crossed behind his back while he was stamping it and told everyone who would listen that it was invalid pretty much as soon as the barons had left the room. Having promised not to challenge their authority, John took them on instead. Wearily the Barons pulled out their list of potential replacement monarchs again, decided that if push came to shove the French Prince Louis might just about be OK, and sent him a letter to say that should he wish to be considered for the soon-to-be-vacant post of king of England, he should arrive in Kent, and please to bring an army.

Getting notice of the moves that were afoot, John and his troops headed south to meet Louis by the coast, only to run into a great storm, which the royal weather forecaster Sir Michael Le Fish had failed to spot. John's troops were battered and beaten by the wind and, thinking that being defeated by the weather didn't augur well for how they might perform in an actual battle against real soldiers, he decided to retreat with them to the north. In King's Lynn in September 1216 King John contracted dysentery. He dropped dead, and the barons' problem with him solved itself. Although he was still a child, the barons invited John's son, Henry, to take the throne, and poor old Prince Louis was left with nothing except a ticket for the hovercraft back to France. The barons were still keen on charters, though, and successive monarchs signed revised versions over the next eighty years.

In law, only three of the original 63 clauses of Magna Carta still remain. The first relates to the freedom of the English Church, the second to the right of every freeman to be judged by his peers or the law of the land, and the third guarantees the freedoms and customs of the City of London, by which I presume they mean the right to have a long lunch and to cock the economy up for everyone else. To be fair, the same clause also guarantees the rights of the so-called Cinque Ports on the south coast, but I am not quite so worried about that. Hastings has a limited ability to bring down the world economy, I think.

Nor should we be too concerned for our liberty that the other 60 sections have now been discarded. Frankly, the Great Charter seems to become less great the further down it you read. For example, Clause 33 called for the abolition of all fish weirs. Clause 48 stated that all evil customs connected with forests should be abolished, although anyone who has eaten a Cumberland sausage at the Leicester Forest Services on the M1 might wish that it was still on the statute.

Clause 50 stated that no member of the D'Athee family, with whom the barons had fallen out, should ever be a royal officer, which seems a bit petty. It's like finding a clause in the United States constitution forbidding George Washington's dentist from ever practising in Maryland. Clause 51 called for all foreign knights to leave the realm, which if still current would prevent Sir Viv Richards from ever commentating on the cricket.

Still, happy accident or not, Magna Carta set us on the course to full representative democracy, and the next few years were crucial.

Because Henry ascended to the throne while still a child, the barons continued to exercise great power, and didn't take kindly to the fact that Henry began to ignore them once he became an adult. So in 1264 they flexed their muscles again, and a rebellion led by Simon de Montfort, Earl of Chester, summoned the first parliament in England ever called without the royal say-so. In a bid to gain popular support for the rebellion, the barons decided the composition of the parliament should be different from all previous ones. It therefore included not only the usual array of bishops, abbots and noblemen, but also knights from the shires and representatives from each borough.

Although De Montfort's rebellion was ultimately defeated, leaving him to be remembered as the name of a university in Leicester and one of the Midlands' most unpleasant rock venues, subsequent monarchs continued to call parliaments involving this wider mix of representatives. The calling of burgesses and knights came to be known as summoning 'the Commons', although calling a knight common to his face would probably have landed you in a certain amount of bother. By 1341 the Commons had effectively separated from the Lords, to make two chambers of parliament, and by 1485 the monarch wasn't a member of either of them.

Yet by the time James I replaced Elizabeth I, the Virgin Queen – so called because she was the first monarch to be owned and operated by Richard Branson – the role of parliament was still advisory. Which was lucky, because there was one key piece of advice it was able to give. In the person of Lord Monteagle, it suggested that James would do well not to turn up for the state opening of parliament on 5 November 1605, because there might be a group of young Catholic boys about wanting to let off some bangers.

As a model of how not to blow up a king, the Gunpowder Plot excels on practically every level. First, the terror cell had no real plan beyond making a massive explosion. Second, in spite of the fact that Guy Fawkes had been hired as an explosives expert, several of the conspirators were injured trying to dry out wet gunpowder in front of a fire. Third, if you are planning to blow up a building, you probably shouldn't write a letter warning your mates not to be there when it happens. And finally, you shouldn't really try to encourage your co-conspirators with the sentence 'If this goes wrong, there'll be fireworks.'

When Charles I, Charles Stuart, came to the throne and began to give the impression that he didn't give a stuff what parliament thought because he had been appointed by God, alarm bells began to ring amongst members of the House, especially as they couldn't really work out which sort of God – Protestant or Catholic – Charles was talking about. Charles's relationship with the Commons was fractious right from the off. They demanded he accept a petition to restore parliamentary rights. So he did, and then dissolved parliament for seven years, only recalling it because he had run out of money and needed to raise taxes to pay for a disastrously expensive war. Finally, he became so hacked off with mere mortals refusing to accept his God-given right to rule that he stormed into the House with a group of soldiers and tried to arrest five MPs for treason. Unable to find them, Charles confronted the speaker of the Commons, who refused to tell him their whereabouts, and said to the monarch eye-balling him, 'May it please Your Majesty, I have neither eyes to see nor tongue to speak in this place but as the House is pleased to direct me, whose servant I am here,' having first prefaced that sentence with the phrase that jobsworths have handed down from generation to generation, 'I don't care who you are, sir.'

The king then stormed off, calling him a pleb. Oh no, hang on, I've got two stories confused there.

In the face-off between royalty and parliament, parliament had won the first round, but the fight was to be a long one. Not long afterwards, England was plunged into civil war, with the Royalists, or Cavaliers, on one side and the Parliamentarians, or Roundheads, on the other.

I should now say that my own view of the Civil War is rather skewed. At my school, when we played football in the playground, we often played as Cavaliers versus Roundheads, but that was because the school was 50 per cent Jewish, and – how can I put this delicately? – the Cavaliers were those of us who still had a full epidermis in the downstairs department. In the Civil War proper, the divisions between the sides were rather more fundamental, and the outcome rather more crucial to the future of British democracy than the silky-skilled football battles that we played out.

Those who know even a small amount about British history will remember that the war was won by the Parliamentarians; that Oliver Cromwell became Lord Protector; that Charles I lost his head; and then, just when we seemed set fair to become a republic, parliament realized that if we didn't have a monarchy,

Colin Firth would never win an Oscar for *The King's Speech*. At which point they decided to invite Charles II to return from exile and reclaim the throne.

For democracy, the relatively short period without the royals was crucial, however, as Cromwell suggested the model for all future parliaments: an elected Commons, an Upper Chamber, and a sovereign who would be subservient to the laws of the land. But, like all problem families, once they were back in the area, the Royal House of Stuart was soon up to their old tricks again.

Charles II, being the son of the divinely chosen Charles I, didn't really subscribe to the idea of parliamentary power any more than his father had, and didn't bother with a parliament for the last four years of his reign. Worse still, the next monarch, his brother James II, was openly Catholic, the very religion the Tudors had got rid of so Henry VIII could get it on, and off, with Anne Boleyn. It was enough to make parliament wonder why they hadn't slapped an ASBO on the lot of them, or had James taken into care by social services.

Alarmed by James II's behaviour, parliament advertised for a new king and, like the FA, was very happy to accept candidates from abroad, so long as they were Protestant. Most impressive in the interview was William of Orange, already married to James's daughter Mary, who then landed in Devon with a boatload of gin, ready to turn the end of the seventeenth century into a nightmare for Alcoholics Anonymous.

So began the reign of William and Mary. But key to the story of British democracy are the terms and conditions that parliament imposed on the new monarchs before they would accept them. The only couple to rule jointly, until Richard and Judy's brief reign at ITV, William and Mary were effectively told to approve a new Bill of Rights, to sign an Act of Settlement sending the royal succession the way of the Hanovers and, most crucially, to agree that they would never ever have a book club.

The Bill of Rights of 1689, thus signed, is another of the great constitutional documents of England. Predating the French and United States equivalents, it sets out certain basic rights for all Englishmen. No taxation by royal prerogative, no royal inter- ference in the law, no royal interference in the election of members of parliament, and no interference from anyone if you decide to spend Sunday afternoon watching the football with your feet up.

At this point, the rather meandering course taken towards full British democracy begins to straighten up a bit. In 1707 the parliament of England and the parliament of Scotland, which had proved an almost equal pain in the side of Scottish monarchs, became joined. Political parties began to be established, as did cabinet government and the role of prime minister.

Originally the cabinet met with and reported to the monarch, but with the accession of the Hanoverians, that all changed. George I, who spoke only German, was apparently so bored by the meetings, and so fed up with ministers trying to explain things to him by speaking more slowly and loudly, that he left everything in the charge of his prime minister, Robert Walpole, and instead spent his time concentrating on his German duchy, where no one thought his accent was funny and everyone had to do what he told them.

It was a time of rapid industrial and social change. There was revolution in France and in Britain's American colonies. Tom Paine wrote *Rights of Man* and in Manchester in 1819 cavalry charged into a crowd demanding parliamentary reform, killing 15 and injuring over 400, in what came to be known as the Peterloo Massacre. And yet the number and types of people eligible to vote remained largely unaltered. This was finally addressed in the Reform Act of 1832

At the beginning of the nineteenth century, the selection of members of parliament was still done on medieval lines. MPs were elected by the counties and the boroughs, even if some of those boroughs were now 'rotten' and had ceased to be important settlements. Old Sarum in Wiltshire, for example, returned two members, although no one lived there, the entire population having moved to nearby Salisbury, while the two MPs for Dunwich in Suffolk didn't only represent a population that had disappeared but a town that had too, the whole place having toppled into the sea. They might as well have been representing Atlantis. Even in the boroughs that were still populated, the method of electing MPs was by no means standard.

In 'open boroughs' all men who happened to be there on the day of the election could vote. In 'potwalloper boroughs' anyone who was able to boil a pot on a hearth, or wallop, could vote, with this right also extended to those who had an electric kettle, while in 'scot and lot' boroughs all ratepayers could vote. In case you are wondering, the 'scot' of 'scot and lot' was a medieval property tax that everyone in the village had to pay, depending on how big their house was. If the house was built away from a water source or somewhere liable to flooding, the tax might be avoided, hence the phrase 'scot free', although anyone building in a flood plain would also find themselves free from any form of insurance cover or payout. In 'corporation boroughs' there tended to be no elections. In 'pocket boroughs', and the clue is in the name, the MP was simply chosen by the local landowner, while in 'freeman boroughs' the vote was restricted to Freeman, without so much as a look-in for Hardy or for Willis.

In Winchelsea – Roman Abramovich's favourite constituency and, like Hastings, one of the Cinque Ports whose freedoms had been guaranteed under Magna Carta – just 11 freemen were entitled to vote. In 1712 each of them was paid £30 to vote for the sitting MP, while in 1811 the returning officer paid himself £200 to count the 11 votes in front of him. In the Cornish constituency of Grampound, which became a byword for electoral corruption, voters boasted of being paid up to £300 for voting the right way. In New Shoreham the voters formed an organization called 'the Christian Club' to sell the constituency to the highest bidder.

The whole borough system was a mess, and in the counties the situation was not much better. Irrespective of size, each returned two members to parliament, known, with echoes of Gandalf, as Knights of the Shire, and the electorate was restricted to men who owned property worth more than 40 shillings, just as it had been since 1432.

The result was massively uneven representation. Manchester, with a population of 200,000, had no MPs, while Devon and Cornwall, with an electorate of just over 1,000 had 53. It was an electoral system rife with abuse and bribery, made easier by the fact that no one had yet thought of making ballots secret.

The Reform Act of 1832 was designed to radically improve things, widen the franchise and rid it of corruption. The rotten boroughs were deprived of their MPs, although rotten boroughs themselves do still exist. Listen, I've lived in Haringey. Seats were redistributed to guarantee better representation for Scotland, Wales, the industrial north and the newly formed London suburbs, and the electorate was increased by up to half a million, although still only one in six adult males was entitled to vote. Voter registration was introduced and the length of time the polls were open was reduced to just two days for each election. Previously, some polls had stayed open for up to 40 days, which irritated Jeremy Vine and meant David Dimbleby could only present *Election Special* if he turned up at the studio with enough pants for a month and a half.

The 1832 Reform Act still failed to give votes to the working man, but whereas in other nations this might have led to out and out revolution, in Britain the governments of the day stood firm, realizing that what the public wanted even more than the vote was something to complain about.

And improvements continued. In 1867 the electorate was doubled again by bringing in those who owned cheaper properties. In 1872 the secret ballot was finally introduced, following the example of Victoria in Australia, and in 1883 the Corrupt Practices Act restricted the amount that candidates could spend on their campaigns, which is why our MPs can only spend about £25k to get elected, while Mitt Romney failed to get elected in the United States with a budget of £1.5 billion.

Actually, I'm not sure Romney would have been elected how-ever much he spent. I suspect that people simply didn't want their president to sound like an oven glove from the Boden catalogue. Thank God Newt Gingrich didn't win the nomin-ation. Who would vote for a man who seems to be using his porn name?

The next major step towards full democracy didn't take place until 1911, however, when, thanks to a dispute over a budget, the Commons finally overturned 700 years of history and gained supremacy over the House of Lords.

In 1906 the Liberal government, which had been elected with the kind of landslide victory they no longer have to worry about, started to introduce welfare reform: children were to be given school meals, old-age pensions were introduced and compulsory health insurance was provided for lower-paid workers. The problem was how to pay for it, so in 1909 the Liberal government introduced a budget that both increased income tax and introduced a new tax on land. When the budget reached the House of Lords, the Lords rejected it, something they were formally entitled to do but had not done for two centuries. A stand-off ensued and the legislation only made it through when the king threatened to create enough Liberal peers to overturn the Tory majority in the Lords. Realizing such a measure would mean there wouldn't be enough seats in the chamber, and that if even only a few of the new peers turned up, there wouldn't be enough space for a nice lie-down, the Tory peers yielded. To avoid the same impasse occurring again, the Liberals then determined to reduce the power of the Upper Chamber and introduced the most unimaginatively named act of parliament so far: the Parliament Act.

Under the act, the House of Lords could only delay legislation rather than overturn it, thereby breaking the stranglehold the Lords had held over parliament for nearly 800 years. As King John doubtless told the barons, 'What goes around, comes around.'

In 1958 life peerages were introduced, and in 1963 an act was passed that enabled those peers, like Tony Benn, who didn't go to the chamber just because it was nice and warm, to renounce their titles and stand for election as members of parliament, if they could find a party and a constituency that would take them.

Which brings us to the present day, as the 19th most democratic nation on earth, although a report covering the last eight centuries would tell us there is still room for improvement and that there were many things we could have done better.

Ninety-five years after the granting of universal suffrage, it seems ludicrous to modern sensibilities that we waited so long to give women the vote, and that they were forced to go to such extreme lengths to get it in 1918. But, frankly, no nation in the world has a record on that issue of which they can be particularly proud. In the United States things looked promising early on. New Jersey allowed women with property to vote as early as 1776, but then went back on it. Kentucky gave some women the right to vote in school board elections in 1837, only to remove it again in 1902, presumably by means of a vote in which women, although they had the right to vote, somehow didn't.

Hugh Dennis

In Europe, like us, most countries allowed female suffrage only in the aftermath of the First World War, although Finland and Norway – who could have guessed? – didn't need the nudge of global carnage. Nor did Australia, which, in spite of priding itself on being pretty much the most macho nation on earth, gave women the vote in 1902, whether they were called Sheila or not

Which isn't to say that in modern Britain women are equally represented. As I write, only 146 of the 605 MPs in the House of Commons are female, and the atmosphere in the chamber can still be that of a rather rowdy boys' boarding school.

Even the prime minister, who should know better, has been forced to apologize to female members for making sexist remarks to them, having told shadow chief secretary to the treasury, Angela Eagle, to 'Calm down, dear' and his own MP Nadine Dorries that she must be sexually frustrated. In Cameron's defence, both incidents happened during the rather gladiatorial Prime Minister's Question Time, but it is to the credit of both women that they didn't retort by asking him if he was suffering from PMQ.

By way of apology, Cameron presumably told them that he didn't think of them as beneath him, he didn't think of them as second-class citizens and that he didn't expect them to do menial things like make the tea, because that is what Nick Clegg is there for. In addition, Cameron promised that he would never let Andy Gray write his speeches again,

In future, David might think it far more fruitful, and less risky, to play on the MPs' somewhat strange names. To me, the Dickensian Nadine Dorries sounds as though she should be the girlfriend of Martin Chuzzlewit , while Angela Eagle could be an evil character from Beatrix Potter. I wouldn't be at all surprised if the referees for her last job were Peter Rabbit and Squirrel Nutkin, as long as she hadn't already eaten them.

We could also have dealt rather better with the problem of parliamentary corruption, but again, it is worth putting our MPs' expenses scandal in the context of what seems to go on elsewhere. In the league table of international financial misappropriation, our politicians are absolutely nowhere.

In 2004 the *Guardian* published a list of the top five most corrupt heads of state over the previous two decades, along with the amounts of money they had purloined. They were:

Mohammed Suharto (Indonesia, 1967–98) : $15–35bn
Ferdinand Marcos (the Philippines, 1972–86): $5–10bn
Mobutu Sese Seko (Zaire, 1965–97): $5bn
Sani Abacha (Nigeria, 1993–8): $2–5bn
Slobodan Milosevic (Serbia, 1972–86): $1bn

Which makes the £1,645 that Sir Peter Viggers, MP for Gosport, claimed on a duck house, the £2,115 Douglas Hogg spent having his moat cleaned, and the £218 that David Cameron had to pay back in wrongly claimed mortgage interest seem rather pathetic, let alone the 88p Jacqui Smith apparently claimed for a bath plug.

Honestly, or rather dishonestly, we need to pull our socks up. Our cash for peerages row produced no evidence conclusive enough to bring charges against any of the individuals concerned, while in France Jacques Chirac and his one-time prime minister Alain Juppé have both been convicted for corruption. In Italy Silvio Berlusconi has been tried and sentenced for tax avoidance.

In Transparency International's Corruption Perceptions Index we are the 16th most transparent, and therefore 16th least corrupt nation on earth, in a table topped by New Zealand, Denmark (this is getting boring now) and Finland (oh, for goodness' sake).

The Westminster model, although not the mother of all parliaments, has certainly been the role model and mentor of many. The principles entrenched within it provided inspiration for many of the colonists in the earliest American states, and the parliamentary system itself provided the template which the colonies were expected to adopt. The first of the Canadian provinces had their versions in 1848, and the Australian from 1855. At the end of the Empire it became the standard parliamentary form for those colonies moving to self-government and is now used throughout the Commonwealth, from Barbados to India, where the two chambers even have the red and green seats we would recognize from the Lords and the Commons.

In some places it has failed. In much of Africa it has been replaced by presidential systems, which seem better suited to the tribal nature of those countries, whilst others, such as Zimbabwe, purport to be democracies whilst rigging their elections and operating under the guiding principle of 'one man, twelve votes'.

Overall, however, we haven't done badly. The circuitous route to full-blown British bicameral representative democracy may be one that has benefited from the self-interested machinations of barons, the delusions of a series of monarchs who believed they were appointed by God and the unwillingness of peers to pay for welfare reform, but it is one which has bypassed bloody revolution, pretty much avoided dictatorship and only produced one relatively short civil war.

True we still have an unelected head of state, who obviously has no actual right to be there, but this seems to have provided a stability which has allowed other greater reforms to be carried out. For republicans, the unfortunate fact seems to be that the presence of a monarch may improve a democracy rather than diminish it – just ask the Danes, the Swedes and the Norwegians.

Plus it is very entertaining. If you were designing a democracy from scratch, the British parliamentary system would be discarded long before it even got to the drawing board. It is a system full of idiosyncrasies, but that is what makes it interesting.

For example, should any MP wish to resign during the life of a parliament, rather than just handing in a letter of resignation, clearing out his or her desk and leaving the building, they must instead apply for the post of steward to the Chiltern Hundreds, a medieval sinecure under royal patronage which prevents the holder from being a member of parliament. Where else would that happen? Answer: nowhere. On one day in 1985 when nine Ulster Unionist MPs wanted to resign in protest at the Anglo–Irish Agreement, each of them held the stewardship of the Chiltern Hundreds for about ten minutes, before resigning it to give the next one a go.

In which other country would the newly elected speaker of the House be physically dragged to his chair by other MPs, as a reminder that in the past speakers could be executed by the monarch and therefore might be slightly reluctant to take the post? And which other nation would go through the ludicrous rituals of our state opening of parliament?

Before the day begins, the Yeomen of the Guard search the cellars of the Palace of Westminster to check there is no one skulking about with barrels of gunpowder, while muttering darkly about Catholics. Then, before the queen leaves Buckingham Palace, a member of the House is Commons is delivered to her as a hostage and is held at the palace to guarantee the monarch's safe return from the ceremony; unless the hostage is someone the government would like to disappear anyway, which may be why Vince Cable has never volunteered for the duty. The queen then sets off for Westminster, but before she gets there, her Imperial State Crown arrives in its own horse-drawn coach, which seems a bit wasteful, seeing as the queen could bring it herself or use DHL. It is then passed to the queen's barge master, a man who has been worried about his job being phased out since about 1600.

The scene is then set for the arrival of the monarch herself, who having alighted from her carriage, then disregards all advice to take one's coat off when one goes inside and instead puts on the Robe of State, meaning that she will never feel the benefit. She then proceeds to the House of Lords, followed by the Earl Marshal and a selection of officials. Once there, and reunited with her crown, which has now been removed from the bubble-wrap, she asks the Lords present to be seated and signals that the time has come to summon the members of the House of Commons. The Lord Great Chamberlain then raises his wand to signal to the Gentleman Usher of the Black Rod who, accompanied by a police inspector, then heads for the doors of the Commons Chamber. As he approaches, these are slammed in his face, the police inspector writes it all down in his notebook and Black Rod bangs on the doors three times with the stick that bears his name. The doors are opened and he requests the Commons join Her Majesty in the 'House of Peers'. This they do, led by the Sergeant-at-Arms, carrying the ceremonial mace, which he will spray if anyone gets too close.

The members of the Commons then process as far as the barrier at the entrance of the Chamber of Lords and have to stand there while the queen reads her speech.

In most countries the head of state probably just cuts a ribbon.

Do you want that?

ANIMAL CRACKERS

What is it with the British and animals?

When I was growing up we had a cat. We had really wanted a dog, but as we lived in the east end of London, right by the docks, and there weren't any obvious places to let a dog run free, my parents felt that probably wouldn't be fair, so we got a cat instead. And then pretended it was a dog. Right down to taking her for long walks on a lead. Well, I say a lead, what I really mean is a 30-foot-long nylon washing line.

She was a pedigree Burmese called Kiska, which, in case you are wondering, is one of the Aleutian Islands that sit between Alaska and Kamchatka in the Bering Sea. Why she was named after an end point of an archipelago, I don't know. It was a name the breeder had given her, and as the breeder was a fairly formidable lady who told us that in her younger life she had been a camel-riding stuntwoman in the 1930s film *The Four Feathers*, I think my parents decided to stick with it rather than incur her wrath.

Hugh Dennis

How we knew so much about the breeder's previous life, given that we were only with her for about 20 minutes, I'm not sure either, but I guess that is what pets do. They make you talk. Anyway, the reason we went for a Burmese cat was that, according to the various books my parents consulted, they were an aggressively friendly breed, and one that was unlikely to scratch the furniture or pull the curtains down. The hope was, I think, that we were getting some kind of feline labrador. From there, it was a short leap to cat-walking.

To be fair, the walks really only happened when we went on holiday. Unwilling, or unable, to leave the cat at home, my parents always brought Kiska with us as we toured the National Parks and beauty spots of Britain in our caravan. And as we seemed to spend most of our holidays walking, the cat did that as well. She climbed Pen-y-ghent, she walked across Dartmoor, she meandered up Dove Dale, and she reached the summit of Whernside, all the while attached by a rather smart red harness to 10 metres of plastic-coated cord bought from our local hardware shop. Most of the time she appeared relatively biddable, and a gentle yank on the nylon rope would encourage her to abandon her search for insects in the grass, or her attempts to stalk birds and climb trees, and rejoin us on the path. When she got tired, or was finding it difficult to walk into a headwind, my father would scoop her up and she would spend the rest of the journey inside his jacket, with her head popping out just above the zip, or if it was warmer, lying on his shoulders with her body wrapped around his neck.

For a long time, I thought this was what everybody did with their cats and that it was completely normal, but as I entered my second decade, the point at which everything your parents do is embarrassing, I became profoundly aware that it was nothing of the sort. I began to notice that on our many hikes we never saw another cat being beckoned by its owner. When I asked my friends, I discovered that the only thing they did with a clothesline was hang clothes from it, and when I enquired if their fathers had scratches on their upper arms from a semi-conscious cat digging in to steady itself, they looked at me very oddly. Eventually, my brother and I decided to walk some distance behind my parents to avoid embarrassment, but that just meant that we started to hear the comments of hikers coming in the opposite direction.

'Did you see that cat? On a bloody lead! Ridiculous!'

'That man had a cat in his cagoule, and blood on his neck. Nutter.'

When we weren't spending the whole day up a cold, wind-swept mountain, the cat came shopping with us. We queued at the tills in local supermarkets with my dad wearing a furry, brown, feline scarf that smelled vaguely of fish. It was hell, the kind of childhood trauma that could very easily have landed me with a very large bill for therapy.

When I left home, the devotion to the cat became even more extreme. Kiska had always slept on my parents' bed, but as her legs began to go, she could no longer jump up onto it the way she always had. So my parents weighed up the options. Should they give the cat a nice basket to sleep in next to the boiler? Should they buy a cat bed and place it on the floor of their bedroom? Or should they think laterally? Which is, of course, what they did. Choosing an option none of us would ever have thought of, my father disappeared to his shed to build two specially crafted, gently sloping cat staircases, each about 4 feet long, which were to be placed on either side of their king-size bed. They were a triumph of engineering, and ingenuity. But cats will be cats, and having looked at the fruits of my father's labour and carefully considered the many hours he had spent sawing, nailing and sanding, Kiska decided that she had no interest in the staircases at all and refused to use them.

My parents would have to think of something else. Back in the shed, my father built the cat a box to sleep in, the dimensions of which were perfect to slot into the gap between two wall-mounted radiators in the kitchen. In the box she lay on a cushion heated by a hot-water bottle, while from above, she had the warming effects of an anglepoise lamp that was permanently switched on. Kiska loved it and lived in it practically all the time, although looking up into the blinding light, it must have felt like the most comfortable interrogation suite ever devised.

I now realize, of course, that although my parents' behaviour may have been a little more eccentric than most, they were by no means alone in it. All over the country, people are equally devoted to their pets. In fact, so committed are they that it barely seems necessary to even pose my next question.

Are we really a nation of animal lovers?

Because the answer is a resounding yes; although, if you asked a badger, they might say something different.

In addition to the human population of 65 million, Britain is also home to 10 million cats, 10 million dogs, 40 million fish, 1 million rabbits, 700,000 guinea pigs, 300,000 hamsters and

300,000 horses. Evidence of our animal obsession is every-where. Meerkats sell us insurance, chimpanzees sell us tea and puppies sell us toilet paper. We love the imagery, although there is no obvious connection with the products. In fact, it's when there is that the campaigns can go wrong. You would have to hope that whoever launched the short-lived toilet tissue called Kitten Soft really hadn't thought it through.

Our chalky hillsides even have pictures of animals etched onto them. There are 14 white horses in Britain. ranging from the stylized Iron Age White Horse of Uffington, to the nineteenth-century Kilburn White Horse on the North Yorkshire Moors, which looks as though it has been drawn by a group of five-year-olds who have discovered which drawer their teacher keeps his vodka in.

We even plan to have a statue of a horse to welcome people to Britain. The White Horse at Ebbsfleet will be a massive 50-metre-high white concrete thoroughbred, visible from the A2 and the high-speed line from Paris. If ever built, it will symbolize Horsa, the mythical Anglo-Saxon who invaded Britain, or more likely will just look like a mutant horse that grew up too close to Dungeness Nuclear Power Station. The project has currently stalled due to lack of funding, and I can't see there being any money soon. At the moment, the government can't even afford a real horse to stand on the site while they think about it.

And if all the animals we voluntarily share our country with aren't enough to persuade you of our national love for them, then you should look at the equally vast number of surveys and research projects into their behaviour, their likes and dislikes and their relationships with us, their owners.

Frankly, some of the surveys are rather alarming. The document that seems to dig deepest is the Petplan Census of 2011, a survey of 10,697 pet owners, undertaken, as you might have guessed by Petplan, the UK's favourite pet insurance provider.

Here are the findings. Brace yourselves.

32 per cent of people find it easier to talk to their pet than their partner.

58 per cent of people felt that their partner was less reliable than their cat.

It really doesn't say much for the state of relationships in Britain, does it, if over half of all pet owners think that their partner is less reliable than an animal whose most reliable attribute is that it simply won't do anything you want it to.

There's more.

31 per cent of respondents would rather tell a secret to their pet than either their partner or their best friend, although they were more likely to tell a dog than a cat.

Very sensible, those cats are notoriously unreliable. Who knows whom they might tell? It also makes you wonder whether MI5 haven't been missing a trick all these years. It wasn't a mole they needed at the heart of the KGB, it was a labrador with a tape recorder. We would have found out everything.

Incidentally, if you are thinking of telling your pet a secret, I have two pieces of advice. First, make it something they don't actually have to retain. You shouldn't, for example, rely on them to remember the password to your computer, or bark your PIN code back to you. Second, and this piece of advice is much simpler, never confide in a parrot.

On with the survey.

55 per cent of respondents let their pets sleep on their beds. This is higher for cat owners than dog owners and owners of rabbits.

Which makes me wonder what happens to people who own all three and want to pass the nighttime hours with them. Do they draw up a rota? Do they share with all three at once? Or do they just hand the bed over and go and sleep in the spare room? Probably they would just ask the animals what they thought should happen, because animal opinions seem to be very important to pet owners. For example:

63 per cent of respondents would consider breaking up with a new partner if their pet didn't like them.

It is a pretty high percentage, isn't it? But one that would surely be beaten by those answering yes to the question, 'Would you dump a new partner if they suggested you con-summate the relationship in their bed, whilst being watched by a rabbit?' In the small survey I conducted, that stood at 100 per cent.

This of course may be why:

59 per cent of pet owners prefer to make friends with other pet owners.

This figure was highest, as you would expect, for dog owners, who like to meet other dog owners out walking. Cat owners seemed less bothered. Take a cat for a walk and the only people you are likely to meet are my parents.

According to the survey pets are also big into social media.

62 per cent of respondents had a picture of their pet on their social networking page. 20 per cent of all 18–24 year olds questioned have a networking page for their pet.

Quite how a pet operates a networking page, I'm not sure.

Perhaps they use a mouse. But there are plenty to choose from. Cats and dogs have Cats Utd, ChampDogs, CatBook, DogBook or Dogster. Rabbits have one called Bunspace.com, which I came across by accident while I was looking for an online version of Greggs. If you have a canary, I guess they use Twitter.

And the stream of pet-based information doesn't stop with Petplan. From other surveys, I discovered that 19 per cent of pet owners will sign cards with their pets' paws, presumably while still attached; that bald cats are the friendliest; and that cat owners are more intelligent than those who own dogs, if you take having a degree as a mark of intelligence, which, looking at many of the cabinet, I don't.

Pets also account for an increasing portion of our disposable income. Every year we spend £4 billion on them, £1.9 billion of it on pet food. The available choice is bewildering. There are scientifically formulated life-stage products for puppies and kittens, health-enhancing foods for the older cat or dog, foods which promise relief from renal problems, shinier coats or livelier eyes, balanced foods for complete pet nutrition, dry foods, moist foods and foods that are succulently slow-cooked in gravy. There are organic foods, whole foods, and foods which are presented as though they are the latest discovery in cat nutrition and form part of a 'raw-food diet'. Yes, I too pity those poor old wild, pre-domesticated cats that wasted so much time cooking everything.

All over the country, our pets are being pampered. We are taking them to pet boutiques and buying them hair treatments, nail treatments and massages. We are employing dog walkers, dog trainers and fitness experts. We are treating them to haute couture, hygienists and sessions with pet psychologists. Yes, hard as it is to believe, pet psychology is an increasingly popular option for owners with misbehaving or over-anxious pets. Dogs, in particular, love it, just for the thrill of being told to sit on the couch, when most of the time they are being ordered to get off it. Does it work? Well, the jury is out.

I had a friend who was mugged on Hampstead Heath while out walking her dog, a rather jumpy labrador called Arthur. She had thought that her dog would protect her, but when the mugger leaped out from behind a bush to demand her mobile phone, Arthur did nothing of the sort and simply ran away, terrified. In her mind, this was a clear case for the services of a dog psychologist.

Arthur was put into analysis. The problem, or so the psychologist said, was that Arthur was too intelligent and had therefore become too aware of the possibility of danger to himself, something a dimmer dog would not even have considered, a brilliantly flattering diagnosis if you are about to charge Arthur's owner several hundred pounds. The answer, though, was clear. Arthur required specific training to overcome this abundance of brains, and should be trained to protect his owner in the event of attack. And so began a period of intensive instruction: Arthur was taught that should his owner utter the code word zebra, he should then stand and growl at whoever the assailant might be. The routine couldn't have been simpler, especially for such an intelligent dog. Zebra, growl. Zebra, growl. Zebra, growl.

After several expensive classes, it seemed time to put the training to the test. My friend took Arthur up onto the heath again. She walked along the same path. The dog trainer jumped out from behind the same bush. My friend cried, 'Zebra!' And Arthur ran away. An expensive lesson had been learned, but not by Arthur.

If the evidence of expenditure and psychology still isn't strong enough to convince you of the British love of animals, then our laws should. In 2006 we passed the Animal Welfare Act, the most far-reaching animal welfare legislation in the world, providing a level of protection for all animals in the UK. As a result, the government produced 'The Code of Practice for the Welfare of Cats', the first in a series of leaflets which will eventually cover all pets. It is a laudable attempt to make sure that we treat our feline friends with the correct degree of respect, although some of the guidelines don't seem to be explicit enough.

For example the instruction, 'You should ensure that your cat receives enough mental, social and physical stimulation to satisfy its own behavioural needs' seems to have been interpreted by most people as an order to tell your cat a secret and give it a Facebook page. On the other hand, 'Your cat should be provided with a suitable toilet area that is quiet and easily accessible' is not open to misinterpretation. It means, quite simply, make sure it goes in next door's garden.

The leaflet also contains the advice: 'Read and be guided by the feeding instructions relating to any cat foods you buy,' which I am not sure was worth including, if I am honest. Anyone who can't be bothered to read the instructions on the side of some cat food is very unlikely to be reading a leaflet sent through to them by DEFRA.

The evidence is clear then. We like animals all right. But say it quietly; it hasn't always been like that.

While we should be proud that the RSPCA is older than other any animal charity on the planet, the fact that it was founded at all is a clue that in the early nineteenth century we treated our animals with less respect than we should have done, and had done so for hundreds of years. Horses had a particularly rough deal.

Prior to the invention of the internal combustion engine, British society relied entirely upon the horse. They charged into battle, they pulled carts, cabs, barges and ploughs, and they carried people and cargo wherever they needed to go. They worked in fields, at factories and down mines, and generally their lives were cheap. Some were lucky and got painted by Stubbs, or ridden by kings, but they were the Ferraris and the Lamborghinis of the equine world. Most horses had as much care taken of them as an X-registration Maestro that the owner knew had no chance of passing its next MOT.

The rapid growth of our cities made conditions for horses even worse. It was in response to those, and the sheer number of mangy cats and dogs found on the streets, that the RSPCA was founded in 1824. The groundwork for such a move had come two years earlier, however, with the passing of the Ill Treatment of Cattle Act, sponsored through parliament by one Richard Martin, MP for County Galway. It was the first substantial animal rights law in the world.

On the face of it, Richard Martin was one of the most unlikely animal rights campaigners you could possibly imagine. Born to a wealthy Irish family, he seems to have had very little regard for human life. He devoted most of his early adulthood to drinking, gambling and duelling. Fortunately for the welfare of animals in Britain, Martin proved only reasonable at the first two activities but exceptionally good at the third.

Duelling had developed in the Middle Ages, and by the end of the eighteenth century seems to have become the leisure activity for young gentlemen with a few hours on their hands. Although technically illegal, duels between gentlemen were used to sort out all transgressions, whether insulting a lady, cheating at cards or owing money and then running away. Often duelling seems to have been regarded simply as a sport, albeit a rather deadly one. So popular were duels that in 1809 two members of the British cabinet duelled to settle a matter of foreign policy. George Canning and Lord Castlereagh had clashed over where troops should be sent in the war against Napoleon, so one challenged the other to settle it with pistols on Putney Heath. It wasn't much of a fight; Canning had never actually fired a pistol before and missed his shot, and Castlereagh, whose aim was not much better, hit Canning in the thigh. The prime minister was furious with their behaviour. It was far below the standards he expected of them. Still, that's politicians for you; they always miss their targets.

Richard Martin, however, wouldn't have missed either of them. Winning over 20 duels without even being scratched himself had earned him the nickname 'Hair-trigger Dick', which to a modern ear sounds like a rather frustrating form of erectile dysfunction. Martin's exploits still form part of Irish folklore, particularly his duel with 'Fighting Fitzgerald', one of the psychopathic Fitzgeralds of County Mayo. OK, I know this is beginning to sound like an episode of *Blackadder*, but honestly it is true. I think.

As keen on duelling as Martin, George 'Fighting Fitzgerald' seems to have been the latest in a long line of the unhinged. At school he had sliced off a boy's nose, and while in Paris on a 'city-break' he had stabbed a man for treading on his dog. But while that kind of behaviour would certainly worry most parents, Fitzgerald didn't need to worry about how it would go down with his. After all, when news had reached Fitzgerald Senior that young George had been injured duelling, his spontaneous reaction had been to run the messenger through with his sword. The Fitzgeralds didn't get many messages after that. In fact, everyone refused to deliver any until the invention of voicemail.

That didn't stop the Fitzgeralds having fun though. Desperate to be violent Fighting Fitzgerald would stand in the middle of narrow Dublin alleyways and knock into people, just so he could challenge them to a fight. Desperate for a laugh, he would dress bears in women's clothes and book them as passengers on the Dublin stagecoach. Desperate to be regarded as the best duellist in Ireland, he hated the current holder of the belt, Richard Martin. It was inevitable that they would meet.

In 1780, angry at having lost an election to the son of Irish nobleman Lord Altamont, Fitzgerald made a slightly unusual loser's speech. He went to the Altamonts home, told Lord Altamont's servant that the family were no longer permitted to have dogs, and then shot their favourite wolf hound.

Martin heard the news, thought that Fitzgerald should be taught a lesson and decided to challenge him to a duel as soon as the opportunity arose. There was only one problem. For

Martin to issue a challenge, Fitzgerald had to insult him directly. So Hair-trigger Dick began to stalk his prey, looking to contrive situations where that might happen. It took four years. Eventually, by chance, he found himself sitting in front of Fitzgerald in a Dublin theatre. So, hoping it might lead to an insult, Martin got up and plonked himself down in the seat next to his favourite psychopath. In the course of the ensuing conversation, Fitzgerald called Martin 'the bully of the Altamonts', which wasn't quite offensive enough for Martin's needs, and then punched him in the head, which was. Once the stars had stopped spinning, Martin could finally challenge him to a duel, and Fitzgerald accepted. Fitzgerald was to choose the time and place, however, and for several days refused to make the necessary arrangements. Eventually, at Martin's urging, Fitzgerald's cousin went to break the stalemate, and with some trepidation knocked on the door of his relative's house. Fitzgerald opened the door, accepted the duel and then, realizing that his cousin was a messenger, followed family tradition and beat him up.

The two duellists eventually met in Fitzgerald's hometown of Castlebar, where Martin stayed at the home of his friend Lord Lucan, who I presume had ridden there on Shergar. Once the duel began, Fitzgerald's initial reluctance to take part seemed well founded. Hair-trigger Dick scored two direct hits to Fitzgerald's body, both of which seemed to make an odd pinging sound. His adversary seemed unhurt, and it became apparent that, contrary to all the codes of gentlemanly conduct, Fitzgerald had been wearing armour.

In the following months, as word spread of his cowardice, Fitzgerald decided he had nothing to lose and went even loopier than before, filling his empty hours by murdering the colonel of the Mayo Volunteers, a regiment in the Irish army dedicated to the manufacture of salad dressing. Fitzgerald was finally tried and hanged in the summer of 1786, leaving Richard Martin to get on with the thing he is now most remembered for, securing the welfare of animals. Because, however happy he was to shoot an iron-plated, messenger-maiming nut-job, Richard Martin could not bear the poor treatment of anything with four legs.

Serving in London as the MP for Galway, Martin saw plenty of animal abuse and recorded the incidents. There were broken-legged horses left to die, 'cat-meat boilers' at Smithfield, dogs rubbed with sulphuric acid as a punishment, and staged monkey-fights just a few yards from parliament at the notorious Westminster Pit. Badger-baiting and cock-fighting were com-mon, and available on pay-per-view.

It was all a long way from *Marley and Me*. As Jacob Marley would have been able to tell you.

On his Irish estate, the solution to the problem had been in Martin's own hands. He was entitled to his own army, his own laws and his own courthouse, from which could dispense his own brand of justice. It sounds great, doesn't it? He simply made animal cruelty illegal within his fiefdom, and anyone found guilty of it would find himself or herself serving a sentence in Martin's very own private prison, a run-down castle on an island in the middle of his lake.

Introducing legislation to the rest of Britain would be rather more difficult. Martin pleaded with parliament, but no one was very interested in his cause and many were violently opposed to his Bill to give animals a better life. At nearby cock-fights, many of the audience were MPs getting light relief from their own fights in the House of Commons, while cab drivers, abattoir owners and horse traders knew that saving animals from damage would cut deeply into their own profits. The fact that his Ill Treatment of Cattle Bill was passed at all was down to Martin's guile. At the first reading, he employed shock tactics, describing the plight of the badgers kept for fighting, and the shamed MPs passed it. By the second reading, Martin reckoned the shame would have worn off and the same MPs would throw the Bill out, so he brought it back to the House at midnight, after a long, tedious debate on army pensions. With everyone comatose, they could be carried into the correct lobby before they realized what was going on. For the third reading, Martin again presented the Bill to a half-empty chamber. He had probably organized a fire alarm or something. The Ill Treatment of Cattle Bill became law on 22 July 1822.

Making a law is quite different from enforcing it though, and 'Martin's Law', as it was now known, became the Georgian equivalent of the one we have about not using a mobile phone when driving. It might be illegal, but no one is prepared to stop dialling for long enough to catch the people doing it. So Martin, to whom the king had now given the even more disturbing nickname 'Humanity Dick', decided to enforce the law himself. Like a tail-coated Dirty Harry, he began patrolling London, looking for cases of animal cruelty and arresting those respon-sible, including horse traders, drovers and costermongers, who were a type of porter or baristas selling venti cappuccinos for £3 a cup. Many magistrates seemed unaware of his new law so, always looking for ways to publicize it, Martin even called a donkey to testify against its owners. This is apparently the only time a donkey has ever been called as a witness in court, although Manchester United fans might unfairly point to Tony Adams in his drink-driving case.

As knowledge of Martin's activities spread, public opinion began to move behind him, and talk began of the need for a society that would also protect animals. In 1824 the Reverend Arthur Broome, the vicar of Bromley-by-Bow, convened a meeting at the appropriately named Old Slaughter's Coffee House in Piccadilly. Richard Martin was there, giving his .44 Magnum a rest for the night, along with others, including William Wilberforce, who was soon to achieve the abolition of slavery. The Society for the Protection of Animals was born. To be honest, it wasn't the first attempt to start a society with the same aims. In 1809, in Liverpool, a group had begun called The Society for the Suppression and Prevention of Wanton Cruelty to Animals, but it failed, the length of the name being considered a cruelty to those trying to say it.

The change in public attitude wasn't entirely down to Martin though. The rights of animals had also become a question mulled over by the philosophers of the age, among them Jeremy Bentham, a man now kept in a cupboard at University College London.

Jeremy Bentham was born in 1748 and devoted his life to reform. A child prodigy, he read history books and spoke Latin from the age of three, which makes you hope that he was terrible with girls and never got picked for the football team. During his career, Bentham addressed the rights of women, for whom he urged equality, homosexuals, for whom he urged tolerance, and animals, for which he advocated far better treatment. Before Bentham had laid out his principles, animals were apparently considered to have no rights at all because, unlike humans, they were held to be incapable of reason. But Bentham argued that if reason was the benchmark for rights, then human babies and many of the elderly should have no rights either, a rule that still operates in many of our care homes. He therefore suggested that it would be far better to offer rights to creatures which could suffer, a definition which would also include animals.

Oddly, for a man regarded as one of the fathers of the animal rights movement, Bentham didn't object to animal experimentation, so long as humans benefited from it, but then he didn't object to experimentation on himself either. And this is where the cupboard bit comes in. In his will, he requested that his body should be dissected for a public lecture on anatomy. The dissection over, and the public having left, his skeleton was then dressed again in his own clothes, which had been padded out with a bit with straw. His head, which was largely intact, was then balanced on top and given a hat and the whole thing was then placed in a glass-fronted wooden box called the Auto-Icon.

In 1860 the box, and its rather macabre contents, was purchased by University College London, an institution Bentham had helped to found, and was put on public display at the end of a corridor. Unfortunately, the mummification of the head proved to be a bit rubbish. Over the years, the skin began to stretch and blacken, until eventually the head had to be replaced by a wax one which would be less frightening to students already terrified by the size of their student loan. On special anniversaries, the body is taken to meetings of the College Council, where it is registered as a non-voting member. If ever the body starts to stalk the classrooms and lecture halls, the plan is to call in Scooby Doo.

Buoyed by Bentham's ideas and a rising tide of public sentiment, the SPCA went from strength to strength. In 1835 the young Queen Victoria gave it royal patronage and a large capital R to stick on their letterhead. The movement spread across Europe and sister organizations became established in Austria, Belgium, Holland, France and Germany.

For Richard Martin, whose commitment to democracy was not quite as great as his commitment to animal welfare, the story didn't end quite so happily. In 1826 he was found to have rigged the election results in Galway and was expelled from parliament. With creditors chasing him, he ran to France, where he died in exile aged 80.

Throughout the nineteenth century, the RSPCA continued its work, educating the public and campaigning for animal welfare legislation. It was also instrumental to the founding of the NSPCC, which would seem to put the two organizations in the wrong order. Certainly the fact that the charity designed to protect animals pre-dates the charity designed to protect children doesn't do much to disprove the idea that the British prefer animals to humans. Anyway, the story is this, and it is set in New York.

One day, whilst visiting a dying woman, a hospital volunteer was told by her that in the next-door room a mother was badly mistreating a child. As a dying wish, the woman asked the volunteer to see if she could help. The volunteer accepted the task and went to the police, who told her that there was nothing they could do, and that they would not interfere between a mother and her child. This is not a thing to tell your misbehaving children, by the way. All those threats to take them to the police station will be pointless.

Eventually, having also been warned off taking action by her lawyers, the volunteer approached a member of the American SPCA, which the RSPCA had helped to found, and spun him a line. The victim of the cruelty, she told him, was 'a little animal'. Only when the SPCA promised to act did she tell them that it was, in fact, a small child. The SPCA, which agreed to continue with the case, then approached a New York court with much the same spin. They argued that children were indeed animals and the court officials, many of whom must have had teenagers, found it impossible to disagree. The case won, the mistreated child was given suitable care. The publicity then started such a flood of similar cases that a society to protect children was founded, and the idea was re-exported back across the Atlantic to Britain as the NSPCC.

The RSPCA and 'Martin's Law' both sought to protect working animals, but the nineteenth century also witnessed an increasing trend for keeping pets. The origins of pet ownership are obviously much earlier. The Chinese had ornamental goldfish in ponds from the seventh century and had invented the goldfish bowl by the fourteenth century. Evidence suggests that the Romans kept cats and horses. English kings also kept menageries. In 2005 archaeologists examined the skulls of two lions that were thought to have lived in the menagerie at the Tower of London. Originally established by King John, in the little time off he had from battling barons, the menagerie is known to have contained both lions and bears, and survived until it was finally closed down in 1830 by the Duke of Wellington. Well, I say he closed it down, but I imagine he probably got someone to round up the lions for him. Having survived the Battle of Waterloo, the last thing he would have wanted was to end up as the raw-food diet for the big cats at his local zoo.

In the Georgian period the menagerie became something of a tourist attraction, with an entry fee of a few pence or a cat or dog that could be fed to the animals. Nice. Mind you, the lions themselves didn't fare much better. When they died, they were just dumped unskinned into the moat. No wonder that MP wanted his cleaned out.

Monarchs didn't restrict themselves to keeping lions, mind you. King Charles II popularized spaniels, while Queen Elizabeth I is said to have had a guinea pig, animals which the Spanish had brought to Europe from South America in the 1500s. Henry VIII was against her choice of pet, because he knew that he would end up looking after it, but relented when Elizabeth promised she would always clean out the hutch.

Nor did zoos restrict themselves to being run by royalty. London Zoo, if you are looking for another source of national pride, was established in 1828 and is the oldest scientific zoo in the world. It also housed the world's first public aquarium, and originated the word, a massive fish tank having been known up until that point as an 'aquatic vivarium'. I suspect a lazy sign-painter.

Initially, pets seem to have been the preserve of the aristo-cratic, those wealthy enough to keep them. But, following the path bordered by exotic plants, they soon became available to all. The first big pet trend seems to have been birds, which were the first animals for which pet food was produced. I've never quite seen the point of a pet bird myself, but they were apparently highly valued in society before the advent of recorded music, as a sort of feathery, Trill-eating iPod. The first commercially prepared dog food was introduced in Britain around 1860. Frankly, it was about time. The French *Enclyclopédie ou Dictionnaire Raisonné des Sciences*, published only a few decades before, had suggested that dog food could be made by mixing up bread, milk and cheese with the heart, blood and liver of a stag. And who was going to want to do that every morning?

In 1859 Britain had its first dog show, and by 1874 we had the world's first kennel club. This is the accrediting council for show-dog breeds, and the body without which we would not have Crufts, dogs with ridiculous names, or any need for the blow-drying of canine hair.

The first Crufts, named for Charles Cruft, the general manager of a dog biscuit manufacturer, was held in 1891 in Islington, later to be the home of the prize-winning American poodle, Tony Blair. Only 2,500 dogs entered that year, but from relatively humble beginnings, it grew, until in 1991 it was officially recognized as the largest dog show in the world, with 23,000 dogs competing for the coveted Best in Show, a title I would love to win as an actor. But never have, understandably.

If early humans were to see us now, you'd think they would be fairly impressed by what we have achieved as a species, but I am not so confident about how a wolf would react to Crufts. Would they enjoy it? Well, possibly about as much as Attila the Hun watching *Some Mothers Do 'Ave 'Em*. The whole show seems to celebrate the softening and over-breeding of the canine species. There are pugs with massive eyes, dachshunds with tiny legs and sad-faced spaniels that look as though they have watched *Tess of the D'Urbervilles* on a never-ending loop.

There are poodles with topiary, Afghans that would win a Rod Stewart lookalike competition and mastiffs with faces so floppy you would swear their whole heads must be melting. There are breeds you have never heard of: affenpinscher, pharoah hound, sloughi, bichon frisé, saluki and chow chow. And there are dogs with names that are so embarrassing, you can't understand why they haven't just run away and had them changed by deed poll: King of Helluland Feel the Win, Puglicious Provocateur, and Pamplona Bring Me the Sunshine. What is wrong with a proper name, like Rover or Spike? The 2009 winner was called Efbe's Hidalgo at Goodspice. Imagine shouting that in your local park. It is never going to be as popular as Fenton.

Fenton!

Fentonnnnnnn!!

But we don't just have dog shows and dog societies. Once the British had decided we were animal lovers, there was no stopping us. In 1886 King Leopold of Belgium gave the British royal family a gift of racing pigeons, which were used to start a royal racing loft at Sandringham, in which the queen, apparently, still shows a great interest. The National Cat Club was formed in 1887, shortly followed by the grandly named

Institute of the Horse, and the British Rabbit Council, where rabbit councillors sit and discuss parking, planning and the general problem of wheelie bins.

By the middle of the twentieth century, an ever-increasing number of suburban gardens meant an ever-increasing number of suburban pets, which was great for families and children, and terrible for suburban birds. Each year, according to the RSPCA, cats kill an astonishing 55 million of them. Whilst not questioning the figure, I do know that our cat had almost nothing to do with it. Kiska lived until she was 21 and the only thing she ever brought into the house was a spent firework the morning after Bonfire Night.

We have also become more and more interested in watching wildlife. The RSPB, which was founded in 1889 to stop the practice of killing birds so their feathers could be used in the hats of Victorian ladies, now has over a million members, and 200 nature reserves bursting with birdwatchers. Twitchers now spend over £200 million a year on cameras, clothing and binoculars, although that figure is lower if you remove those who claim to be birdwatchers, but are simply stalkers, who use the same equipment.

And for those who love wildlife but find the outside far too cold and wet, there are plenty of shows to watch in the comfort of your own home. David Attenborough's programmes on animals of whatever sort, size or shape are consistently amongst the highest-rated on British television.

The trends in animal love are, however, changing. Exotic pets have become popular, and a bit of a problem. According to the Reptile Trust, which is badly named because, frankly, I wouldn't trust any of them, Britain has a 'plague of iguanas', many of which need re-homing because people aren't expecting them to grow to 5 feet long. Unable to cope, exotic pet owners are letting their pets go, or leaving them in inappropriate places. By repute, Britain's moorlands are chock-full of abandoned panthers, while at the Beamish North of England Open Air Museum, an unwanted python was unexpectedly added to its exhibits of industrial life.

Meanwhile, cats and dogs, pets which used to be the preserve of families, are now becoming more popular with couples who have put off having children for a while, or perhaps for ever, when they realize how much easier it is to clear up after a tabby or a labradoodle.

But are we the greatest animal-loving nation in the world? Well, the honest answer is that there is no real way of telling, but Japan would certainly run us close. In fact, if anything, they seem rather more obsessed than we are.

In Tokyo, where high-density living makes keeping your own pet rather difficult, there are 39 Cat Cafés, where, for an hourly fee, you can get coffee, pastries and a cat to play with while you are there. Each café may have up to 20 resident cats, wandering free, delighting the customers and terrifying the environmental health inspector. If you don't like cats, Japan now offers 2,000 pet rental companies, where you can hire dogs, cats, hamsters, rabbits, ferrets, turtles, guinea pigs and squirrels for a fee as low as £6 an hour, although it is more if you go for the collision damage waiver, or bring the animal back without a full stomach. If you don't like animals at all, they will probably rent you a Tamagotchi.

Perhaps Britain is heading in the same direction, although I hope not. Renting a pet seems like a rather soulless way of doing things. Despite the fashion for pet pampering and dogs that can fit in the celebrity handbag, the most popular dog in Britain remains the labrador, and for good reason. I asked my dog-loving wife why she thought that was, and her answer was concise and unsentimental. Labradors, she said, are straightforward. They come in just three types: yellow, black and chocolate. They are good-natured, they don't mind if children blow up their nostrils, and they don't smell too much. Aaah. The perfect pet.

THE FATHER OF INVENTION?

For those of you still wondering who Kenneth Branagh was meant to be in that stovepipe hat during the Olympic opening ceremony, this is the chapter for you. Because this chapter is about British inventiveness, and that chap was Isambard Kingdom Brunel, the Victorian engineering genius who came second to Winston Churchill in the BBC poll to find the greatest-ever Briton, and the man who more than any other symbolizes what we all now know about our nation, but had forgotten: that we are good at stuff. Inventing stuff, discovering stuff and getting stuff done. The Olympic Stadium was completed on time and within budget, so we are even good at building stuff too, which comes as a surprise to those, like me, who thought that British builders based their working practices on God. That is, they tell us they are coming back, but they give us no indication of when that will be.

But how inventive are we? Well, if you ask David Cameron, the answer is: really inventive. In fact, he thinks we have invented stuff that wasn't even invented. In an interview on *The Andrew Marr Show*, he said, 'We are brilliant inventors in this country. You can run through; we invented the jet engine, DNA, the World Wide Web...'

Honestly, David, I would stick to Magna Carta. No one 'invented' DNA. The jet engine and the World Wide Web, I can go with, but just because we have David Attenborough as a national icon that doesn't mean we can claim to have invented the building blocks for all life on earth. DNA is not an invented thing. It was a discovery, a massively impressive and important discovery, but we did not invent it any more than people discovered the computer or Branston Pickle, although of course that last example is a bad one. Everyone discovers Branston Pickle, at the back of a cupboard, usually two years beyond its sell-by date. Anyway, the point is simple: there is a difference between inventing something and revealing the true nature of things you have observed, as the evidence in the Plebgate inquiry clearly shows. To confuse the two is a basic error. Goodness knows what Andrew Marr thought of Cameron's list. He probably couldn't believe his ears. I'll leave that one there...

Forgive my nitpicking. David Cameron is essentially right, if conceptually wrong. As a nation, we do indeed have an impressive record for both inventing things and discovering them. If you don't believe me, just check out Wikipedia for the lists of inventions and discoveries by the English, Scottish, Welsh and Irish.

First, though, a word of warning: for three years, my own Wikipedia entry had my date of birth wrong, not to mention a fair number of the statistical details, so there are reasons to doubt how definitive this list is, but in the absence of any other easily accessible run-down, I am going with it. It is certainly more accurate than a list provided by Number 10 would be.

OK. Get ready. It is quite long. You might want to make a cup of tea or something before you settle down to read it. No? All right, here goes.

Oh, remember, this doesn't include the stuff we already know about: the lawnmower, the macintosh, the corkscrew, the self-emptying tipping rain gauge and the process to make the world's most tasteless bread. We've already got those. Those are safe. Those are ours to keep.

So off we go. The British are responsible for inventing or discovering: the seed drill, the steam-driven ploughing engine, the spinning jenny, the power loom, the flying shuttle, the pencil, the mechanical pencil, the clockwork radio, the tin can, shorthand, the Christmas card, the postage stamp, the first computer, the first computer program, the first computer game, the flip flop circuit, the universal Turing machine, the MP3 player, the balance spring, iris recognition, the World Wide Web, the first web browser, disc brakes, the first coke-consuming blast furnace, the internal combustion engine and the marine chronometer, which allowed us to work out longitude. Someone should write a book about that . . .

Do you need a break? No. OK, on we go . . .

The gas turbine, the microchip, the slide rule, the screw-cutting lathe, the iron bridge, the vacuum diode, the steam turbine, the universal joint, cathode ray tubes, the pendulum governor, the light bulb, the two-stroke engine, the wind tunnel, the pram, the collapsible buggy, the fire extinguisher, stainless steel and the mouse trap.

Still all right? Good.

The clinical thermometer, antiseptic for surgery, the typhoid vaccine, Viagra, diagnostic ultrasound, blood transfusion, blood pressure measurement, general anaesthetic, radar, the television, the torpedo, the self-powered machine gun, the depth charge, the hovercraft, the jet engine.

Just let me know when you are getting bored . . .

The tuning fork, the ballbarrow, the concertina, the motion picture camera, the electrical generator, calculus, holograms, argon, helium, hydrogen, the proton, the electron, the neutron, the symbol for multiplication, the Harrier jump jet, the cat's eye, the seat belt, the theory of evolution, traffic lights, the lifeboat, the steam hammer, tarmac, the screw propeller, the submarine, the hydrofoil, scuba equipment, the diving bell, the sextant, the gas mask, plastic, Plasticine, penicillin, the spirograph, the friction match, linoleum, Meccano, the cross-word puzzle, the Venn diagram, the bicycle, the pneumatic tyre, wire rope, cordite, the Higgs boson, the telephone, hypnotism, the oil refinery, the teleprinter, the refrigerator, the flush toilet, the piano foot-pedal, lime cordial, the kaleidoscope, the hypo-dermic syringe, the percussion cap (whatever that was), the typewriter, the ejector seat, the spare wheel, the ball bearing.

And I am sure I have forgotten one . . .

Ah, yes.

Gravity.

It's an impressive list, isn't it? Although, obviously, some things are more impressive than others. Much as I like James

Dyson, I'm not sure that his ballbarrow is really up there with penicillin, or that the Venn diagram was as great a leap forwards, or indeed upwards, as the jump jet, or that lime cordial should be on the same stage as the discovery of hydrogen. Although the invention of lime cordial is very important in my family; on their first date, which was a picnic, my mother gave my father a glass of it undiluted, not realizing that you had to add water. My father drank it without complaining or even mentioning it, a sort of proof that he was in love, and a pretty important step on the way to me being here and able to write this book. So it may not seem much to you, but I would like to take this opportunity to thank Lachlan Rose and his 1867 method of preserving citrus juice without alcohol.

That apart, I may not be the best judge of the list, because, if truth be told, I don't really know what some of the inventions are, or what they do. The flip flop circuit, for example, sounds like it should be a short, circular walk sunbathers make to the beach bar and back, but it turns out to be a type of electronic circuit, without which we would not have been able to develop microprocessors. I tried to read an article about our development of the language protocols on the World Wide Web, and frankly didn't understand a word. Actually, most of it wasn't in words. It seemed mostly to be in code, which I guess is the point.

The question is, though: is the list an accurate reflection of our achievements as a nation?

And the answer is: yes.

And then again: no.

It comes with a number of caveats. First, actual British people didn't necessarily invent or discover everything listed.

Sometimes they were invented or discovered by people from overseas who happened to be working here. Or are working here now. For example, iris recognition, the system whereby thieves will no longer be able to steal your PIN number, but will instead have to thrust your head into the cashpoint, or steal your eyes, seems to have been co-invented by an American whilst working in America, and before he took up the post at Cambridge University that he currently holds. I could be wrong though. My eyes may be deceiving me. Secondly, we can't necessarily claim the full credit for many of the inventions and discoveries included. Often, we just helped them on their way, with a nudge here and poke there.

So, yes, you are right. Essentially, it is a list of things that Britain, or the British, have just been involved with, in some way, for a period of time, perhaps very short, but that's fine. We were in the room, or just on the other side of the door. Come on, everybody embellishes their CV a bit, don't they?

Here's why we need to be cautious. The typewriter is said to have had 52 contributory inventors before we reached its modern version, which is two for every letter of the alphabet. In other words, most of them smudged and many missing letters altogether, it took 52 attempts by separate people to end up with a machine that worked, even vaguely. Our claim to involvement is that a Briton seems to have submitted the first patent application anywhere describing a machine 'for the impressing or transcribing of letters'. Which is not much of a claim at all, frankly. There are no surviving pictures of the typewriter patented by Henry Mill in 1714, and he didn't even leave a typewritten note saying how great it was. For all we know, it could have been a series of potatoes with the alphabet cut into them. After that, and there seems to be a gap of several decades before an Italian thought he might have a go, the typewriter seems to have been a European–American co-production. We had no influence on the shift key, or the QWERTY keyboard, or on the development of all those ancillary products, like carbon paper and correction fluid, although it is tempting to include the last one in our list and just blank it out afterwards.

As an aside, correction fluid, so-called liquid paper, seems to have been invented by a not very good American typist called Bette Nesmith Graham from Dallas, who made it at home from paint and used it to correct all the mistakes in her work at the Texas Bank. The bank didn't like either the fluid or her mistakes and, sick of the errors littering every page of the documents she typed, they gave her the old heave-ho. Without a job, and with a son to feed, she made more of her liquid paper, to see if she could sell it commercially. Good move; she eventually sold her company to Gillette for $47.5 million, although you can't help wondering if the contract originally said $4.75 million and no one had noticed the small white bottle she had smuggled into the lawyer's office. As for her son, well, he inherited her fortune, but didn't really need it, because in the interim he had become Mike Nesmith of the Monkees, which should have a Y in it. The name of the band must have been typed by his mother.

Like the typewriter, the claim that we invented the pencil is also contentious. The principle of the pencil goes back thousands of years. The Egyptians, for example, used metal sticks, or styluses, to scratch incomprehensible writing into papyrus every time they were delivered a part for the pyramids by

Parcelforce. No one thought to use graphite until the sixteenth century, however, when we discovered the world's largest solid deposit of it at Grey Knotts in the Borrowdale Valley of Cumbria. But even then we didn't advance the design much. The locals just cut the graphite into sticks, which they called 'leads', because, without chemistry to tell them any different, that is what they thought they were made of. We didn't even put wood around them. That innovation came much later, in Italy. To make our misnamed 'leads' easier to handle, we simply wrapped them with cloth or animal skin. Once draped in the hide of a dead cow, we didn't even use the pencils properly. Instead of using them to draw in sketchpads or write great thoughts in notebooks, local farmers decided that the very best use of the pencil was to shade in patches of wool on sheep, so they would know which of the animals were theirs, a practice they were happy with until other farmers discovered the rubber, which incidentally we did invent. Possibly.

Let me take you through it.

Traditionally, the method of removing pencil marks from paper, and presumably sheep if they needed it, had been to rub them with breadcrumbs, which must have looked very suspicious on the Cumbrian hillsides, but in 1770 Edward Naime, an English engineer, made a lucky mistake. Instead of picking up breadcrumbs to correct a mistake in his writing, he inadvertently picked up some fragments of rubber that happened to be lying around, and thereby invented the eraser. I am not so sure that story is true. Who keeps rubber in the bread bin? No one. Unless, of course, their bread has been made by the Chorleywood Process.

But our rubber achievements don't stop there. Hyman Lipman, the man who first thought of putting a rubber on the end of pencils, was also British. Well, he was born in Jamaica and lived in Philadelphia, but he had British parents. Don't look at me like that. Listen, he could have played cricket for England, and no one would have raised an eyebrow, especially if they had read George Washington's book on etiquette. Anyway, he had a patent for the pencil eraser. At least he did until it was declared invalid by a court that said he had just lumped the pencil and the rubber together, and that it wasn't really an invention at all. The patent was erased from the records, leaving Lipman wishing he had written it in ink. Still, not all was lost: Hyman was also the first man to combine his first name with a casual greeting so as to make the whole process of saying hello that much quicker.

The whole question of what constitutes an invention is tricky. The right to be seen as the inventor of something often seems to depend on what you think its defining characteristics are. For example, toilet paper seems to be Chinese – they have been using it since the sixth century – but if you only use two-ply, then the British are in with a shout. Who gets the bicycle depends on what you think makes it a bicycle; is it the fact that there are two wheels? Or the fact that you pedal it? If you were to choose two wheels in a line as your definition, then the bicycle is German. In Mannheim, in 1818, an inventor called Karl Drais produced what was essentially a sit-on children's scooter: a frame with two wheels and a saddle, which you had to walk along the street while you were sitting on it. It was terrible going up hills, because of the effort required, and terrifying going down hills, because it had no brakes. It was also called the 'dandyhorse', which, had it stuck as a name, would surely have put off our entire current crop of cyclists, whether dandyhorsing in a peloton, riding a mountain dandyhorse, or competing in the dandydrome.

If your criterion is two wheels powered by pedaling, the bicycle may be Scottish, however. In 1839 a Scottish inventor, Kirkpatrick Macmillan, may, and I only say may, have produced the first one with pedals, although I am guessing without brakes, as he seems to have been fined five shillings for colliding with a small girl while riding it. At least she wasn't crossing at traffic lights, as those hadn't been invented yet.

The first chain-driven bicycle, and therefore arguably the first recognizably modern bike, was produced in Coventry in 1885, and was an improvement on a French chainless design that had been brought to Britain 20 years earlier. So does that make the bicycle British? Well, no, not entirely. If we discount the dandyhorse, it sounds more like an Anglo–French design project, of which there have been many since. The most famous, of course, was Concorde, the supersonic passenger jet with the tilting aerodynamic cockpit cone, designed, I am told, so the French plane could turn its nose up when it arrived at a British airport.

Likewise, many countries claim a crucial role in the development of the internal combustion engine, because, like many inventions, it was dependent on numerous small technological steps that had come before, such as the sparks produced by Alessandro Volta, the use of cylinders and the development of the carburettor. Our claim stems from the fact that a British inventor named Samuel Brown may have been the very first person to drive a vehicle powered by such an engine. In May 1826, some 60 years before Karl Benz introduced his 'Patent Motorwagen', Brown set off up Shooters Hill in south-east London, in what was effectively a gigantic 40-litre, gas-powered cart. That Brown's feat has been largely ignored in the annals of motoring seems unfair. By the time Benz first drove his elegant four-stroke, wire-wheeled, tubular-framed vehicle in 1886, Brown was very nearly at the top of the hill and looking forward to seeing the view back towards Greenwich.

Don't worry, though, because there are bits of the car in which our input has been far more essential. Pneumatic tyres were definitely a British development. Twice. They were first patented by Robert Thomson in 1846, and then, having been forgotten about, patented again in 1888 by John Dunlop, a Scottish vet working in Belfast. And for Dunlop's patent we must once again thank poor medical advice. Dunlop's son, apparently, had a heavy cold and it was suggested by a local doctor that the perfect remedy would be to go for a ride on his tricycle. Of course, it makes perfect sense. If you have a cold, what could be better for it than extreme physical exercise, especially if your water bottle is also brimful of health-giving gin or port?

Anyway, Dunlop must have been a little worried, because having heard the doctors suggestion, he decided that the very least he could do was to make his son's ride smoother; not metaphorically, by sending him to private school, or calling in a favour from a cousin who could give him a start in a bank, but actually, by improving his son's tyres, which, like those on all bikes at the time, were made of solid rubber. Given that it is almost too much to put batteries in the toys you buy the kids for Christmas, Dunlop's devotion to the well-being of his son was remarkable. He got some canvas, which he rolled into tubes and glued together to form a circle. He then stuck one of the tubes on each wheel of the trike, filled them with air, called his son and told him to get cycling. God knows how long it took him. It might have been quicker just to invent Lemsip.

Loath as I am to mention it, doubts also cloud our claim to have invented the television. In Britain we all know the story. Television was invented by a Scot called John Logie Baird, who, along with his assistant Boo Boo, successfully transmitted moving pictures in front of a journalist and members of the Royal Institution in 1926. From that point on, thanks to the wizardry of Baird, who had constructed his early equipment in the British style from biscuit tins, cardboard and ladies' tights, these islands were at the forefront of televisual technology. It was but a small step to the BBC becoming the world's pre-eminent broadcaster, producing programmes like *Grandstand*, *Newsnight* and *Sir Prancelot*, and broadcasting them by a system based on Baird's great breakthrough.

Right?

Well, no. Wrong

Although Baird definitely made both the first private television transmission – of a ventriloquist's dummy called 'Stooky Bill', who I imagine looked quite like Michael Gove – and the world's first public one, he was just one of many scientists involved in research in the area. Indeed, his own ideas were based on a patent for spinning perforated disks filed in 1884 by a German inventor called Paul Nipkow. Others working on the transmission of pictures included a full-blown American called Philo Farnsworth, who sounds like a character from *The Archers*, and a Russian working in America called Vladimir Zworykin. What is more, the systems pioneered by the Americans worked much better than ours, as they used electronics rather than mechanical spiralling lenses. Crucially, they had far better picture quality; an electronic system gave misty pictures, whereas those produced mechanically came with an instruction to watch them carefully with your fog lights on.

In 1936 the new BBC Television service tested the two systems against each other, and the electronic variety, running on 405 lines rather than Baird's 240, won hands down. At least that is what the BBC said. On Baird's system, you couldn't really make out the hands, wherever they were.

So although the story of John Logie Baird has moved into British folklore, it took just a decade to realize that his method of broadcasting was a technological cul de sac. His equipment at Alexandra Palace was dismantled and the development of television continued elsewhere, on fully electronic lines.

Ask anyone in America who invented television and Baird doesn't get a look in. Whether he is known there for any of his other inventions, I don't know. Have Americans heard of his pneumatic shoes, for example? It is unlikely, I guess, because the balloon-filled prototypes didn't really work and burst in use. I say burst, I am actually rather hoping that they let air out in a long farting sound, and that John flew randomly round the room he had been standing in before hitting a wall and falling to the floor.

Baird also had an unsuccessful dabble with turning graphite into diamonds, which would have made pencils a lot more expensive, and a slightly more successful one with thermal under-socks – socks with an extra layer of cotton inside them. Apparently, he suffered from cold feet, although not when he was telling people about the weird stuff he was inventing. No, he was perfectly happy to do that.

Sometimes, however, fortune worked the other way round, and in favour of the British. According to the patent, the telephone is a British invention and Alexander Graham Bell is its inventor. Again, the story is well known. Bell made the first telephone call in March 1876 in his laboratory in Boston, Massachusetts. When the call was answered, Bell heard a voice telling him that he was held in a queue and that he should hold to speak to the next available operator. After a click, there was a snatch of Vivaldi's *The Four Seasons*, the voice told Bell that his call was important to them and the line went dead for no apparent reason.

But it nearly wasn't like that. Bell was in a race to the patent with an American inventor by the name of Elisha Gray, who was developing a telephone in his laboratory in Illinois. Both inventors were neck and neck, but on 14 February 1876 Bell beat Gray to the patent office by just a few hours, leaving Gray to wish he hadn't wasted so much time calling chat lines when he should have been working. In spite of legal challenges and the suggestion that he had stolen Gray's ideas, Bell was awarded the patent and his place in history.

Incidentally, it was not the first telephone invented by the British. In the seventeenth century Robert Hooke, best known for his work in elasticity and his rivalry with Newton, apparently invented the tin-can telephone loved by science teachers at primary schools, whereby sound is transmitted down a string, and all without having to pay a tariff. This is also known as the 'lovers' telephone', although it isn't really that suitable for lovers who don't want the world to know that they are lovers, or are worried about journalists discovering their identities by following the pieces of string. Still, we shouldn't discount the achievement. As we also invented the tin can, or at least patented it, it is an all-British invention, apart from the string. God knows how many people would lay claim to inventing that. Well, I suppose it depends on how long it is.

We also can't be too jingoistic over the development of the SMS message and the geostationary satellite, the ones that stay in exactly the same position overhead. The first SMS message was certainly sent in Britain, over the Vodafone network, but the idea itself seems to have been developed in France and Germany. As for geostationary satellites, well, any claim we make to have invented them seems a bit farfetched, frankly, and is based on the fact that Arthur C. Clarke mentioned the possibility of them in an article for *Wireless World* magazine in 1945. Listen, that isn't inventing them. When he was seven, my brother drew a picture of a passenger jet that was powered on milk. There was no design as such, just a drawing of a plane and an arrow pointing to each of the engines, above which he had written 'milk'. If someone does now invent a plane that works that way – for example, a desperate dairy farmer who is fed up with Tesco and has a background in aeronautical engineering – there is no way we could nip off to the patent office to stake our claim. It would be ridiculous, but it would still be stronger than the claim Arthur C. Clarke has over geostationary satellites. It is weak, and made even weaker by the fact that Clarke seems to have forgotten that he had ever mentioned them at all until he was reminded of the fact a year after the first one was launched. And yet, based on this single mention, Clarke seems to have a geostationary orbit of the world named after him. Why is a mystery: The Mysterious World of Arthur C. Clarke.

OK, that is enough caveats. We have undoubtedly invented a lot of stuff, and discovered more. All I am trying to say is that we shouldn't get carried away; inventions and discoveries are often the work of many, and if other countries were to put together the same sort of lists, you would probably find pretty much the same inventions on them. Apart from Luxembourg, which doesn't seem to have any. This isn't to say that some things aren't ours alone. The discovery of gravity seems to have been 100 per cent British, for example, and what's more, it was the work of a man whom many consider the greatest scientist who ever lived: Isaac Newton.

Isaac Newton was the son of a Lincolnshire farmer, also called Isaac Newton, who, if baby-naming is anything to go by, was considerably less imaginative than his offspring. Isaac Junior has been an inspiration to generations of scientists, including Albert Einstein, who had a picture of him on his study wall, next to ones of electrical pioneer Michael Faraday, theoretical physicist James Clerk Maxwell and that girl in a tennis dress who is touching her own buttock.

And the high regard for him isn't misplaced. Newton not only weighed in with gravity, but also the laws of motion,

calculus, the principles of optics and the reflecting tele-
scope, while his monograph *Philosophiae Naturalis Principia
Mathematica,* published in 1687, provided the foundation for
classical mechanics.

And those were just the things that worked. He also spent a
lot of time trying to work out the principles of alchemy, which
George Osborne might do well to have a go at, and looking
through the scriptures to try and work out when the world
might end; apparently we are fine until 2060. With the little
time he had to spare, he also suggested that coins should have
the ridges round the edges to make them less easy to counter-
feit and invented the cat flap. Well, the flapless cat flap. All right,
it was a cat hole. Not wanting to break off from his important
work – or break his fourth law of motion, the one everybody
forgets, but which states, 'Never go to the door to let the bloody
cat in' – he designed it so the animals that had previously
scratched at the door of his laboratory could come in all on
their own. In fact, he is supposed to have cut two holes next to
each other, one for a mother cat and one for her kitten, but the
kitten just followed its mother through the bigger one and
never used its own, a story Newton proudly told on the cats'
Facebook page. At least he didn't cut a third hole for aristocrats.

Fortunately, Newton also ventured outside occasionally, or
he might have missed his greatest discovery, for famously he
found the inspiration to develop the laws of gravity whilst in an
orchard. Whilst watching an apple drop from an apple tree, he
found himself asking why apples always fall perpendicularly to
the ground, rather than fly off in some other direction. In some
accounts, including, I think, the Ladybird book from which I am

half-remembering this story, he was sitting under the tree and the apple actually fell on his head. If so, he deserves further congratulation for developing the theory at all; most people would have ignored the gravity bit altogether and gone straight to a lawyer to claim for an accident that wasn't their fault.

You will be relieved to know, however, that Newton's story is not one of uninterrupted greatness. He wasn't particularly outstanding at school, or as an undergraduate at university, but he did like to experiment at home. As a teenager, he also got on very badly with his parents, and on at least one occasion threatened to burn their house down with them in it.

How comforting is that? Those results in the mocks, all that storming off to their rooms, the taking no notice of anything you say – it means nothing. Or at least it could mean nothing. Your child could be up there with the curtains drawn and the iPod dock at full volume, changing science for ever. They might even end up with their head on a twenty-pound note, and not just because it is rolled up and they are snorting something. It is more likely they are playing FIFA, or posting how much they hate you on Facebook, but you never know.

OK, time for another angle. Why have we invented the things we have?

Well, to state the bleeding obvious, it depends, of course, on what the thing is. Some inventions are down to moments of inspiration, while some are the end points of long, incremental advances, each slow step leading to the next. The development of the computer would be the latter type, while the invention of the cat's eye was the former. Its inventor, Percy Shaw, was driving home from the pub one night in thick fog, and, unbeknownst to him, was about to steer over a precipitous drop when his car's headlights were reflected back to him by the eyes of a cat that was watching him from the roadside. It was, quite literally, a flash of inspiration. Realizing that what he had seen could save thousands of lives, but that training actual cats to sit in the middle of road would be almost impossible, he decided instead to experiment with reflective beads that did the same thing, and the cat's eye reflector was born. It was, as far as I know, the only thing Shaw ever invented, and made him into a multi-millionaire, although he really didn't live the life. When he died in the 1970s, aged 86, he was still living in his childhood home, from which, for some unknown reason, he had removed all the curtains and carpets. His one luxury was to have four televisions permanently on, one for each of the three channels then available, with the last as a spare, to stop any malfunction robbing him of a crucial episode of *World of Sport* or *It's a Knockout*. Luckily, he died before multi-channel television made it as far as Halifax, or he wouldn't have been able to move for Samsungs.

There do seem to have been particular golden periods of British inventiveness. For a start, there was our Agrarian Revolution, which, as it lasted several hundred years, was a revolution even slower than the one you get on the London Eye. By the end of the seventeenth century, everything seemed to be in place for advances in agriculture. With parliament strong, landowners were more secure that they wouldn't just be turfed off their holdings on the whim of a monarch or nobleman; the Bank of England had been founded and land-owners and inventors could raise funds for improvements; and literacy was increasing, so there was more and more information available to farmers on the nature of soils and crops.

In a largely rural economy, it was inevitable that much of the inventive spirit of the age would be focused on farming, and it was. In 1701 Jethro Tull, a Basildon-born lawyer, took a technique used by the Chinese for centuries and developed his seed drill, which improved yields by planting seeds at the correct depth, rather than just throwing them onto the soil and hoping for the best. This guaranteed Jethro Tull's place in agricultural history, alongside other pioneers such as Black Sabbath, Saxon and REO Speedwagon.

One advance soon led to another, as anyone who has taken out a pay day loan will already know. Ploughs were improved, techniques of crop rotation and fertilization made better, fields were enclosed and agriculture, which until that point had struggled to feed the population, moved into surplus. The number of labourers required on the land was reduced, releasing people to start cottage industries and, with time, to populate the factories and mills of the Industrial Revolution.

In both agriculture and industry, improvements in one area seemed to spur faster and faster improvements in another. In northern mills, the weaving of cloth by hand was mechanized by the invention of the flying shuttle. Cloth could be produced far more quickly, but was often held up by a bottleneck in the supply of yarn, which was still hand-produced. So inventors set to work. The yarn problem was solved by the invention of the spinning jenny, a wheel that meant that it could be produced up to eight times as fast. And so it went on. The flying shuttle was replaced by the power loom, and the spinning jenny was improved by the spinning mule, which I think was a very early version of Buckaroo. Soon the northern mills were the pre-eminent cloth producers in the world.

New problems produced new solutions. Competition spurred people on, as did a general dissatisfaction with things not being quite as good as they could be. Unlike the contributors to *Grumpy Old Men*, the inventors of the age didn't just moan about how crap things were, but did something about it. It wasn't all done for the good of society, though, far from it. There were profits to be made, and with cash to be made from patents, even the heroes of the Industrial Revolution don't seem to have minded nicking ideas and claiming them as their own.

For example, I had never heard of Thomas Highs, a manufacturer of spinning engines, but knew all about Sir Richard Arkwright, inventor of the water frame, the machine that revolutionized the manufacture of English cottons in the 1770s, but which sounds like it was used to torture inmates at Guantanamo Bay. And that may be wrong, because it now seems extremely likely that Arkwright had stolen Highs' idea by taking his machine-maker to a pub and persuading him to hand over the industrial secrets. He might even have threatened to water-frame him. In a trial, Arkwright's patents for the machines were subsequently overturned, but that wasn't enough to stop Highs becoming destitute and dying in obscurity, while Arkwright made a fortune and got a knighthood.

The Industrial Revolution inspired invention. In textiles, new machines upped output a thousand-fold. Steam engines by Newcomen and Watt not only made coal mining easier, but were put to use in factories the length and breadth of the country. Improvements in iron-making made its use far more widespread and cost-effective for machinery, while the Bessemer process made steel a mass-market material. Cheaper and more effective ways were found to make acids and bleaches, and machine tooling became common. Our technology made us the most advanced nation in the world. We had struck down the old methods, and it had made us more powerful than you could possibly imagine. Sorry. And as Britain became richer, so there was more money available for inventors.

But this story isn't just about massive industrial processes. We seem to have other specialities. For example, we seem to be very good at breakfast.

Yes, that's right, we seem to have led the world in the technology that produces the most important meal of the day, and are responsible for the electric kettle, the toaster and the Teasmade. Obviously I am exaggerating a bit. The kettle had been around for years, even in electric form, before Bill Russell and Peter Hobbs – actual people, just like William Hoover and Laszlo Biro – came up with the idea that kettles might switch themselves off when they started boiling, rather than just whistling rudely at you until you switched them off yourself.

The electric toaster was first marketed by the Crompton Company in Glasgow, while the Teasmade doesn't seem to have any other nation claiming it at all, and who can blame them? It is a ridiculous contraption, based on the idea that you would want something gurgling and spluttering by your bed to make you a cup of tea by the time you wake up, rather than sleeping on undisturbed for another ten minutes and then make a cup of tea all by yourself. The Teasmade does at least show the problems faced by many British inventors; an early version, marketed as the Teesmade, was apparently refused a registered product licence because the product was not manufactured near the River Tees and the authorities were worried that the public might get confused. Perhaps the patent officer involved had recently been to Oxford Circus and wondered why he couldn't find the university.

The British also seem to have developed an expertise in house-cleaning, and well before the Dyson Bagless. The Hoover might be an American trademark, but we were there first. In 1901 Hubert Booth of London produced a massive vacuum cleaner called 'the Puffing Billy'. Admittedly, it was petrol-driven, kept in the street and pulled around on a cart, but it sucked stuff up, and that is enough.

Prior to Booth's invention, household cleaning had been the subject of many patents in America. In 1876 Melville Bissell of Michigan had produced a push-along beating sweeper which could remove sawdust from carpets and stop his wife complaining about him doing DIY in front of the telly, while in 1898 a John Thurman of Illinois patented a 'pneumatic carpet renovator', using compressed air. For many, Thurman's device is regarded as the first vacuum cleaner, and it would have been, but for the absence of one small feature: it didn't suck. Well, it did suck as a cleaner, because all it did was blow. The user simply pointed a jet of air at the offending household dirt and tried to blast it into a receptacle. It must have been rubbish at cleaning, although quite good if you wanted to beat your children at blow football.

Having seen a demonstration of a similar cleaner in London, Booth decided to reverse the action, so the dust was sucked into the machine. He patented his idea in 1901. Ideally, he would probably have liked to sell small versions of his cleaner to every household in the country, but houses had no electric sockets or other means of powering them. So instead of making his fortune from sales of his invention, Booth started a cleaning service, using a vacuum the size of a dust cart, which he pulled around town with a team of horses. Not surprisingly, such a device had drawbacks, not least of which was where to buy the bags for it. On arriving at a house, Booth and his staff would unroll a massive hose, drag it across the pavement and push it through the windows, thereby bringing in more dirt than the machine could ever suck up. It was, however, successful for a while and Booth's company was asked to clean the carpets of Westminster Abbey for the coronation of Edward VII. In time, Booth did begin to manufacture smaller domestic cleaners, including a Dustbuster-sized one, pulled by a team of ponies, but when Hoover introduced their small, electric-powered household cleaners, also using suction, Booth found himself behind the technological curve and unable to compete. His company still exists as a manufacturer of industrial cleaners.

Having developed macadam road surfaces, tarmac and the first steam trains, we also seem to have a pretty good record in transport, and not just for adults.

The first pram may have been designed in 1733 by William Kent, the garden designer, who was probably as good at his job as Capability Brown, but didn't have as memorable a name. And, unlike his name, it would have been hard to forget – it was pulled by a goat, which isn't a bad idea. Using one in the aisles of Tesco would certainly divert attention from how badly your children were behaving, although you might end up with quite a bill for the things it had eaten whilst in the shop, like vegetables, fruit and the skirts of other shoppers.

More recently, having seen his daughter struggle off a plane with a full-sized pram, Owen Maclaren – granddad, engineer and designer of the undercarriage for the Spitfire – invented the collapsible Maclaren buggy. Which is what Jenson Button might just as well have been pushing in last year's F1 World Championship.

I know. Prams, Hoovers and breakfast are all important, especially if you have a tiny, hungry baby that throws up a lot, but you are wondering if there are other areas of greater import to which the inventors of Britain have made a significant contribution.

Yes, medicine. In 1928 the often very untidy researcher Alexander Fleming inadvertently discovered penicillin by leaving a petri dish uncovered when he shouldn't have done, thus ushering in the greatest medical advance in history: antibiotics. These were the first effective cure for gangrene and tuberculosis, as well as those conditions brought on by things we shouldn't have done. The principles of radar helped Godfrey Hounsfield develop the CAT scanner, while the search by Pfizer in Kent for a cure for angina by increasing blood flow had the unintended consequence of producing Viagra, a cure for an entirely different condition. To protect modesty, perhaps we should just say that Pfizer's share price wasn't the only thing that rose steeply.

But if the quest to preserve life has been a stimulus to discovery and invention, so has its polar opposite, the quest to cause death, in the form of war. And as a regular wager of war, Britain has been there to play its part. We developed radar in parallel with the Germans, although it is fair to say that we weren't really cooperating at that point. In the person of the Reverend George Garrett, a clergyman who can't have been that peace-loving, we took early steps to develop the submarine as a weapon, while in 1866 a Briton called Robert Whitehead developed the first prototype of the modern self-propelled torpedo, albeit for the Austrian navy. By way of an aside, Whitehead's granddaughter married a Von Trapp and had seven children, who became the Von Trapp Singers.

And that brings us back to Do. Tor-pe-do.

We built the first aircraft carrier, developed depth charges, and invented the jet engine and the jump jet. Perhaps most significantly though, our inability to break German communications in the early 1940s forced us to develop the computer. Colossus, designed by Post Office engineer Tommy Flowers, at Alan Turing's Bletchley Park, was the world's first electronic, digital, fixed-programme, single-purpose computer with variable coefficients, using thermionic valves to perform Boolean operations and calculations.

Don't worry, I don't know what that means either. I just got it from Wikipedia.

More recently, at CERN, Tim Berners-Lee simply took the existing hypertext idea and connected it to the transmission control system and that for domain names, to create the World Wide Web. Honestly, I think any of us could have done that.

Fortunately, British involvement with the computer goes back to the far more comprehensible days of the early nineteenth century, however.

Charles Babbage was a mathematician and philosopher who was so bright that half his brain is now stored at the Royal College of Surgeons and the other half at the Science Museum. The reason he was so admired was that in the 1820s and 30s he produced the world's first mechanical computer and provided the blueprint for a successor capable of yet more advanced techniques. These were the difference and analytical engines, and were inventions of such magnitude that, unlike the other engines, Thomas, Gordon and Percy, they were never given first names. The analytical engine, although never built, theorized that calculations could be undertaken by a machine pro-grammed by punched cards, and would have been the first machine capable of all and any type of calculation. Or so the Fat Controller told me.

The development of the computer also gives us an insight into the personality of inventors, and perhaps a clue to why we have produced so many. As a nation, we seem to have a high tolerance for the unconventional, and that is precisely what many seem to be.

Take, for example, Ada Lovelace, collaborator with Babbage and the person sometimes given credit for writing the first computer program. She was the only legitimate daughter of the poet Lord Byron, and was introduced to mathematics by her mother, as a way of warding off the insanity she thought that Ada might inherit from her somewhat potty dad. Why mathematics should ward off insanity is unclear. In my experience, it tends to be the other way round, especially if you are not very good at it and only ten minutes into a double period. Ada put her brilliance at mathematics to good use. Not only did she correspond with leading scientists of her day, but as an avid gambler, she also started a betting syndicate and tried to build a model guaranteeing the success of large bets. It didn't work; she went into massive debt and was blackmailed by another syndicate member. She died aged 36, having managed to fall out with her husband on her deathbed. It is supposed that she admitted her adultery to him, although she might simply have told him that she had put the last of the family fortune on an accumulator at Haydock Park.

Dionysius Lardner, who was Professor of Natural Philosophy and Astronomy at University College London, a popularizer of science and one of the scientific celebrities of the age, rather diminished his reputation by running away to Paris with the wife of a cavalry officer, who, on discovering the affair, followed them to France and beat him up. To be fair, his reputation, even scientifically, hadn't been that high to start with, due to his somewhat hasty pronouncements that railway passengers might suffocate in tunnels if the trains went too fast, and that no steam ship would ever cross the Atlantic because the voyage would require too much coal, a statement he must have been praying was wrong while fleeing to New York in 1841.

And Lovelace and Lardner weren't the only ones refusing to settle for a comfortable life. Newton was a potential arsonist, and Frank Whittle, the inventor of the jet engine, almost didn't get that far because he loved stunt flying. At the RAF College at Cranwell, he was banned from the end-of-term gala for having taken too many risks, and later destroyed two aircraft during rehearsals for a 'crazy flying' competition at RAF Hendon.

Nor have our great inventors been deterred by failure. Instead of sulking, they have often just got up and had another go. Baird's pneumatic boots and Newton's dabbling with alchemy make them part of a long list of inventors who have got it precisely right in one area of their research, and 100 per cent wrong in another. Richard Trevithick, inventor of the steam engine, made his locomotive too heavy for the tracks, which snapped. Lord Kelvin, the first British scientist elevated to the House of Lords, and the man who defined absolute zero in the temperature scale, predicted that 'no balloon and no aeroplane will ever be practically successful'. He thought that the announcement of X-rays was a practical joke, and is reputed to have stated, in 1900, that there was nothing new to be learned in physics. At which point, Einstein removed his picture from his office wall.

Great American inventors also had patchy records, mind you. As Thomas Edison said when struggling for a breakthrough, 'I have not failed. I have just found 10,000 ways that don't work.' Which is what I shall say next time my children make me do a Rubik's cube.

There were also some inventors that never got much right at all, but became famous because they were expert at playing the press.

In the period between the wars, one of Britain's best-loved men of science was a charlatan called Harry Grindell Matthews, whose habit was to announce an invention, try to sell it to the government and then fail to prove that it actually worked.

In 1911 he claimed to have invented the 'aerophone', a radio-telephone which could communicate across two miles. It couldn't. In 1914 government officials foolishly paid him for a 'beam' which he told them would be able to stop Zeppelins. It didn't.

In 1923, though, came his greatest triumph. The novels of H. G. Wells had captured the public's imagination by suggesting that one day a 'death ray' might be able to destroy objects and people at a distance, and now Matthews claimed to have invented one. He gathered the press and demonstrated his invention for them by stopping a motorcyclist who miraculously fell off as soon as the ray was fired at him. The journalists loved it, and even more so when Matthews told them that with more powerful equipment, he could stop an aeroplane in flight and destroy the air surrounding it, which seems a bit of a wasted effort if the aircraft had already blown up.

Understandably, the government was wary of the claims for his invention, but with the press suggesting that Matthews might sell it to a foreign power unless they showed some interest, officials from the War Office finally asked him to demonstrate its awesome power to them. So, in his laboratory, in front of invited guests, Matthews unleashed the 'death ray' in two experiments. First, having signalled to an assistant standing suspiciously near a trip switch, he used it to stop a small motor that was sitting at the other end of the room. That done, he then used its previously undreamt of power to switch off a small bulb, a feature which would really only have been useful to the RAF if they had left the light on in the hangar after they had taken off. Not surprisingly, the War Office was unconvinced.

And so it went on. Infuriated that the government wouldn't buy his invention without more proof, Matthews told them that testing it had cost him the sight of one eye. In 1924, having unsuccessfully tried to flog the ray in France, the frustrated Matthews made a newsreel-style film to showcase his invention and finally silence the doubters. In it, as the machine is turned on, a rat falls over in its cage and a bicycle wheel stops turning. Powerful stuff.

Matthews ended his days like an Argos Blofeld, living in a fortified bungalow on a Welsh hilltop, surrounded by alarms and fences he had designed himself. To be fair to him, he did invent some things that worked, including cinematographic equipment used in Hollywood and a projector for advertising on clouds, which could be useful, although probably only in Britain.

Although Matthews' invention had proved as effective as a horsemeat detector in a lasagne factory, the idea of a death ray as a weapon of war remained powerful in the imagination. Indeed, it was crucial to the development of radar. In the early years of the Second World War, scientists were asked to investigate whether such a ray might bring down enemy aircraft. The answer from the experts was no, but that radio waves could be used to work out where those enemy aircraft were.

At least Matthews tried to make money from his inventions, because many British inventors don't seem to have been that bothered. It is an oft made criticism of Britain that we fail to exploit the ideas that we have, and, to be honest, the list of our inventions seems to bear that out. Obviously there are exceptions. I bet James Dyson's house is quite nice – completely dust-free and without a hand-towel anywhere – but our talent does seem to be coming up with the ideas, rather than making fortunes from them. Given the number of cat's eyes on British roads, Percy Shaw left a surprisingly small estate. John Dunlop sold his company before it had really achieved anything, and Kane Kramer, the man who invented the technology behind all MP3 players, including the iPod, over 30 years ago, failed to renew his patents and had to sell his house in 2007 after the closure of his family furniture business.

Joseph Swan, a British physicist, demonstrated the first incandescent light bulb to an audience in Newcastle upon Tyne in 1878. Thomas Edison, who was working on the same idea, then submitted patents in the United States, claiming that the invention was his. The case went to court, but because Swan was more interested in the science than money, he allowed Edison to keep the rights in America, while he retained them in Britain. Last year Americans spent $2 billion on a product they think Edison invented. The light bulbs he manufactured may have worked perfectly, but the one in Joseph Swan's brain didn't come on at all.

Frederick Lanchester, the automotive engineering genius who first patented the disc brake in 1902 and invented both the pendulum governor to control engine speeds and an early form of carburettor, had to rely on charitable help in his later years to stay in his own home. Sir Clive Sinclair would need a pocket calculator to work out how much he lost from failing to dominate the market for pocket calculators, and the list goes on. From kaleidoscopes to computers, we haven't proved that good at making our inventions work for us. Perhaps that is why we are so keen on the man in the stovepipe hat, because, more than anyone else, he put our inventions to work in an age when we led the world. Except in hats – those Victorian ones were ridiculous.

Isambard Kingdom Brunel was born in Portsmouth in 1806, but very nearly wasn't British at all. His father, Marc Isambard Brunel, was a French engineer and royalist sympathizer, who had felt it wise to leave France when someone heard him make disparaging remarks about the guillotine-happy revolutionary leader Robespierre. Initially, he fled to New York, where three years later, he became chief engineer for the city. However, on discovering that the Royal Navy were having problems hand-making all the pulley blocks they needed for their vessels, he set off for England with plans for a machine that could manufacture them far more quickly and efficiently. Brunel's choice of destination may also have been influenced by the fact that, whilst still in France, he had fallen in love with an English girl called Sophia Kingdom. Why else would you swap 'chief engineer, New York City' for 'pulley manufacturer, Portsmouth'? Still, the ending was a happy one, and the clue is in the names.

Brunel Senior became an eminent engineer; his pulley machinery was much valued by the armed forces, as was his method of manufacturing military boots, and he became a fellow of the Royal Society. In fact, so valued was he that when the fallout from a failed business venture meant he was thrown into debtors' prison and he let it be known that he was considering offering his services to Russia as a means of getting out of trouble, the British government, urged by the Duke of Wellington, paid the £5,000 to have him released, on the understanding that he would stay in England. I'm not sure if that would work if you missed a payment to Wonga.com, but it might be worth a go. Just phone them up and make sure that your talking Alexander the Meerkat toy is audible in the background.

Isambard Brunel first began work with his father on the Thames Tunnel between Wapping and Rotherhithe, at the age of 20. He is best known, however, for his work as chief engineer on the Great Western Railway, the jewel in the crown of Victorian engineering, which ran, as the name suggests, west from London to Bristol, and subsequently Exeter. In the BBC project to find the greatest Britons, each candidate had a modern champion. Brunel's was Jeremy Clarkson. Why a petrol head would support the king of railway builders, I have never fully understood. Perhaps he is grateful to Isambard for keeping so many people out of the fast lane of the M4.

The Great Western Railway was a massive project that utilized many of the advances of the age. Tunnels were dug, viaducts built, bridges suspended, stations constructed and locomotives manufactured, all to Brunel's specifications. The Box Tunnel, near Bath, was the longest railway tunnel in the world, while the vast Ivybridge Viaduct took Brunel's locomotives across the wilderness of Dartmoor. Nothing stood in the way of the railway, neither hills, valleys, nor marshes, and certainly not modern planning laws. As if the railway itself wasn't enough to be going on with, Brunel then intended to continue his transport network across the Atlantic to the United States. To fulfil his dream, he built what was then the world's longest ship, the *Great Western*, which trundled from Bristol to New York, driven by two gigantic paddle wheels, looking for all the world like a massive steam-driven pedalo. So successful was she that soon a sister ship was needed and Brunel set about designing the first iron-hulled, propeller-driven ship to cross the Atlantic, the SS *Great Britain*, which is what Himmler would have been in charge of had the Nazi invasion been successful a century later.

And Brunel's work didn't stop there. He extended the railway along the hillier and trickier Devon coast beyond Exeter, by using the principle of atmospheric traction. Without locomotives, the carriages were sucked along the track by a big pipe placed between the rails. Unfortunately, it didn't work; the vacuum required had to be maintained by leather flaps, which proved to be very tasty to local rats, but at least he had tried. And he never seemed to let up. In 1831 he designed the Clifton Suspension Bridge in Bristol, and in 1854 the Royal Albert, the grey, snake-like bridge in Plymouth that carries the railway over the Tamar and into Cornwall. He was a remarkable man.

Although, on the downside, he is also responsible for Swindon. The railway decided it needed somewhere on the line to build locomotives, and settled on the small attractive Wiltshire village as the perfect place. No damage done there then.

He also made other mistakes. For example, he decided that all his rails should be broad gauge rather than narrow, which meant that, after his death, when the railways nationally adopted the narrower form because there was a greater mileage of it, his tracks were ripped up and his locomotives and carriages replaced. A recent biography has even suggested that he might not have designed the Clifton Suspension Bridge after all. But, if anything, his failures and failings make him more attractive. He never rested on his laurels, was willing to have a go and, in life, as on the route for his railway, never let anything get in his way. He was a man to whom the debate over HS2 and the current state of our railways would be entirely inexplicable, and one who simply wouldn't have understood my favourite announcement from a guard ever: 'We apologize for the delay outside Bath. This was due to two decades of chronic under-investment in the railways.'

Brunel would have turned in his grave, if he's still in there. To be honest, I think he will probably have tunnelled his way out. He died in 1859, after a stroke, partially caused, it is thought, by his heavy smoking. Perhaps that explains the constant presence of his stovepipe hat; engineering genius that he was, he may have used it as a sort of funnel.

So where does all that leave us? Well, with one final query: are we as inventive as we were?

Well, if you go into Google and enter the admittedly rather childish question, 'Which country has invented the most things?' you will find that it has been the subject of some debate. Satisfyingly, most forum respondents answer Britain, closely followed by Japan, and America. One blogger also included Iran, because she thought that they had invented mathematics, which I think the Egyptians, Greeks and Iraqis might argue with. I can't imagine the Iranians would want to be in the list anyway. They don't seem keen on claiming the credit for anything very much, especially their nuclear weapons programme, which they want us to believe was invented by America.

As you would expect, most people seem to say Britain because they are impressed with our achievements during the

Industrial Revolution, which are indeed the most obvious. Yet dig further into the web of Berners-Lee, and you will find a claim in a UK newspaper that Britain has been responsible for over half of the world's most significant inventions since 1945. Which is fantastic, and entirely wrong, because the Japanese government report on which it was based had been misquoted.

But listen, I think things are fine. We still have *Dragons' Den*, there are people out there developing covers for cucumbers, gloves that tell you when you are driving on the wrong side of the road and suction clamps you can take on holiday, in case the showerhead has come loose in your hotel room. In other words, we still produce people with the essential characteristic of inventors – the willingness to fail.

And even if we are not inventing quite as many things as we thought we were, our papers are inventing figures about how inventive we are. And how inventive is that?

WHISTLEBLOWING: BRITAIN AND SPORT

At 9 a.m. on the morning after the London opening ceremony, the first full day of Olympic competition began with the Great Britain men's archery team taking on Ukraine in the elimination round at Lord's Cricket Ground. By 9.45 a.m. it was all over. Ukraine had trounced us 223–212. Britain's Olympic archers had trained for four years, and their dream had lasted 45 minutes.

Which is bloody typical. At Agincourt, we had led the world in the use of the longbow; no one could match the English bowman. We had taught everyone else the game and now, a mere 597 years later, we had been humiliated in our own backyard by a country fabled for its production of tractors. The rest of the world had stuck their two fingers up at us. Somewhere, somehow, we had forgotten how to win. Henry V would have been livid.

So runs, in a somewhat extreme example, the most common complaint by those who like to moan about British sporting achievement: that having given sport to the world, we now never win at it, and worse, don't seem that bothered if we lose. Which is why, from 9.46 a.m. on the first day of the Games, it became a very difficult summer for those moaners, because we did win, at practically everything, and with a ruthlessness which seemed completely counter to our national image. Medals poured in from every corner: rowing, running, swimming, riding, cycling, gymnastics and canoeing all provided their share, as the nation settled down to a fantastic fortnight of sport. By number of gold medals won, we finished third in the overall medal table, behind the United States, a nation four times bigger than us by population and about ten times bigger by weight of population.

I watched almost every minute of it. I was doing *The Now Show 2012* series for Radio 4 and had to watch it for work, or so I told my wife when she began to wonder why I hadn't moved from the sofa since the lighting of the flame. Eventually, she gave up trying to get me to move and bought me a pair of socks to prevent deep vein thrombosis. I was hooked and was watching sports which, even as a keen sports watcher, I had never even thought of watching before: handball, shooting and weightlifting became unmissable television. I watched events as they were happening, I watched the highlights and then I watched the round-up the next morning. I got the BBC Olympic App for my iPhone, and I became an expert on the favourable lanes at Eton Dorney in the event of a crosswind, the course layout at Weymouth and the rules of the team pursuit. I knew the names of our boxers, pentathletes and even our canoeists. My favourites were Florence and Hounslow in the slalom C2, not only because they took the silver, but also because they sounded like the most unlikely town twinning in history.

'So, Hounslow, we have the Uffizi Gallery and the works of Michaelangelo. What do you have?'

'Us? Well, we've got a big branch of Staples.'

I became incensed by poor decisions, unable to understand why, after my three hours of viewing, the judges didn't agree with the score I had given Tom Daley for his forward 4½ somersault with tuck, or his reverse with pike, although perhaps in the second instance they were upset that he wasn't actually carrying the promised fish. In fact, the scoring system in many sports became something of an obsession. In the show jumping, the customary four faults, which are applied if the horse and rider hit a fence, seemed to have been replaced by four points. Why had it been changed? I decided it was probably because the original scoring was open to misinterpretation, and you wouldn't want a commentator going, 'So, Beaurivage there with four faults; he's got bad hair, he's self-opinionated, he loves the sound of his own voice and, worst of all, he's French,' because that might give the wrong impression of our openness, friendliness and fairness.

As a British sports lover, I found that fairness mattered to me quite a lot. I became upset for certain competitors, because I felt that they weren't being properly rewarded for their efforts, particularly if they had four legs and neighed a lot. The equestrian events at the Olympics are the only ones in which men and women compete directly with each other, and the only Olympic events in which there are animals involved, unless you count clay pigeon shooting, which is just a name anyway, and has been since they discovered that dipping pigeons in clay stops them flying properly. Yet, however well the horses perform and wherever they are placed in the competition, they do not get a medal. How unfair is that? To be honest, to me, it looks as though the horse is doing most of the work. It isn't the rider jumping over the fences, or trotting sideways for no apparent reason, is it? No wonder they hit those poles so often; they are thinking, 'Yes, I could jump that, but what is in it for me? Nicer hay?'

Their rider is urging them onwards but they can't see the point. 'Even if we win gold, I won't get a single vote in Sports Personality of the Year.'

To be honest, I am surprised that more of them don't stop abruptly, throw their rider into the fence and neigh, 'There you go. Jump it yourself if it matters so much!'

No, the Olympics didn't seem quite fair to our equine friends, until I discovered another quirk of the equestrian rules, namely that although the rider has to be a national of the country he or she is riding for, the horse can come from anywhere. It doesn't seem quite right, does it? At the very least, you would expect a British horse to need a British ancestor of some sort, a grand-stallion or something, but no. Horses can even swap countries between competitions. The American rider Karen O'Connor had a mount called Mr Medicott, who, according to the commentator, used to be a German horse. And he had been; I looked Mr Medicott up on the internet and discovered that not only had he been German, but that he had been a member of the gold-medal-winning German eventing team at the Beijing Olympics.

How he had got his Green Card, I simply don't know. It is like Wernher von Braun all over again.

Sorry, I'm rambling. I'm going off at an Olympic tangent, which is dangerous, especially if you are a hammer thrower and they haven't adjusted the netting correctly. The fact is, we had a fantastic Olympic summer, and our sporting achievements didn't stop there. In spite of the fact that we haven't got any mountains to practise on, Bradley Wiggins majestically won the Tour de France; Andy Murray won his first grand slam; our cricketers beat India in the subcontinent; and just when it looked as though the glory would end in the Ryder Cup, we pulled it out of the bag on a miraculous final day. I say we; inspired by the spirit of Seve Ballesteros, and captained by José Maria Olazábal, the British team of Garcia, Molinari, Colsaerts, and Kaymer brought it home for queen and country. By then, for most of us, Europe was Britain, and Britain, Europe. I hope, for his health, that Nigel Farage was watching another channel.

Finally we seemed to have shaken off decades of underperformance and regained our rightful place at the top of sport, most of which we had invented in the first place. What is more, we had done it unapologetically and without the vertigo which seems to assail us as a nation whenever we get near the top step of the podium.

But have we always performed more poorly than we should have done? Have we always preferred defeat to victory? And does the world really have us to thank for most of the games it plays?

Perhaps it is time for a quick whizz through the history of sport.

Hugh Dennis

OK, first up, let me say that we did not invent sport as a whole, obviously. Even just 30 seconds of research shows that sport has been around since the Ark, when Noah and his three sons, Ham, Shem and Japheth – who would have been called Jeremy had Noah not been slightly pissed at the Christening – arranged the animals in a 2–2–2–2–2–2–2–2–2–2 formation. Every civilization has had its form of sport, especially the Greeks, which is why we copied their Olympic Games.

Not that the all the Ancient events made it into their modern equivalent. In 1895 Pierre de Coubertin, the founder of the modern Olympics, asked the Archbishop of Lyons to agree which of the various events might be revived in the Games to be staged in Athens the next year, and the archbishop agreed to all of them except one: pankration, and you can understand why.

Pankration was a mixture of wrestling and boxing, with no particular rules, in which the death of an opponent could be counted as a win. Theseus was very keen on it, and used his skills to defeat the Minotaur, which is very impressive. The Minotaur was deeply scary; not only did it regularly eat Athenian children, but as the torso of a man on the body of a bull, it was the undefeated all-time Cretan bucking bronco champion. In pankration, almost anything was acceptable, with the exception of gouging out the eyes of your opponent, or biting them, which must have been difficult for Theseus, who apparently liked his beef rare. Common moves included picking your opponent up and driving him head-first into the ground as hard as you could, and the charmingly named 'tracheal grip choke', where one fighter would grab the other's windpipe and

Adam's apple and squeeze them as hard as he could. Essentially, it was like rugby, but without worrying about the referee, and it is obvious why the archbishop was nervous about sanctioning its comeback. Quite why de Coubertin asked him to adjudicate in the first place, I don't know; perhaps he was hoping the archbishop would allow a version with a sin-bin.

Not everybody would have been against pankration though. In an interview during London 2012, Boris Johnson said he would like to see it revived, although possibly he was just thinking of no-holds-barred naked wrestling with other people's wives.

To fill the pankration-sized hole in the running order, the Olympic organizers have subsequently included events that the Ancient Greeks didn't bother with at all. The shot put may seem like the kind of thing that would have been very popular in the Peloponnese, but it isn't. It could either be Scottish, a variation of the ancient Swiss game 'steinstossen', or based on the habit of English sailors of throwing their cannonballs, in what must have been the least effective method of warfare ever invented. Likewise, the pole vault appears to have its origins in the low-lying Frisian Islands between Holland and Denmark. Perhaps the islands were so low-lying that the locals really fancied seeing what they looked like from higher up, and while they were there, upside down.

Always admiring of Greek culture, the Romans had sporting events too. Indeed, they were so important that they built massive stadia to hold them in, like the Colosseum and the Circus Maximus, which, if they weren't being used for sport, would be used to hold concerts by young up-and-coming musical performers like Cliff Richard and the Rolling Stones.

Hugh Dennis

Roman sport was used as entertainment, emphasized athletic prowess and, if anything, was even bloodier than the sports the Greeks liked, with slaves and criminals often fighting to the death against each other or wild animals. And it happened throughout the empire. At an amphitheatre near York, bodies have been discovered with what are described as normal gladiatorial injuries, namely tiger bites and hammer blows. Shame they found them in such an obviously Roman context really; it would have made a terrific episode of *Waking the Dead*.

Such events may well have been the first organized sporting gatherings in Britain, but even though they staged the Games, the Romans seem to have had paid very little attention to legacy, a trait they share with the organizing committees for Sydney and Beijing. Once they abandoned these islands, there was very little sport at all. It was the Dark Ages, and no one had invented floodlights.

By the later Middle Ages, however, sport in Britain was in full swing, amongst serfs and nobility alike. For those at the royal court, it often consisted of hunting or tournaments where knights would battle against each other to prove their prowess. A favourite pursuit was jousting, where two knights holding lances would charge at each other on horseback, in an attempt to unseat their opponent, or worse, impale them, like a receipt on an old-fashioned bill spike. As is obvious, it was quite dangerous, yet even kings enthusiastically took part in the fun. In 1536 Henry VIII was knocked from his horse at Greenwich, and the horse landed on top of him, giving him serious head injuries. To test for concussion, the physician held up his wives and asked him to count them.

In France, jousting went out of fashion after 1559, when King Henry II died from wounds he had received in a tournament celebrating his victory, and survival, in the Italian War. It finally faded out in England in the reign of Elizabeth I, when, thanks to health and safety, they got rid of the horses and the armour, and turned it into the pole vault, although the people of the Frisian Islands would beg to differ.

Once jousting was removed from tournaments for being too macho, its place was gradually taken by what was termed 'horse ballet' or 'carousel', which frankly wasn't macho at all. Essentially, it was synchronized dressage, in which knights on horseback performed highly choreographed dance routines to musical accompaniment, whilst both they and their horses were decked up in elaborate fancy dress. Bathed in torchlight, each knight would cross, turn, swivel and form shapes for the amusement of the crowd, before Bruno Tonioli and Craig Revel Horwood gave them their score, or accepted their hand in marriage.

But sport wasn't just restricted to the upper classes. It was essential for the lower classes too, because medieval peasants seem to have had an enormous amount of time off. One estimate I read put it at eight weeks a year, not including Sundays, which was already a day of rest. So, in the absence of daytime television, the internet, or joining their partner on the weekly trip to Sainsbury's, that left serfs with a lot of time to fill. And if royal sports throughout the Middle Ages were heading for greater sophistication, the sports for the masses don't seem to have joined them on the journey. The peasants of the Middle Ages seemed to like violence.

Extreme violence. And the sport that best provided that violence was football.

It is hard to believe it when you watch clips of Joey Barton on YouTube, but football has actually calmed down a bit. In the Middle Ages no one would have described it as the beautiful game. In fact, it really wasn't a game at all, and feet only seemed to be used for kicking people. It was a massive brawl between the men of neighbouring towns, during which they struggled to wrest control of an inflated pig's bladder and then score with it by fighting their way through the opposition defence, past an array of wrecked shops, pubs and houses, to a marker at the end of a street. With no limit on numbers, there were often hundreds on each side. There were no real rules, there was no pitch and there were no goals, except trying to injure as many of the opposition as possible.

There are very few images of medieval football, but that is hardly surprising; you wouldn't want to be painting it, or looking even vaguely artistic, with a crazed, testosterone-fuelled mob rushing towards you. In 1928 the Prince of Wales, later to become King Edward VIII, went to watch one of the few surviving examples of such a game in Ashbourne, Derbyshire, and even he was given a nosebleed. It was a lucky escape really, given that the only absolute rule of that match was that no player should commit murder. The game of the Middle Ages might have been called football, but it would be unrecognizable to modern fans, unless they had been hooligans in the 1970s.

The masses loved it, both here and in Europe. In France the equivalent was called *la soule*, and may have been slightly gentler. There, the village teams often included clergymen, the goals were set up in front of the local parish churches and on occasion the ball was decorated with woollen 'pom-poms'. As in Britain, there were regional variations. A record of a game at a village called Bellou-en-Houlme suggests that they played with a ball that was 3 feet wide and weighed 13 pounds; it doesn't say whether the local child was ever given back her space hopper. In Italy, too, football was popular, although even by 1555 they seemed to have the jump on us technically, the laws stating that the ball could not be thrown by hand. By 1600 they were advocating the sweeper system, they had set up academies and were vowing never ever to play route one.

In fact, so popular was the misnamed football across the Continent that there were several attempts to ban it, both in Britain and across the Channel. Edward II had a go in 1314 because he thought the fighting over the balls – the *grosses pelotes de pee* – was too noisy. He prohibited it in the City of London, thus beginning the great British tradition of banning ball games from grass anywhere near a block of flats.

Shortly after the Black Death, in 1349, Edward III had another go. With all the death and pestilence, he probably thought the remaining half of the population were enjoying themselves too much. And, with far fewer people around to be noisy, it wasn't the decibels of football that he was worried about; it was that the young men playing it were forgetting to practise their archery. If the French were to invade, he reasoned, it wouldn't be much good just kicking a football at them. Further attempts were made to stop it in 1389 and 1401, although not in 1500, even though, for purists, that is the correct time to start a football match.

Even Henry VIII had a go, in spite of the fact that he seems to have played it himself. Evidence for his participation in the sport comes from a royal shoe order, in which he seems to request a pair of leather football boots and an Arsenal shirt with 'Henry 8' printed on the back of it.

Royalty weren't opposed to all sports, however, and by the seventeenth century there were many that both they and the aristocracy were positively encouraging, mainly those involving betting. In 1605 James I had spotted that Newmarket would be brilliant for horse racing and built stables and a race course there. Soon others were springing up all over the country, as the aristocracy indulged their love of match racing, where two horses were pitted against each other for a prize. Even the rather dour William of Orange kept racehorses, including one called Stiff Dick, suggesting that in his spare time William had the headphones on and was listening to *Derek and Clive Live*.

By the early eighteenth century, boxing, or prize fighting, had became a popular pursuit of the wealthy, although it was strictly illegal. Rich patrons funded their own fighters, provided the money to be boxed for and kept the winnings if their man won. By the early nineteenth century, the whole sport seems to have become like a rave. Promoters dared not advertise fights for fear of ending up in court, so the location of a bout would only be divulged a few days before, in local pubs. On the day itself, punters would gather in a secret location, often under cover of darkness to avoid attracting attention, before heading off in a convoy of coaches, horses and sedan chairs to the field or clearing where the fight was to take place. On occasion, crowds were as high as 30,000, although the police put the figure closer to 300.

Perhaps it was all the gin they had consumed, but the British seemed to go gambling crazy. They bet on lawn bowls, they bet on which waterman would row them fastest across the River Thames, they bet on cricket, and occasionally fixed matches – so nothing changed there then. People even gambled on walking.

By the start of nineteenth century competitive walking, or 'pedestrianism', was a major spectator sport, in spite of a rather pedestrian name, which certainly wouldn't pull the punters in now. Initially, aristocrats would bet on which of their footmen would be the fastest if they made them walk beside their carriages, until they realized that the fastest was usually the one who saw the highwayman coming first. But, as has happened with modern marathons, the sport then developed into more extreme forms. When I was in my twenties, running a marathon as an amateur athlete was thought to be pretty full-on. Now you get no credit at all unless you have done a triathlon, or had a go at an Iron Man, a ridiculous event where you run a marathon, cycle a road race and then swim several miles, all the while clad in iron. Silly.

In pedestrianism, the walking distances became longer and longer, until in 1809 Robert Barclay, 'the celebrated pedestrian of Stonehaven' – which makes him sound like he was famous for being knocked down on a zebra crossing or something – walked 1,000 miles in 1,000 hours for 1,000 guineas, singing a

Proclaimers song the whole way. Bets on the event totalled over £5 million in today's money. Barclay himself became rich through his exploits, which was handy; he was a member of the Barclay's bank family, and they needed the money, so they could lose it for us all later.

But pedestrianism wasn't simply about speed and endurance. Punters also liked to bet on novelty events. In the 1940s the American sprinter Jesse Owens raced against horses, but 300 years earlier, the events staged for the gamblers were even more bizarre. Men with wooden legs hobbled against each other; men on stilts raced against those without them; and in what must have been some form of time trial, a fishmonger raced from Hyde Park Corner to Brentford carrying 56lb of fish on his head, hopefully in a basket. Given that Brentford is on the river, he also seems to have been running in the wrong direction, which is the kind of thing that can happen if a shoal of whiting is obscuring your view. Either way, it makes running a marathon dressed as a deep-sea diver look a little half-hearted.

Now, so far in this rundown of sports, there is one thing you will obviously have noted: the British haven't been exclusively responsible for any of them. People have always walked, boxed, rowed, run, kicked things, wrestled and charged around on horses, and they have done it for as long as anyone can remember, in all cultures and all around the world. Furthermore, when taking part in them, we don't seem to have shown any sign of the most oft-cited criticism of our sportsmen and women: that is, a willingness to lose. Indeed, 200 years ago, Britain seems to have been awash with professional sportsmen who relied on prize money and their own ability to attract a crowd. Losing simply wasn't on their agenda. They were full-on ruthless professionals, and the public loved them for it.

On the River Tyne, the burning desire of the professional oarsmen to beat their London rivals led them to develop the outrigger and modern-shaped rowing eight. When the best of them, Harry Clasper, died in 1870, 130,000 people attended his funeral. He had been pretty well unbeatable in a scull for years, so in races with more than two boats, rivals would discuss whose turn it was to ram him and take him out. Sport was well on the way to becoming a business, and our best sportsmen did whatever it took to win. It doesn't sound at all British, does it? So what on earth happened? How did we go from a nation of cold-blooded Michael Schumachers, to a nation who idolized Eddie the Eagle because he was so bad at ski jumping? And how come we think we invented modern sport?

The last question is the easiest to answer, so I'll start with that: we invented modern sports by establishing the rules.

Obviously, there are some rules that aren't helpful at all to the development of sport – 'keep off the grass' being a prime example – but if you want teams from different places to play against each other, or if you want fair contests on which people can safely bet, then rules are what you are after. And we were pretty much the first nation to do it. In some sports, it just happened naturally. In horse racing, the Jockey Club was established in 1750 as a club for gentlemen interested in horse racing, and fairly quickly starting writing rules to counter the corruption and bribery that was ruining a sport based on gambling. It set the weights that horses would carry and made most races shorter and the fields running in them larger. Admittedly, it didn't entirely work as a means of stopping scandal. Running Rein, the winner of the 1844 Derby, was eventually disqualified for being a year too old to run in the race and using an assumed name. He had previously competed in the Olympics for Germany.

In the mid-nineteenth century boxing introduced rules endorsed, if not written, by the Marquess of Queensberry, covering the length of rounds, the size of the ring and the type of gloves to be worn. And at roughly the same period, football began to work to a rulebook pushed for by the former pupils of Britain's unexpectedly violent public schools.

Prior to the nineteenth century, public school and university sport didn't really seem to be that different from the regular punch-ups over a pig's bladder that happened in Ashbourne. As now in schools, the ideal sporting activity was one that involved the greatest number of pupils, and the smallest amount of supervision. The ideal for teachers was to get as many pupils as possible on a field where you could see them, and then just let them get on with it. In fact, effective supervision of any sort seemed to be fairly rare in the schools of the time.

In 1793, at Winchester College, the pupils rebelled against their masters and, mimicking the French Revolution, flew the red flag of liberty from one of the towers. In 1818 the pupils were at it again and started a full-on riot, having taken against their treatment by one of the teachers. They pulled up stones from the school courtyard to use as ammunition and the local militia was sent in to sort out the uprising, with their bayonets fixed. Rioting obviously went down well with future employers though. Three of the pupils involved became generals, one a distinguished diplomat and one a Church of England bishop, ready to join the incomprehensible battle against women taking his job.

Strangely, none of the pictures of the riot made it into the Winchester prospectus. With similar uprisings at Rugby and Harrow, where the young Lord Byron tried to blow up the new headmaster with explosives, it isn't surprising that the schools liked to offer mob-style football as a way for the boys to let off steam without the staff having to call the army in. None of the parents seemed to object to the horrific injuries the game might inflict on their children, and anyway these could be halved simply by playing against other schools. A fixture list would be a way of spreading the mutilation around a bit. The problem was that no two schools played quite the same game.

Charterhouse, in the City of London, had no grass at all, and the game was played in their cloisters, on paving slabs. According to the school rules, you were allowed to pick the ball up, but not run with it, and the main way of getting it forward was to dribble it while the opposition aimed kicks at your shins. Rugby School allowed catching the ball and running with it, while at Winchester College, the rules were different again. Originally, the game there was played along a main street in the town, but too many windows got broken. It was then moved to the top of a nearby hill, those playing being supplemented by a group of younger boys whose job it was to stop the ball rolling down the slope. Finally, they decided to change venue again, this time to the attractively named 'Palmer Swamp'. And this, ladies and gentlemen, is at one of the most academically successful schools in Britain. Each school also had different footballing terms. At Winchester, the talk was all of worms, ropes and tag, while the forwards called themselves hot-men, which seems a bit self-regarding; surely only girls can really decide whether boys are hot or not?

At Eton, Marlborough and Shrewsbury, the laws and language were different again. Schools couldn't play each other, but, more significant for the development of the game, when they met at university, pupils from those different schools couldn't agree on which version they should play.

To sort out the mess of rules and regulations, it was obvious that there should be one unified code. Various attempts were made throughout the 1840s and 50s, but there were major stumbling blocks to agreement. First, it had to be established whether the game was about running with the ball or dribbling with it. And secondly, there was the vexed question of 'hacking', the technique of kicking lumps out of your opponents' shins wherever the ball happened to be. For some, hacking was the very essence of football. It simply wouldn't be a game if you were not allowed to kick away mercilessly at the shins of the opposition players. Some schools, like Rugby, took a middle position; you could kick an opponent as much as you liked, but taking great chunks out of his tibias wasn't allowed if your teammates were holding him down while you did it. Other schools thought the practice entirely unnecessary, largely on the grounds that if people were randomly kicking whatever happened to be in front of them, it would make a 'spot the ball' competition almost impossible.

The clubs established by old boys didn't have much more success in defining the sport either. Until, in 1863, a group of London clubs you have now never heard of, including Blackheath, Forest, the War Office, Crusaders and No Names from Kilburn, met at the Royal Geographical Society to hammer something out.

It wasn't a simple negotiation; some of the delegates were 'runners' and some were 'dribblers', while some barely used their handkerchiefs at all and were just interested in sorting out the rules of the sport.

After weeks of debate, the dribblers won the day. The final draft of the new rules banned hacking, tripping and running with the ball. Blackheath, a club run by old pupils of Rugby School, for whom all such activities were the very essence of manly Saturday entertainment, was incensed. They withdrew from the newly formed Football Association to carry on with their own thing, soon to be covered by the rules of rugby football. One meeting had created two separate sports. Britain was on a roll.

After the division between those who wanted to handle the ball and those who wanted to kick it, clear rules for each game were swiftly standardized, although Luis Suárez occasionally confused them. The footballers, who could now reasonably be called that, introduced crossbars for the goals and worked towards an offside law, changing it deliberately every time their wives had understood it. The FA Cup was started, and the number of clubs began to expand, particularly in the north, where new legislation on factory hours left working men with time on their hands. Englishmen abroad soon began to establish clubs too, Peñarol in Uruguay and AC Milan among them. Leagues were established across South America, and the game spread across the globe. Not all nations were fans though. In Germany, where nationalist gymnastics was in vogue, football was thought to be a very inferior activity and was described as 'the English disease'.

To be fair, at first, the English game was lacking something. After the initial split between running and dribbling, the latter meant just that. The skill of the game was thought to be dribbling past your opponents, and no one even thought to pass the ball. It took Scottish football to put its English counterpart on the right track. The Queen's Park Club in Glasgow became the Barcelona of their era, and their eleven McMessis developed a short passing game with which the dribbling southern clubs could not compete.

Rugby developed rapidly as well, and within a decade it too had a unified code. The RFU was established, and after the intervention of a doctor, who said he was fed up with crippled boys cluttering up his surgery on a Saturday afternoon, hacking was banned. In the main, the laws reflected those in use at Rugby School, hence the name of the sport. Disappointingly, though, there seems to be little truth in the story of William Webb Ellis, the boy who picked the ball up and ran with it, thus inspiring a whole new game. Webb Ellis never mentioned the incident, which you'd think he would have done. Possibly he just had no memory of it, having been hacked in the head by his outraged teammates shortly afterwards. Like football, rugby spread across the country and the English-speaking Empire.

The development of rules in cricket followed a similar path. Cricket had been played in the south-east of England since the sixteenth century at least. Originally, it may simply have been a country game played amongst friends or villagers. Like football, there would have been few rules, but those playing it seemed less set on violence, which is lucky, because at least two of them would have been carrying a large wooden bat. By 1700 matches were being regularly played between teams put together by landowners, who chose players from their own staff, some having been employed specifically for their cricketing prowess. Clubs grew up, like those at Hambledon in Hampshire and Slindon, to the south of Chichester. Cricket was already semi-professional and attracted huge crowds. And as its popularity grew, so the matches attracted larger and larger wagers, many of them from Malaysian betting syndicates. To keep things fair, some laws for the game were needed. There was, for example, no stipulated maximum size for a bat, which could be twice the size of the wicket, if you fancied it, and no clear rule as to how the arm should be held when bowling. The laws were worked out between the clubs, until eventually one of them, the Marylebone Cricket Club, became dominant and the regulatory body for the game as a whole.

Andy Murray's sport of choice got its laws at roughly the same time. Tennis, a game of hitting a ball with a bat in a court, had been popular for centuries and was played by monarchs such as Henry VIII. Lawn tennis, however, began in the 1870s as the brain-child of one Major Wingfield, an army officer who just liked inventing things, including a sport for family entertainment which could be played in your own garden. His original tennis sets – a box containing a net, some rackets and rubber balls – sold the new game under the name 'sphairistike', which meant nothing, although it was better than the alternatives, 'accenture' and 'Timotei'. As it was also unpronounceable, it was quickly shortened to 'sticky', before people sensibly abandoned the name altogether and decided to call it tennis. As its popularity grew, a court was set aside to play it at Wimbledon. The All England Club was born and a rulebook was developed so the game could be exported around the world.

So keen were we on writing rules that we couldn't stop ourselves. Table tennis, aka 'ping pong' or 'wiff waff', as it is still known in Boris Johnson's house, was another parlour game, and we wrote the rulebook for that. Rowers in Henley got on with writing one for their sport, as did the hockey players of the clubs around London.

For golf, the journey was slightly different. In origin, golf is Dutch, or Belgian, or Greek, or all of them, all nations and all people being equally keen on smashing stones about with a stick, but it wasn't until the end of the nineteenth century that the game, which had already been played in Scotland and throughout Britain for centuries, adopted the same rules everywhere, those produced by our dominant club, the Royal and Ancient.

By the end of the nineteenth century, the British had codified most of what are now the world's major sports, although, to be honest, it is quite difficult to work out which the world's major sports are, as it depends entirely on the criteria you use to measure their popularity. Participation, the size of television audiences, the number of global federations devoted to that sport and the visits to websites about them all produce different results, and many of them are ridiculous. Based on the number of federations, an indication of the number of countries in which is it is played, the most popular sport in the world is badminton. See what I mean? It's madness, even though we did write the rulebook for it in 1893.

If you take television audiences as your criterion, the most popular sport is football, which seems more reasonable, although, according to the *Economist*, the second most watched sporting event in 2008 was a volleyball match between China and Cuba. Still, whichever way you slice it, our influence is there for all to see. Top in every list is football, for which the rules are ours, followed by cricket (ours), and then variously by hockey (ours), tennis (ours), badminton (ours), baseball (not really ours, except that it is quite like rounders) and volleyball (not ours at all).

So, with all the rules defined and a winning mentality deep within the DNA of all our sportsmen, Britain seemed set up for global sporting domination, which is why it is now time to address the question we haven't answered yet.

How did we go from believing that winning was everything to thinking that practice was practically cheating, and that altitude training should simply be running up and down the plane a bit on the way there?

Well the example of W. G. Grace provides some of the answer.

As the rules of cricket were being written, it was still a game in which making money was a key motivation for the players, and many of them played for several different sides all at the same time, just to make as much as they could. Even cricket's first sporting celebrity, W. G. Grace, exploited every commercial opportunity going, charging fees for playing and putting teams together and claiming expenses for his wife and family on overseas tours that would make an incarcerated MP blush with embarrassment. Nor was W. G. averse to bending the rules to his advantage. Apparently, on one occasion, the ball being bowled at him lodged in his shirt and rather than allowing the fielders to retrieve it, he just ran between the wickets accumulating runs until he became bored and stopped. So ruthless was his gamesmanship that the Australians actually complained about him.

Unfortunately for the survival of the winning mentality of British sport, the Australians seemed to have natural allies in the administrators of the game. At some point in the nineteenth century, those running cricket, the landed gentry from the counties with time on their hands and no particular need to earn a living, seemed to go through a kind of conversion. Sport should not be about just winning, because that was somehow, well, you know, a bit common. It shouldn't be about making money, or even about having fun. No, sport should be about the higher ideals. It should be about building character, manliness and virtue. And the change wasn't just felt in the battle of leather and willow.

With rapid industrialization across Britain, the Anglican Church began to worry about the evils that change had brought with it: poverty, crime and a slow decline of Godliness among the urban poor. To counter them, clergymen such as Charles Kingsley, of *The Water-Babies* fame, developed the concept of muscular Christianity, the idea that Christians could turn back the rising tide of sloth and sinfulness by setting an example of religious belief, manliness, athleticism and devotion to their country. These were a set of ideals that sat very poorly with playing sport to win a few quid, gambling or doing whatever it took to win. For muscular Christians, sport was about moral health. Sadly, turning the other cheek was unlikely to be a successful tactic in any sport, particularly boxing.

The new ideals became something of a national obsession, particularly in the public schools preparing pupils for a life of duty to God and Empire, and for clergymen operating in the rapidly growing cities of Britain. The YMCA was founded in London in 1844, with the aim of keeping young men on the path of righteousness by promoting 'a healthy mind, body and spirit'. The organization offered classes in boxing, self-defence, moustache-growing and wearing construction helmets. In America, the organization invented both volleyball and basketball to keep their members on the straight and narrow.

And as the idea of making money from sport came to be looked down upon, amateurism spread through all the sports we had just sorted out with rules. In rowing, the Henley Regatta debated whether they should allow crews made up from non-amateurs, and their definition of amateur became tighter and tighter as time went on. Initially, they banned professional watermen. Eventually, they banned crews containing any type of tradesmen. By 1874 even northern regattas were banning ordinary working men from taking part, because they didn't fit the new code. In 1920 Henley's rules had become so strict that they banned an American oarsman called Jack Kelly, who went on to be a triple Olympic gold medallist, because he had once worked as apprentice to a bricklayer. It was a bad move – Jack Kelly was Grace Kelly's father, a woman most men in Henley would have wanted to show their sliding seat to.

In some sports, the attitude to amateurism was even more extreme, if not bonkers. In hockey, a decision was made that all matches should be friendlies. There were to be no competitions and no leagues. Hockey was to be a game untainted by money and played by friends; friends who, in my experience, would charge at you and try to hit you in the ankle with their sticks. They certainly weren't amateur at that. A friendly 'bully off' at Cubs gave me my first experience of A&E.

The first proper leagues only appeared almost a century later, in the 1960s, and were founded by those fed up with how badly we were performing internationally and determined to do something about it.

In athletics, the amateur ideal was even included in the title of the governing body, the Amateur Athletics Association, or 3As, an organization originally known as the AAC, but changed when they sent it back for a re-mark. Founded by public school boys, athletics had a problem with what being amateur actually meant too. In their first attempt, the bar was set at 'someone who had never competed for money or earned a living from athletics', but feeling that would be far too easy to clear, they raised it by excluding anyone who had ever been a mechanic, artisan or labourer.

In rugby, the authorities' unbending attitude to amateurism led to the development of Rugby League. Right from kick-off, there had been differences in the structure of the game in the north and south. In the south, the clubs were dominated by former public school boys, determined to maintain what they viewed as the noble ethics of the game, while in the north, the game was increasingly played by working men and the clubs run by industrialists, to whom muscular Christianity seemed less important than muscular players.

When the southern-dominated RFU decided they wouldn't hold a cup competition because people might gamble on it, the Yorkshire clubs started one anyway. When the RFU discovered that the some northern clubs had started to pay their players, in order to attract the best ones and to compensate them for the work they had lost whilst playing, they suspended them. Eventually, the differences became so great that the majority of clubs in the Northern Union resigned to form the Rugby League, which soon threw off the shackles of amateurism to become fully professional. The self-governing northern clubs then took the opportunity to make their brand of the game distinctive, more exciting and safer; in Yorkshire, in the 1890s, even without the dangers of widespread hacking, it wasn't unusual for more than 20 players to die every season, which made attracting younger players necessary and impossible all at the same time, especially if you had to convince their mothers that playing would be good for them. The League therefore changed their rules to reduce the amount of brawling, the number of players on each side dropped to 13, the line-out and ruck were abolished and we had invented yet another game.

In football, the rise of northern industrial teams also challenged the amateur ethics of those clubs founded by the public school pupils. The Old Etonians, Carthusians and teams from Oxford and Cambridge began to lose their dominance to rivals like Aston Villa, Woolwich Arsenal and Newton Heath, the team that would become Manchester United, although most of their fans lived hundreds of miles away. These were clubs to whom winning was everything, although Arsenal, in particular, seemed a bit confused between actually winning and coming fourth. Aware that schism was possible and keen to avoid it, the FA therefore took their commitment to amateurism in a different direction. They said the players could be professional, but those that ran the sport could not be.

And so, across all our major sports, we ended up with a system that meant that we were hideously hampered by our sporting code, while those players overseas, to whom we had explained the rules, were not. The results were fairly inevitable.

In hockey, we refused to join a European or world federation, because other countries didn't adhere to our values for the game. At the time, we had more hockey clubs than the rest of the world combined, so it didn't seem to matter much. By the time we did join an international hockey federation, after the Second World War, we were shocked to find that other countries were better than us.

In rugby union, the strict adherence to amateurism meant that it got left behind by football in popularity, whilst in football itself, the amateur ethic of those running the game meant that we didn't notice what was happening abroad. We had invented the game, and simply weren't interested in what the rest of the world was doing. We didn't bother to enter the first World Cup in Uruguay in1930, because we assumed we would win, and when we finally agreed to go in 1950, we lost to the United States. In 1953, at Wembley, Puskas and his Hungarians astounded us by being able to kick a ball. Into our net, six times.

Of course, every major sport is now professional. Not only does football take what is happening overseas seriously, but practically everyone in the Premier League, from owners to players to coaches, is from overseas. But attitudes take a long time to change, and even if it has affected our national results, most of us still cling quietly to the ideal of gentlemanly sport. That is why we like Bradley Wiggins, who slowed down for Cadel Evans to catch up when tacks on the road had left him with a puncture. That's why we value the victories of canoeists who combine capsizing in the River Lee with working in a bank, and that is why we object to footballers diving at the slightest touch. There is something fundamentally un-British about pushing the rules that far, even if it might mean winning the game. To us, winning by cheating isn't winning, and losing because you haven't cheated is some form of victory, even if it isn't reflected in the number of points you get at the end of the season.

Of course, in some of the sports we invented, our lack of success has nothing to do with our self-defeating sporting code. Tennis has obviously been run by those strapped firmly to the ideals of Victorian sport; the amateur ethic is everywhere, from the ball boys and girls at Wimbledon, chosen from local schools, to the line judges, who, for no payment, willingly stand stock-still by the court for hours staring at a set of white lines, as though in training to be human speed cameras. It doesn't matter how exciting the match is, they don't get to see any of it.

They just listen and hope for the thrill of an occasional puff of chalk.

Yet it isn't lack of a killer instinct that, Andy Murray apart, has done for our success in tennis. No, the problems in tennis are two-fold. First, no one plays it at school, because team games like cricket occupy more pupils for longer, on facilities that are cheaper to provide. And secondly, the courts at Wimbledon and other major tournaments are not like the ones most British players are used to. No one in this country plays on grass or decent courts. If we want a winner, we shouldn't try and improve the national facilities and coaching programmes, because that is expensive and pointless. We should just change Wimbledon. We are far more likely to win if those courts are cracked black tarmac with some weeds growing out of them. And if that doesn't work, we should restrict each match to a supply of just four balls, one of which is flat, do away with the ball boys and make the players fetch them themselves.

Anyway, things are changing, as the Olympics shows. We are now winners, and not just in the sitting-down sports. Our sailors and rowers and cyclists may be among the best in the world, but so are our athletes, cricketers and rugby players, and our footballers may eventually get to a World Cup final that doesn't have 'quarter' written in front of it. In fact, in football, we are probably doing rather better than we should expect. In 2006, FIFA, the world governing body, found that, globally, 265 million people play football. Of them, 26 million are in China, 24 million in the United States and 20 million in India. Germany has 16 million players in total, accounting for 20 per cent of their population. The FA, meanwhile, has just 1.4 million male players registered, putting us just behind South Africa, and just ahead of Japan, and no one is thinking that *they* should be winning the World Cup every time.

To be honest, I am rather sad that we seem to be changing our ways. There is a lot to be said for being slightly amateur at sport. My own amateurishness at it is one of the things that set me off down this particular career path. Two days after the end of my A-levels, I played my first round of golf, with some mates at school. We were mucking about and I got hit on the head by a golf ball, a lofted eight iron, hit by one of my friends. I was standing on the green and once the ball had split my head open, it bounced off my cranium to within two feet of the hole. Even though I obviously needed to go to hospital, and the green was rapidly turning red, my friend displayed admirable ruthlessness by refusing to take me until he had putted for his birdie. Once in A&E, the doctor shaved half my head and gave me five stitches. The next day was my school's prize-giving day, at which I had to give a speech. It was meant to be a rundown of the school's achievements for the year, but slightly concussed, and aware that the state of my head required some explanation, I devoted most of it to taking the assembled parents and staff through why I was looking like a before and after photograph for Wayne Rooney's hair clinic. It was the first time I had spoken in public, and I liked the fact that people laughed.

Secretly, I'm hoping that our slightly amateurish attitude doesn't disappear too soon, and I'm fairly confident it won't. Apart from watching Jessica Ennis and Mo Farah win gold, it gave me my favourite athletic memory of the Games.

Hugh Dennis

Having failed to qualify for the next round of heats, one of our 1500 metre hopefuls, Ross Murray, was interviewed trackside by the BBC. Asked how he felt about his performance, he said he thought it had probably been easier for the African runners who had qualified from his race. They had been training hard for four years. Whereas he had really only been at it for six months, after 'two years on the lash'.

Magnificent.

AND THE WINNER IS...

When I started this book, one of my worries was that our new British winning streak would somehow be paid for with our reputation for creativity and comedy. You see, British comedy isn't about winners, or those who are successful; it is about losers, the unsuccessful, those who simply can't overcome whatever life throws at them. The theme runs right through our sit-coms. David Brent is a self-deluded man who thinks he is far better at his job than he is. Basil Fawlty is a man battling with the frustrations of an unfulfilled life, and Reggie Perrin is a man who runs away from the tedium of a suburban corporate career.

Porridge is set in a prison and *Dad's Army* in a church hall, where a group of incompetents aim to provide our last line of defence in case of invasion. *Some Mothers do 'Ave 'Em* is all explained in the title. *The Inbetweeners* is about a group of hopeless teenagers. In *Only Fools and Horses*, Del Boy never wins, and nor do the parents in *Outnumbered*. In *Peepshow*, two dysfunctional thirty-somethings struggle to cope with modern life, and in the final episode of *Blackadder*, they all go over the top of the trench to certain death. There are exceptions, of course, but I won't mention *The Vicar of Dibley*, because it doesn't fit my argument.

In the main, winning simply isn't funny. Well, not to British audiences anyway. We like people whom life has defeated, people clinging on to the backs of buses on roller skates, people falling through the bar in pubs, people beating their cars with saplings because the engine has refused to start. We like the incompetent staff at holiday camps, the man who says, 'I don't believe it' when some misfortune befalls him, the rag and bone man who dreams of the better life you know he will never have, and the Norwich Radio presenter with no sense of his own crassness.

Our comedy relies on things that don't work properly, the unexpected open manhole in the pavement, the moose head that won't stay attached to the wall, trains that are delayed – 'Sorry I'm late, C. J. Wildebeest on the line at Penge.'

Perhaps that is why some Germans seem to have no sense of humour; they simply don't need one in a country where everything works. What is there to laugh about if your car always starts, the builders are competent and the buses arrive when the timetable says they will? And we shouldn't worry that there are countries like that, because that kind of thing really isn't for us. We might complain about it, but, creatively, there is a lot to be gained from a transport network that collapses under the wrong kind of snow, sat-navs that direct us into lakes and customer care centres that never ever answer their phones.

I know I became addicted to the Olympics, but when *The Now Show* accepted the offer of a series to cover them, we took it because we assumed that, this being Britain, things would go wrong, that when the contractors finally handed over the stadium, they would do so with the words: 'Track? No. No one said anything about there being a track.'

We imagined that the gathered spectators would admire the velodrome, feel one of the great steel supporting struts and say, 'Is it just me, or is this a bit wobbly?'

We were hoping, purely for the purposes of comedy, that the hurdles would be too tall, that the swimming pool would spring a leak and the starting pistol wouldn't work. We were certain that some athletes would get the wrong size kit to wear, that the hammer would fly off the end of its chain and that the cycle road race would be disrupted by emergency road works. We were convinced that a commentator would go, 'Yes, he's wearing spikes, and that is why he has punctured the kayak.' Or, with one lap to go, we would hear, 'There goes the bell! Someone has stolen the bell!'

None of it happened, and it made the programme much more difficult to do, because comedy often comes from disaster. For comedy writers, even personal embarrassment is welcomed as a source of anecdotes.

The moment of my greatest personal embarrassment was whilst having a colonoscopy, a procedure I opted to have at a small local hospital, on the basis that the fewer people you meet, or who recognize you, the less explaining you have to do about why you are there. If you are on the television and need a camera fed up your posterior, UCH or Guy's is not

Hugh Dennis

going to be the place for you. And in the small, quiet local hospital, all was going well. No one seemed to have clocked me. I had stripped naked, was lying on the operating table in my backless gown, gently slipping into unconsciousness and thinking I had got away with it, when the nurse turned to me and said, 'I'm a very good friend of your next-door neighbour.'

And even as I heard it, I thought, 'Oh, that'll make a good story.'

The British get the funny side of disaster. Steve Punt and I used to do a series for Radio 2 called *It's Been a Bad Week,* which was designed to cheer people up by finding stories of people who had had worse weeks than they had. The audience would vote for the story they liked most in the series, and the winner illustrates my point exactly. It was the story of a first-time bank robber who was so nervous that, once faced with customers and staff, he had held his gun aloft and shouted, 'Freeze, mother-stickers! This is a f**k up.' After which, he ran back out of the bank in embarrassment, and empty-handed.

Failure, frustration and an appreciation of the finer points of being a loser seemed to me to be one of the things that spurred British creativity, and if we were about to turn into a nation of winners, that might go, which would be a national disaster, about which being funny might be quite difficult.

Because Britain is undoubtedly a nation of very creative people. In 2010 British musical artists were responsible for nearly 12 per cent of global sales of recorded music. Between 2007–10 the British won 23 Grammies; in 2012 Adele won six on her own. The Beatles, Elton John, Led Zeppelin and Queen have each sold more than 300 million records, while Pink Floyd, the Rolling Stones and the Bee Gees are not far behind. Nearly half of the world's computer games companies are based here, and we produce nearly a quarter of the games themselves. We have over 100 film studios, nearly 5,000 film production companies, 2,500 post-production companies and some of the world's largest visual effects studios. Our actors are winning Emmys and Golden Globes, even if Hugh Laurie and Damian Lewis are both pretending to be American when they do it. Our films are winning Oscars, along with our directors, our producers and our writers. Our artists are feted globally, even if some of our own are confused by who they are. 'Hirst?' a friend of mine said. 'Oh yeah, he's good. He got a hat-trick in the World Cup final.' Yes, and if the linesman had said that the ball hadn't crossed the line, he would have cut him in half and preserved him in formaldehyde.

Our adverts often dominate the top prizes at the Cannes Lions Advertising Awards, although it is hard to believe it when you see the ads for DFS or Harveys; last year they gave top awards to Lynx and the *Guardian*. And our authors top the global bestsellers list. It is obviously difficult to work out overall sales for writers who have been dead for 400 years, but the best estimate seems to be that for fiction authors, to date and writing in any language, Britons take the top three spots, with William Shakespeare, Agatha Christie and Barbara Cartland. Enid Blyton is also up there, although she didn't necessarily write the books herself, while God, who may not have written the whole of his book either, isn't included because he isn't British, apparently. I find that hard to believe.

J. K. Rowling is just ahead of Tolstoy, and in the top 50 we also have Edgar Wallace, J. R. R. Tolkien , C. S. Lewis – not to be confused with CSI Lewis, a show about criminal pathologists in the Outer Hebrides – Charles Dickens, Beatrix Potter, Alastair Maclean, Catherine Cookson, Roald Dahl and Roger Hargreaves, aka *Mr Enormous Royalties*. Lewis Carroll, Ian Fleming and Ken Follett make the list, as does Jeffrey Archer, with global sales of around 120 million copies, although he could just have made that up. In E. L. James's *Fifty Shades of Grey*, we can also lay claim to the publishing phenomenon of the decade, and the fastest-selling book of all time. So far, 40 million copies have been sold worldwide, although only ten people will admit to having bought it. The book, part of a trilogy detailing the relationship between student Anastasia Steele and businessman Christian Grey, deals with themes of bondage and domination, and the way it is written, is the perfect book for masochists.

Admittedly, there do seem to be some gaps in our creative Hall of Fame. Our classical music, for example, doesn't seem to be as globally popular as that coming from our rock and pop stars. Our instrumentalists seem to be very highly regarded, as are our orchestras, particularly the LSO, but in composition, we don't seem to have been able to keep up with our continental cousins.

Obviously, all these things are subjective, and I willingly admit that I may not be the best judge musically. I have only ever played one instrument, the recorder, on which I could only play one tune, 'Darby Kelly'. And I was thrown out of the church choir, rather unfairly I thought, for being unable to sing treble after my voice had broken. In fact, I lasted rather longer in the choir than I should have done; for the first month or so after my voice had dropped an octave, I just mimed along to the songs, hoping that no one would notice and consoling myself with the fact that had we ever sung Beethoven's 'Ode to Joy', I would be singing it exactly as he would have heard it himself.

Don't get me wrong, we've got some great composers in our team, but compared, say, with Italy (which gave us Puccini, Verdi and Vivaldi), Germany (which gave us Bach, Wagner, Strauss and Beethoven) or Austria (Mozart, Haydn, Mahler and Schubert) our canon of classical music is not that exceptional.

If you go on About.com – I know, it is hardly going to be definitive – and search for famous British classical composers, they give you a list of seven: William Byrd, Thomas Tallis, Henry Purcell, Ralph Vaughan Williams, Benjamin Britten, Gustav Holst and George Frederick Handel, who, as a court favourite of the Hanoverians, became a British citizen at the age of 42, enabling us to claim national ownership of *Messiah*, which I mouthed at a church concert in 1973.

I have no argument with the credentials of any of them. I listen to Tallis, I think Ralph Vaughan Williams' *Dives and Lazarus* is one of the most hauntingly beautiful pieces of music I know, and I admire the work of Handel, although I often thought that, for health and safety, the movements of his *Music for the Royal Fireworks* – Ouverture, Bourrée, La Paix – should really be: Keeping the pets indoors, Lighting the fireworks with a taper, Not returning to the lit firework.

The Planets by Gustav Holst is also very stirring and may have been the first piece of classical music I ever heard, although I can't help thinking that Holst should be glad he isn't alive now. When he composed it, between 1914 and 1916, we thought that there were only seven planets other than Earth, the farthest out being Neptune. Writing movements for the 786 we have now discovered would have been almost impossible. By the time he got to planets like Gliese 581d or Kepler 22b, he would have had been composing a variation on 'Chopsticks' or something.

But however much I, or the listeners of Radio 3, like the work of British classical composers, the fact remains that, as a nation, we have so far been comprehensively outshone by many of those nations that UKIP wish to have no political union with. There seem to be various theories why this is this case. The first suggestion is that when Henry VIII – footballer, jouster, be-header and serial monogamist – got rid of the Roman Catholic Church, he also inadvertently got rid of church music. By robbing the churches of their wealth and dissolving the monasteries, he left them insolvent (something wrong with the chemistry there) and unable to commission great choral works, thereby stopping our musical creativity in its tracks. Another theory is that we just aren't a very musical people, that we preferred to play football, and that the two just don't mix, which would seem to be disproved by both the German and Italian traditions in both.

There also seems to be a school of thought that we have actually had great composers, but with the dictates of fashion, no one has ever felt able to say so, for fear of being laughed at. Obviously, as someone who thinks of Delibes' 'Flower Duet' as the British Airways music and who is quite keen on Rossini's

'Music from *The Lone Ranger*', I am in no position to judge the merits of any of the arguments, but I do know that, at the very least, there were some British composers who got away.

Thomas Linley, for example, appears to have been the Duncan Edwards of Georgian music. Born in 1756, he was sent as a child to Italy to develop his musical talent. Aged 14, he met and became friends with Mozart, who thought of him as a genius. He died at the age of 22 in a boating accident in Lincolnshire. Who knows what might have happened had he lived? He could have been the kernel from which we developed a great musical tradition, the inspiration for generations of composers. Or, more likely, he could have collapsed under the weight of his own fame, fallen in and out of nightclubs, developed a coke habit and spent his fortune on rehab at the Priory clinic.

I personally think that we may also lack great music because we are not quite triumphal enough. Tchaikovsky, for example, wrote the *1812 Overture* to celebrate Russia's defeat of Napoleon's Grande Armée outside Moscow in that year. We had an equally great victory over Napoleon at Waterloo, but our instinctive reaction was to name a railway station after it. It is a nice one, with lovely platforms and everything, but there is really nothing triumphal about Waterloo Station, least of all the service of South West Trains.

Art too may represent a slight hole in our creative curriculum vitae. There seem to be some doubts about how many of our artists have been world class, and whether some of them are more like Wayne Rooney. That is, good in our terms, but never likely to win The Ballon d'Or.

Again, it is not a question I can answer. You won't find me arguing against the merits of Blake, Turner, Hogarth, Gainsborough, Reynolds, Moore, Hepworth, Spencer, Hockney, Bacon, Freud or Banksy, largely because I would have no idea how to argue against the merits of them. Art is one of those subjects where you feel a bit of an idiot if you don't have anything particularly intellectual to say about it, where it isn't enough just to like something without being able to explain why.

I enjoy the equine paintings of Stubbs, but know they are often derided because they are simply pictures of horses, which isn't enough for many art critics. Why, I don't know; horses are bloody difficult to draw. They have twice as many legs as a human and the head is a lot trickier to get right. Not even artists can agree on what constitutes great art. Sir Alfred Munnings, who was thought of between the wars as one of Britain's greatest artists for his depiction of sporting scenes, famously hated modernism, and even went on radio to say so. In his final speech as the president of the Royal Academy, he claimed that Matisse, Cézanne and Picasso had corrupted art. Not true. Although Citroën have possibly corrupted the legacy of Picasso. It isn't that you shouldn't name a car after a great artist – although perhaps the fact that there is no Ford Gainsborough or Land Rover Constable shows that our artists aren't in the top echelon – it is just that if you do, the car should reflect the spirit of the artist involved. The Citroën Picasso is a relatively conventional car – surely a car named after a cubist and surrealist should at least have square wheels and eight doors, all in the wrong places?

And to match his periods of painting, the early models should all have been blue.

In judging great art, everyone has his or her own opinion, and no two people seem to agree. Andrew Lloyd Webber, for example, loves the Arthurian fantasies of the Pre-Raphaelites, whereas I can't bear them. In fact, I think that Arthur's whole obsession with a round table was a mistake in the first place. Round tables are a nightmare, especially for 13, as anyone who has been to a wedding reception will tell you. No one can reach stuff put in the middle, and you can only have a conversation with the people on either side of you. I think the court of King Arthur would have lasted a lot longer if he had gone for a long, thin table and told people to swap places before dessert.

But, look, we shouldn't let minor doubts about classical music and great artists detract from the satisfaction we feel about how creative Britain is. We might complain about the ever-diminishing size of our manufacturing industry, the fact that we no longer really build ships, or make textiles, or mine coal, but according to the Foreign and Commonwealth Office, our creative sector is the largest in the world relative to the size of our population, and that must mean something.

Now, obviously, before we get too carried away about how brilliant we all are, certain things are working in our favour. First and foremost, we speak English, the major international language, so overseas sales, for our music artists say, are always going to be easier than for artists who don't normally sing in English like Stromae, Françoise Hardy or Chas and Dave. In fact, the only foreign stars you are likely to have heard of are the ones who have opted out of their own language to sing in ours, like Abba, Kraftwerk, and Ah-ha.

Yes, I know 'Gangnam Style', a song which was bizarrely hailed by Ban Ki-moon as 'a force for world peace', is mostly in Korean, but the title is English. Well, one half of it is the name of a suburb in Seoul, but the other half is English, sort of. Anyway, the point is, singing in the world's most influential language has helped our musicians. If the most influential language happened to be Mongolian, we might all be listening to Hurd, the Ulan Bator heavy metal band who have no idea of the damage that naming themselves after Margaret Thatcher's foreign secretary will have done to their chances of success in the UK. If that language was Hindi, we would all be downloading the mix-metal of Euphoria. If it was Mexican Spanish, we would have posters of Panda and their album *Arroz con Leche*, and if it was Serbo-Croat, we would all be getting down to the rhythms of Ceca and her Latin–Serbo–Oriental fusion. Or, more likely, we wouldn't, because you are not going to feel that good about yourself dancing to music performed by the widow of Arkan, the Serbian warlord who was indicted for crimes against humanity, the title Ceca hasn't chosen for her new album.

For our writers and journalists, it can also only have helped that we have been able to say pretty much whatever we want to, without censorship, for nearly 350 years, and we haven't really needed to worry about it unless we were threatening to blow up an airport or incorrectly tweeting the name of a former Tory cabinet minister.

Britain has effectively had press freedom since the end of the seventeenth century. Prior to that, having a printing press needed the permission of the Stationers' Company, a Restoration version of Ryman, and all printing was licensed by the crown, to stop people writing nasty things about them. After 1679, this approach was abandoned in favour of a libel law to be used once something had been published. It was a win-win situation. From that point on, newspapers could print what they liked, while lawyers and libelled celebrities got richer.

We do still have some print restrictions, of course, among them the Obscene Publications Act, which was designed to prevent certain types of printed pornography and to shelter our youth from the corruption it might cause. It was introduced in 1857, and was used a decade later to try and ban the publication of an exposé called 'The Confessional Unmasked: Showing the Depravity of the Catholic Priesthood'. That was only 150 years ago; good to know the pope has dealt with it all so quickly.

Beyond the printed word, freedom of speech in other areas wasn't so quick to emerge, although, strangely, this may have helped our reputation as a nation of novelists. In 1737 parliament passed the Theatrical Licensing Act, which meant that the lord chamberlain had to approve any play before it was staged. And it might never have been passed had it not been for a play called *A Vision of the Golden Rump*, which is fantastic and should be used as the new name for Rear of the Year.

Throughout the early eighteenth century, theatre had become more and more satirical, with plays such as *The Beggar's Opera*, *The Dragon of Wantley* and *The Spitting Image* increasingly attacking the Whig government. Those in power didn't much like being mocked, and having been tipped over the edge by the content of *A Vision of the Golden Rump*, they decided to close down all plays that might be critical of them. The key mover was Prime Minister Robert Walpole, who claimed not to like lampooning at all, although he did write to *Spitting Image* and ask if he could buy his puppet. Sadly, no manuscript of *The Vision of the Golden Rump* has survived, and as it never made it past the censors, no one is quite sure which vision of the rump we would have seen. In fact, there is now a theory that it was not a genuine play, and that the manuscript had been sexed up by Walpole in order to get his way in parliament. Thank God no modern prime minister has thought to do the same thing. The lord chamberlain retained the function of approving all plays until 1968, although, for the century before that, he had only been allowed to veto a production if he thought it might threaten the preservation of decorum, good manners or public peace, or if, like *Bad Girls – The Musical*, it was so bad the audience might riot while trying to get out.

And how did it help novelists? Well, before the Licensing Act, the fashion was apparently to write for the theatre, where the greatest number of people would see your work. After the act, those who wanted to be satirical or witty started writing books instead.

Of course, the United States also has a commitment to free speech, enshrined in the First Amendment. I only mention it because one of its legal tests was a case called Dennis versus the United States. Eugene Dennis was the leader of the American Communist Party in the 1940s and was convicted of 'conspiracy for the destruction and overthrow of the United States government'. I don't approve, obviously. I just think it is pretty cool when the only other Dennises I've been aware of in public life are Les and the bloke who runs Maclaren.

In addition to being able to say what we want to say in this country, we also have the advantage of enjoying the words we are using to say it. Playing with words is a national hobby. We love puns, we love Scrabble and it was an Englishman, albeit one who had emigrated to America, who invented the crossword as we now know it. The first one in Britain was published in 1924 by the *Sunday Express*, squeezed between two articles, one on immigration and the other on the death of Princess Diana. The cryptic type, for many the only proper version, originated here, and is therefore sometimes known as 'the British crossword' in the United States. In some ways, it was our love of words that saved us in the Second World War; faced with German codes that the military couldn't break, Turing and his team at Bletchley Park turned to those at Oxford or Cambridge who did crosswords faster than anyone else in the common room.

Where our love of words came from, no one knows for sure, but it seems that we have been at it for centuries. The Anglo-Saxons enjoyed word play too. Their poets whiled away the hours by lumping old words together to create new ones. For example, the Anglo-Saxon for the human body was 'bone-house', and for a ship, 'wave-floater', a magnificent description that simply doesn't apply to the *Costa Concordia*. The sea was variously called 'whale-road', 'seal-bath', which sounds like an entry on a DIY to-do list, or 'fish-home', which is very fitting, unless the sea has just been scoured by a Spanish trawler. These new words were called 'kennings' and make up about one-third of the words in *Beowulf*.

Hugh Dennis

Unlike the French, we seem to enjoy the constant changes in our language, and don't regard them as a threat. In France, the Académie Française gets very upset about the creeping anglicization of their tongue. A Canute-like section of their website, called *'Dire, ne pas dire'* offers pure French alternatives to the rising tide of foreign words which are flooding their language. For email, they offer *'courriel'*, for networking they offer *'travail en réseau'*. We, by contrast, simply don't care. In fact I may pop into Pret A Manger in my culottes and grab a panini to stuff in the rucksack I won at a fete, just to show them how little we need such diktats to maintain our national linguistic *esprit de corps*. We have no need of a *cri de coeur*; we simply don't have that angst.

Words and wit mean a lot to us. I had a Swiss–German boss once who was amazed that British newspaper headlines had verbs in them, because verbs could denote bias. Apparently, in Swiss newspapers, and admittedly I only have his word for it, headlines excluded verbs for that reason. They would just be a selection of nouns like 'Train Crash', 'UN Vote' or 'Benefit Cuts'. How boring is that? It may be why Swiss newspapers have sold so badly in Britain. We need wit, we need banter, we need 'Stick It Up Your Junta'.

In advertising in Britain, the crime is not to be creative enough, and in that we seem to differ from the rest of Europe. All those perfume ads at Christmas are the essence – excuse the pun, it's a national failing – of French advertising. It is glamorous, seductive, luxurious and utterly ridiculous when done as a meaningless monologue by Brad Pitt. By contrast, German advertising is all about efficiency, technology, engineering and performance. Except for Lidl, which is all about rather unappealing cheapness; and that is why, for Tesco, every Lidl helps.

In Britain, though, we go for wit and weirdness. It is almost as if we are scared that no one will buy anything if the ads aren't clever enough. Occasionally, of course, even our best creative teams do run into trouble. For several years I was the voice of the Hovis ads – no, not the ones where the kid rides his bike down the cobbled hill, I was barely even born then. At the time, the brand was introducing a whole series of new range extensions: Best of Both – brown bread that looked white – and a new loaf with a crust that had been baked slightly longer than normal in the oven. The new ad had to explain what the new crust was like, but in spite of the fact that the ads had won a whole selection of awards that year, no one, me included, could think of a new word to describe succinctly what the difference in the bread was going to be. So, eventually, I read a voiceover script which said, "New Hovis Crusty, with a brand new "crusty" crust'.

Don't worry yourself, though, this is Britain, and it won't happen again. In a few years we will have nicked a word for it from German, French, Dutch, Danish, Ukrainian, Lithuanian, Bajan, Street or Sanskrit, because that is what we do.

It is a consequence, dare I say it, of being an island nation, a phrase that brings me back to where I began.

I wasn't really intending to come to any conclusion in this book. It wasn't meant to be a work of great scholarship, or read by children for their GCSE coursework. In fact, if there are any children reading, please don't rely on this at all – I don't want to be responsible for your failure to get to the university of your choice. This book was simply an attempt to get to know the country I live in rather better, to understand our obsessions and our achievements, and perhaps to work out why we are the way we are. And I have learned things, not least of which is that there is a limit to the number of times you can read sections out to your wife before she has to start feigning enthusiasm, and that if you endlessly regale your children with the phrase 'You'll never guess what I have just found out about the . . .', they will eventually start trying to avoid you.

I wasn't necessarily expecting common themes to emerge, but as the weeks have gone on, one thing has become clear. Being an island nation really has made a difference to Britain, even if we are cracked into more than 6,000 pieces. Not because it has made us isolationist, but exactly the opposite. Our position has made us a stopping-off point for traders and travellers, and some of them liked it so much they decided to invade. The Vikings popped in and the Anglo-Saxons took a trip over, bringing their word puzzles. The Romans brought us wine and under-floor heating, and when the Normans came to dinner, the gifts they brought were architecture, the French language and, less impressively, the name Norman.

Being surrounded by the sea seems to have made us desperate to see what lies beyond it, and frantic to get off these lumps of rock. Having a sea view has widened our horizons; our lack of plants made our plant hunters and horticulturalists want to find others; our lack of real hills, at least in this geological epoch, made our explorers want to find some proper ones elsewhere.

Our position between the Atlantic and the Continent

explains our ever-changing weather and the need of our sailors, and cloud-watchers, to understand its patterns, if indeed there are any.

The sea has made us into a trading nation, living on our wits to provide those things that others might want to buy. And our need to trade has driven the innovations and inventions in our manufacturing.

The fact that we have had to travel to pay our way seems to have made us open to other cultures and ready to plunder them for ideas better than those we could come up with ourselves, whether they be in food, philosophy, manners or the best way to plant seeds.

As a result, British culture, like the British sausage, contains bits of everything. Britain is a melting pot that has benefited from every wave of immigration and every bout of exploration. To outsiders, watching only the Changing of the Guard, a royal wedding, or the state opening of parliament, we might appear to be a land where traditions are stultifying and paralysing, but in fact nothing could be further from the truth, I think. So far as I can see, there is no Great British tradition, other than to be constantly adaptable.

In language, we have absorbed and embraced new words and phrases, regarding them as a means of strengthening the richness of our mother tongue. The etiquette that we imported from France was adapted and changed to meet our require-ments; not for us the rigid system of status that led to the beheading of so many aristocrats. In fact, I'm not sure that there has ever been any completely rigid class system at all. We might appear to be a regal state, but it is centuries since the royal family had any real power. It is nearly 800 years since the barons challenged the power of the king with Magna Carta, and nearly 400 since a monarch, frustrated by the fact that some MPs didn't agree with him, last entered the Commons to try and threaten them. For centuries, this has been a country where the individual has known his rights, where people have known that, by and large, they can rely on the protection of the law. This is a country where the emphasis on rights has naturally extended to animals, and where the emphasis on individuals, and thus individuality, has made us more embracing of the eccentric, the unconventional and the creative.

In Britain no one, it seems, has ever really known his or her place. In fact, one of the more realistic aspects of *Downton Abbey* to me is that a chauffeur could marry into a great family. I don't know if it ever happened, but certainly, if you were successful, you could be given a title whatever your social background, to which Thomas Cromwell and Lords Kelvin and Archer would give testimony.

Democracy has been stable for centuries and that has given us time and the inclination to get on with other stuff. It may even explain our willingness to queue. It is an odd thought, I know, but it seems to me that queuing is a manifestation of our deeply held belief that if we were there first, neither wealth nor status gives anyone the right to go in front of us. By queuing, we are exhibiting our membership of a free society. Well, that is what I am going to tell myself when I am on the line to BT Broadband, or in the bank behind the man paying in all those bags of coins.

I hope this book is helpful in those pub quizzes and helps

you understand Britain a little better. It seems to make more sense to me, but if I have got things wrong, I'm not going to mind too much. I will simply do what our great inventors and scientists have always done. I shall dust myself down, have a think and then give it another go.

Oh, before I go, I've realized that there is a car called the Land Rover Constable. One stopped me for speeding on the M25.

Acknowledgements

In particular, I would like to acknowledge the following sources:

The website of the Cloud Appreciation Society – www.cloudappreciationsociety.org/

The Automatic Rain Gauge of Sir Christopher Wren F. R. S. – Asit K. Biswas (Notes and Records of the Royal Society of London, 1967)

Considerations for Sustainable Irrigation Development in Asia – Asit K. Biswas (Water Resources Development, 1994)

Meteorological Phenomena in Western Classical Orchestral Music – Karen L. Aplin and Paul D. Williams (*Weather*, November 2011)

The Perils of Plant Collecting – A. M. Martin (lmi.org.uk)

The Urban Back Garden in England in the Nineteenth Century – The University of Cambridge: Department of Geography

The Petplan Pet Census – Petplan, 2011

Code of Practice for the Welfare of Cats – DEFRA, 2009

Creativity is Great Britain – Foreign and Commonwealth Office

United Kingdom: Tipping and Etiquette – www.tripadvisor.co.uk

15 Countries That Consume the Most Alcohol – www.CNBC.com

Global Status Report on Alcohol and Health – WHO, 2011

Grindell 'Death Ray' Matthews – Dr. D. Clarke and Andy Roberts Forlean Times Oct 2003

Corruption Perceptions Index 2011 – Transparency International

Democracy Under Stress 2011 – *Economist* Intelligence Unit.

How Long Is the Coastline of Britain? B. B. Mandelbrot (*Science*, 156, 1967)

As my Amazon account will testify, I have also consulted many books and heartily recommend the following for those whose interest has been tweaked:

Can We Have Our Balls Back Please?: How the British Invented Sport – Julian Norridge (Allen Lane, 2008)

Humanity Dick: The Eccentric Member for Galway – Peter Phillips (Parapress, 2003)

Predicting the Weather: Victorians and the Science of Meteorology – Katharine Anderson (University of Chicago Press, 2005)

The Wrong Kind of Snow: How the Weather Made Britain – Anthony Woodward and Robert Penn (Hodder, 2008)

Inventing the 19th Century: 100 Inventions That Shaped the Victorian Age – Stephen Van Dulken (The British Library, 2001)

Inventing the 20th Century: 100 Inventions That Shaped the World – Stephen Van Dulken (The British Library, 2000)

The Garden: An English Love Affair – Jane Fearnley-Whittingstall (Weidenfeld & Nicolson, 2002)

The Geology of Britain: An Introduction – Peter Toghill (Swan Hill Press, 2000)